# THE LIMITS OF PRIVATE GOVERNANCE

Is there a future for the law? In this book, Florian Grisel addresses one of the most fascinating questions raised by social scientists in the past few decades. Since the 1980s, socio-legal scholars have argued that governance based on social norms (or 'private governance') can offer an alternative to regulation by the law. On this account, private governance could be socially efficient and even optimal compared with other modes of governance.

*The Limits of Private Governance* supplements this optimistic analysis of private governance by assessing the long-term evolution of a private order in the fishery of Marseille. In the last eight centuries, the fishers of Marseille have regulated their community without apparent means of legal support from the French state. In the early 15th century, they even created an organisation called the *Prud'homie de Pêche* in order to regulate their fishery.

Based on archival evidence, interviews and ethnographic data, Grisel examines the evolution of the *Prud'homie de Pêche* and argues that the strong social norms in which it is embedded are not only powerful tools of governance, but also forces of inertia that have constrained its regulatory action.

The lessons drawn from this book will appeal to academics, policy-makers and members of the general public who have an interest in the governance of our modern societies.

# The Limits of Private Governance

## Norms and Rules in a Mediterranean Fishery

Florian Grisel

·HART·

OXFORD · LONDON · NEW YORK · NEW DELHI · SYDNEY

HART PUBLISHING

Bloomsbury Publishing Plc

Kemp House, Chawley Park, Cumnor Hill, Oxford, OX2 9PH, UK

1385 Broadway, New York, NY 10018, USA

29 Earlsfort Terrace, Dublin 2, Ireland

HART PUBLISHING, the Hart/Stag logo, BLOOMSBURY and the Diana logo are
trademarks of Bloomsbury Publishing Plc

First published in Great Britain 2021

A catalogue record for this book is available from the British Library.

Library of Congress Cataloging-in-Publication data

Names: Grisel, Florian, 1982- author.

Title: The limits of private governance : norms and rules in a Mediterranean fishery / Florian Grisel.

Description: Oxford ; New York : Hart, 2021.   |   Includes bibliographical references and index.

Identifiers: LCCN 2021025981 (print)   |   LCCN 2021025982 (ebook)   |
ISBN 9781509938148 (hardback)   |   ISBN 9781509953981 (paperback)   |
ISBN 9781509938155 (pdf)   |   ISBN 9781509938155 (ePDF)   |   ISBN 9781509938162 (EPub)

Subjects: LCSH: Fishery law and legislation—France—Mediterranean Coast—History.   |
Fish trade—Law and legislation—France—Marseille Region—History.   |
Trade associations—Law and legislation—France—Marseille Region—History.

Classification: LCC KJV5822 .G75 2021 (print)   |   LCC KJV5822 (ebook)   |   DDC 343.449/1207692—dc23

LC record available at https://lccn.loc.gov/2021025981

LC ebook record available at https://lccn.loc.gov/2021025982

ISBN:   HB:        978-1-50993-814-8
        ePDF:      978-1-50993-815-5
        ePub:      978-1-50993-816-2

Typeset by Compuscript Ltd, Shannon

*A mon filleul Côme*

# PREFACE

My peregrinations in the field of private governance began with an interest in the evolution of international arbitration. Over the years, I have become increasingly fascinated by self-governance and its wide-ranging consequences for the study of law.

The case study that I present in this book came my way by chance, as I was strolling along the port of Cassis with Alec Stone Sweet back in 2014 and happened upon an old building with the following words engraved above the door: *Tribunal de Pêche* (Fishing Tribunal). The discovery of rich archives pertaining to an even more ancient institution located in Marseille, the *Prud'homie de Pêche*, further convinced me to undertake this project.

I was fortunate to obtain a grant from the *Agence Nationale de la Recherche* (Grant No ANR-16-CE26-0012-01), which allowed me to travel to Marseille on a regular basis. The ANR grant also enabled me to hire a team of graduates of the *Ecole nationale des Chartes*, who helped with the review and translation of medieval archives. I am very thankful for their assistance and great work.

The massive amount of empirical material upon which this book is based was gleaned from various sources over a period of six years. Due to the generosity of Thomas and Aude Eisinger, I found a second home in Marseille, from which I was able to carry out ethnographic research, conduct a large range of interviews and consult the rich archival records of the *Prud'homie*. This book would never have come into being without their friendship.

Another friend, Maxime Riché, was by my side as I explored the fishery of Marseille. I thank him for his artistic skills, displayed on the cover of this book, and for his help.

My research owes a great deal to numerous institutions, colleagues and friends who have shown unfaltering support over the past few years. I owe special thanks to those who have offered useful suggestions and help at different stages of the project: Jérôme Baudry, Robert Ellickson, Daniel Faget, Jean-Louis Halpérin, Azélina Jaboulet Vercherre, Chad Jorgenson, Madhav Khosla, David Nelken, Thibaud Marcesse, Catherine Minahan, Lauriane Mouysset, Linda Mulcahy, Fernanda Pirie, Mikaël Schinazi, Thomas Schultz, Esmé Shirlow, Alec Stone Sweet, Elisabeth Tempier, Jorge Vinuales, Patrick Weil and Luping Zhang. Thank you.

Some of the material presented in chapter 3 led to publication in *Fish & Fisheries* ('Managing the Fishery Commons at Marseille: How a Medieval Institution Failed at Accommodating Changes in an Age of Globalisation') and the *Law & Society Review* ('How Migrations Affect Private Orders: Norms and Practices in the Fishery of Marseille').

My interviewees have offered me fascinating insights into the daily life of fishers. I have learned so much from my discussions with them, and they have helped me discover a trade that I have come to admire. Antoine Ciccarelli, his wife Marie and their daughter Babeth have been particularly gracious with their time and assistance. The story of Antoine's life is a true inspiration. I am thankful that he accepted to appear on the front cover of this book. His fight against the sea is an apt metaphor for an old institution that has been struggling to fulfil its functions.

I was also able to rely on my academic institutions, the *Centre national de la recherche scientifique*, King's College London and Oxford University (Centre for Socio-Legal Studies), throughout the project. I am grateful for their unfaltering support.

My wife Nicole has been my anchor throughout this project. Her love and patience gave me the strength to write this third book.

Last but not least, my editor at Hart Publishing, Roberta Bassi, has been incredibly supportive. Her open-mindedness and confidence in the project have been both a relief and a delight.

# CONTENTS

PART III
COLLAPSE

# PART I

## Genesis

# 1

## Social Order in the Fishery of Marseille

## I. Introduction

In November 1622, Louis XIII planned a visit to the city of Marseille. His goal was to reaffirm the ties between Marseille and the Kingdom of France, and to dissuade the city from seeking political autonomy from the royal state.[1] A fervent hunter and weapons master, Louis XIII allocated time in his busy schedule to fish tuna in the natural harbour of Morgiou, located in the south-east of Marseille. Since 1452, Morgiou had been the property of the fishers of Marseille, who elected their representatives, raised taxes and exercised their own jurisdiction over the disputes that invariably arose in their fishery. In other words, Morgiou was part of an enclave of private governance within the Kingdom of France.

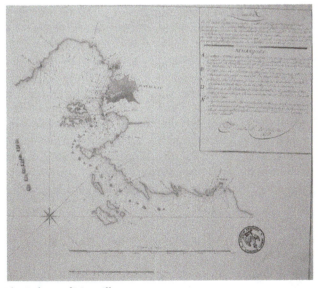

**Figure 1.1** The Fishery of Marseille

*Source*: Archives nationales (France), Cartes et Plans, G212 no 51 (20 October 1812). Morgiou is located on the right side of the map, near Cassis.

---

[1] MC Canova-Green, 'L'entrée de Louis XIII dans Marseille le 7 novembre 1622' (2001) 212 *Dix-septième Siècle* 521, 522.

The king's visit was critical for the fishers of Marseille, who were hoping that Louis XIII would confirm the rights and privileges that they had accrued since the Middle Ages. According to legend, the fishers dug stairs into the stone of the cliffs surrounding Morgiou in order to enable Louis XIII to descend safely to the beach. Four hundred years later, curious visitors can still see remnants of these 'stairs of Louis XIII' in Morgiou.

The fishing party took place on 8 November 1622, in a special tuna trap called a 'madrague', a source of immense pride for the local fishers. The *madrague* was the latest fishing technique originating from Spain, which could catch up to 1,000 tuna and had just been installed in Morgiou. Archival documents report that Louis XIII killed more than 25 tuna with a golden trident and that he 'had never seen anything that pleased him so much during his trip'.[2] It was not long before Louis XIII expressed his satisfaction through concrete acts. On 30 November 1622, around three weeks after the fishing party, the king confirmed all of the rights and privileges that the fishers of Marseille enjoyed over a vast territory encompassing more than 20 miles of coastline.[3] These rights included the opportunity to elect their own representatives in the *Prud'homie de Pêche* (or simply the *Prud'homie*), an organisation that exercised broad powers over the regulation of the fishery, its policing and the settlement of disputes among fishers.

Fast-forwarding 400 years to the present day, the *Prud'homie* still exists and is still endowed with similar powers. This, in itself, represents a remarkable story of private governance and institutional survival. The truth is, however, that it has survived in name alone: the *Prud'homie* rarely, if ever, uses any of the powers that it has accrued over the centuries. Today, it is an empty shell that fishers cherish as a symbol of their past glory. Morgiou also still exists: it remains the same amazingly beautiful harbour where Louis XIII fished for tuna in the seventeenth century. However, bluefin tuna have almost entirely disappeared from the area and Morgiou has been incorporated into a natural park, where fishing activities are strictly regulated. This book tells the story of the *Prud'homie*, a private order that had successfully operated for centuries before entering into decline. In other words, it is the story of the life and death of a system of private governance. Before telling this story, however, I will first present the theory of private governance and explain why the case of the *Prud'homie* matters in this context.

## II. The Rise of Private Orders

Over the past few decades, an emerging stream of scholarship has developed a theory of so-called 'private orders' (also known as systems of 'private governance'

---

[2] M Lapierre, *Les Prud'hommes Pêcheurs Marseillais* (Aix-en-Provence, F Chauvet, 1938) 38.
[3] Decision of the Council of the State (30 November 1622), MA HH370.

or 'private legal systems'). These private orders are usually defined as systems that promote long-term cooperation among individuals on the basis of social norms.

The emergence of this field of scholarship has not come as a surprise to sociologists, who have traditionally paid attention to the norms that are frequently emerging in human societies. One pillar of legal sociology is that state law does not exhaust the wide range of mechanisms regulating social life and that legal rules must consequently be read in conjunction with social norms. The fathers of sociology, Emile Durkheim and Max Weber, converge in their analysis of why legal relations cannot be studied independently from social norms.[4] One of the first scholars to examine the relevance of social norms in the context of a sophisticated legal system was Stewart Macaulay, who identified the importance of non-contractual norms in the operation of businesses based in Wisconsin.[5] Sally Falk Moore, for her part, aptly captured the complex interactions between social and legal norms using the term 'semi-autonomous social field'.[6] Through the study of 'legal pluralism', socio-legal studies have further analysed how different forms of normativity coexist and intermingle in society.[7] The term 'private ordering' itself was used for the first time by a prominent socio-legal scholar, Marc Galanter, who noted the need to explore what he calls 'indigenous law', that is, a set of norms that develop outside of state law.[8] However, socio-legal scholars (also called 'law and society' scholars) have not attempted to theorise an object with which they have always been very familiar. Efforts to provide a theoretical framework for the study of 'private orders' have instead originated from another branch of legal scholarship called 'law and economics'.[9] Unlike socio-legal scholars, scholars of law and economics traditionally paid little attention to the emergence of norms beyond

---

[4] See, eg, E Durkheim, *The Division of Labor in Society* (Chicago, IL, The Free Press of Glencoe, 1960) 211; M Weber, *Economy and Society: An Outline of Interpretive Sociology* (Berkeley, CA, University of California Press, 1978) 311, 312.

[5] S Macaulay, 'Non-Contractual Relations in Business: A Preliminary Study' (1963) 28 *American Sociological Review* 55.

[6] SF Moore, 'Law and Social Change: The Semi-Autonomous Social Field as an Appropriate Subject of Study' (1973) 7/4 *Law & Society Review* 719, 720. See also J Fishburne Collier, *Law and Social Change in Zinacantan* (Stanford, CA, Stanford University Press, 1973) (showing the coexistence of various normative levels for the resolution of disputes in Zinacantan).

[7] See, eg, SE Merry, 'Legal Pluralism' (1988) 22/5 *Law & Society Review* 869; BZ Tamanaha, 'Understanding Legal Pluralism: Past to Present, Local to Global' (2007) 29 *Sydney Law Review* 375; PS Bermann, 'The New Legal Pluralism' (2009) 5 *Annual Review of Law and Social Science* 225.

[8] M Galanter, 'Justice in Many Rooms: Courts, Private Ordering, and Indigenous Law' (1981) 19 *Journal of Legal Pluralism* 1. The term 'private ordering' appears to have been coined by MA Eisenberg, 'Private Ordering Through Negotiation: Dispute-Settlement and Rulemaking' (1976) 89 *Harvard Law Review* 637. This term echoes the analysis of 'spontaneous orders' suggested by Friedrich Hayek in order to capture the ways in which certain social systems achieve self-regulation without interference from 'organisations' (see FA Hayek, *On Law, Legislation and Liberty: Rules and Order*, vol 1 (London, Routledge, 1982) 41–52).

[9] See M Granovetter, *Society and Economy: Framework and Principles* (Cambridge, MA, Harvard University Press, 2017) 39.

the state, at least until a few academic pioneers elaborated an analytical frame-work for the study of these norms. I will retrace the efforts of law and economics scholars (among others) to analyse the mechanisms of private governance, before examining the building blocks upon which they have based their theory.

## A. The Pioneers of Private Ordering: Two Main Strands of Scholarship

One of the first and most important pioneers of the theory of private ordering is Robert Ellickson. In his important book *Order without Law*, Ellickson offers a broad and enlightening analysis of the ways in which ranchers in Shasta County, California regulate the issues arising from cattle trespassing.[10] His findings are at once straightforward and highly consequential: while lawyers usually consider legal rules to be the reference point for the settlement of disputes, Ellickson shows how Shasta County ranchers rely on social norms to resolve disputes arising from cattle trespassing. The key reason proposed by Ellickson is the following: because transaction costs are too high for ranchers to identify and rely on the law, they prefer instead to turn towards social norms of cooperation and reciprocity (what he calls the 'live-and-let-live' philosophy) in order to regulate their interactions. Based on this case study, Ellickson introduces what he calls a 'hypothesis of welfare maximizing norms', according to which 'members of a close-knit group develop and maintain norms whose content serves to maximize the aggregate welfare that members obtain in their workaday affairs with one another'.[11] In a separate article, Ellickson presents similar findings in relation to New England whalers, who relied on three main norms ('Fast-fish, loose-fish', 'Iron-holds-the-whale' and 'Split ownership') to regulate whaling in the nineteenth century.[12] In another book, Ellickson observes yet again how 'households' can achieve 'welfare maxi-mization' through social norms.[13] Ellickson's scholarship has come to represent a reference point for the literature on private governance. His plea for social norms has inspired numerous scholars and encouraged them to look more closely at the inner workings of societies when assessing the strength of legal mechanisms.

---

[10] RC Ellickson, *Order without Law: How Neighbors Settle Disputes* (Cambridge, MA, Harvard University Press, 1991).

[11] ibid 167.

[12] RC Ellickson, 'A Hypothesis of Wealth-Maximizing Norms: Evidence from the Whaling Industry' (1989) 5 *Journal of Law, Economics, and Organization* 83, 84: 'This essay advances the hypothesis that when people are situated in a close-knit group, they will tend to develop for the ordinary run of prob-lems norms that are wealth-maximizing.'

[13] RC Ellickson, *The Household: Informal Order Around the Hearth* (Princeton, NJ, Princeton University Press, 2007) 94: 'An implicit utilitarian pact of this sort promises to enhance shareable surplus. By embracing the Kaldor-Hicks calculus, participants will not only incline toward adopting rules that minimize deadweight losses, but also succeed in simplifying their decision-making process.'

Another important study of private ordering has reached similar conclusions, on the basis of a study of diamond traders. In an important article, Lisa Bernstein analyses the organisation of the diamond trade in New York City.[14] She argues that diamond traders rely on the mechanisms offered by their private club (the Diamond Dealers Club) to govern what she calls 'extralegal' contracts. These traders rarely, if ever, turn to the 'official' legal system when making contracts and settling their disputes. Bernstein identifies the taste for secrecy among diamond traders and the inadequacy of the damages awarded in the official legal system as key reasons for their preference for 'extralegal' contracts.[15] Although her analysis is less focused on social norms than that of Ellickson, Bernstein notes that social norms must be 'Pareto superior to the established legal regime' in order to survive.[16] In other words, both Ellickson and Bernstein seem to consider that social norms prevail over the existing legal system and persist over time if and when they are more 'efficient' than the law. Bernstein has extended her analysis to other systems of private governance, such as those found in the cotton industry.[17] She claims, in particular, that the 'private legal system' in this industry creates 'important benefits' that 'improve on aspects of the public legal system' (by providing, for instance, efficient procedural rules and substantive rules to facilitate contracting).[18] In line with Ellickson's findings, she emphasises how this system of private governance can 'maximize the value of transactors' legally enforceable and legally unenforceable commitments'.[19]

Other scholars active in the law and economics tradition have arrived at similar conclusions. In *Private Governance*, Edward Stringham emphasises the 'superb' track record of private orders on the basis of several case studies.[20] In *Stateless Commerce*, Barak Richman tracks the worldwide evolution of the diamond industry, drawing on his study of diamond traders in New York, Indian merchants and the integration of the diamond business by DeBeers.[21] On this basis, Richman revisits Bernstein's conclusions through the lens of transaction-cost economics and offers a 'positive theory of private ordering'.[22] He suggests that 'private ordering is comparatively superior to both firms and public courts' in circumstances where 'difficult to enforce' transactions are sensitive to 'high-powered incentives' and do not suffer from high entry barriers.[23] Richman's study

---

[14] L Bernstein, 'Opting out of the Legal System: Extralegal Contractual Relations in the Diamond Industry' (1992) 21 *The Journal of Legal Studies* 115.

[15] ibid 134 et seq.

[16] ibid 117.

[17] See L Bernstein, 'Private Commercial Law in the Cotton Industry: Creating Cooperation through Rules, Norms, and Institutions' (2001) 99 *Michigan Law Review* 1724.

[18] ibid 1739–44.

[19] ibid 1761.

[20] EP Stringham, *Private Governance: Creating Order in Economic and Social Life* (Oxford, Oxford University Press, 2015).

[21] BD Richman, *Stateless Commerce: The Diamond Network and the Persistence of Relational Exchange* (Cambridge, MA, Harvard University Press, 2017).

[22] ibid 75.

[23] ibid.

can be considered the culmination of the theory of private governance and the most recent product of 30 years of scholarship on the subject.

Law and economics scholars are not alone in their analysis of private governance. At approximately the same time as Ellickson and Bernstein (and without any apparent contacts with them), a second strand of scholarship emerged and reached similar conclusions, this time at the intersection of political science and economics. In *Governing the Commons*, Elinor Ostrom identifies several case studies of 'long-enduring, self-organized, and self-governed common-pool resources' that preserve shared resources and ensure 'long-term economic viability'.[24] Drawing on similarities among these case studies, she distinguishes a set of eight design principles that characterise these 'common pool resources',[25] arguing that these institutional arrangements offer a credible alternative to the state and the market by building 'collective-choice arrangements' that rely on long-term cooperation between social actors. Although she does not place the role of social norms at the centre of her analysis, Ostrom still mentions the 'strong norms of acceptable behavior' that often emerge in these 'common pool resources'.[26] Ostrom became the first female laureate of the Nobel Prize in Economics in 2009, a sign of the broad influence of her scholarship.[27] Although law and economics scholars rarely refer to Ostrom's writings in their discussions of private governance,[28] these two strands of scholarship overlap not only in their conclusions but also in their theoretical background.[29]

In short, the theory of private governance is rooted in the work of various authors whose analysis of different social groups crystallised around the same time period (the first half of the 1990s). The success of this theory has inspired

---

[24] E Ostrom, *Governing the Commons: The Evolution of Institutions for Collective Action* (Cambridge, Cambridge University Press, 1990) 1: 'What one can observe in the world, however, is that neither the state nor the market is uniformly successful in enabling individuals to sustain long-term, productive use of natural resource systems. Further, communities of individuals have relied on institutions resembling neither the state nor the market to govern some resource systems with reasonable degrees of success over long period of time.' ibid 60: 'What one can observe in the world, however, is that neither the state nor the market is uniformly successful in enabling individuals to sustain long-term, productive use of natural resource systems. Further, communities of individuals have relied on institutions resembling neither the state nor the market to govern some resource systems with reasonable degrees of success over long period of time.'

[25] ibid 88 et seq.

[26] ibid 206.

[27] Ostrom has further developed and refined her conclusions following the publication of *Governing the Commons*, see, eg, E Ostrom, R Gardner and J Walker, *Rules, Games, and Common-Pool Resources* (Ann Arbor, MI, University of Michigan Press, 1994); E Ostrom, *Understanding institutional diversity* (Princeton, NJ, Princeton University Press, 2005).

[28] See, however, RC Ellickson, 'Property in Land' (1993) 102 *The Yale Law Journal* 1314, 1391; ZCM Arnold, 'Against the Tide: Connecticut Oystering, Hybrid Property, and the Survival of the Commons' (2015) 124 *The Yale Law Journal* 1206, 1214–15.

[29] It has been suggested that scholars of private ordering applied 'the ideas underlying *Governing the Commons* to the study of the law'. See E Berge and F van Laervohen, '*Governing the Commons* for two decades: a complex story' (2011) 5 *International Journal of the Commons* 160, 170. See also C Rose, 'The impact of *Governing the Commons* on the American legal academy' (2011) 5 *International Journal of the Commons* 28, 30–31.

a number of scholars, who have noted the existence of private orders in a range of communities, including lobster fishers in Maine,[30] traders in Mexican California,[31] rating agencies,[32] international commercial arbitration[33] and even organised crime.[34] Contemporary scholarship continues to be deeply influenced by the hypothesis of 'welfare maximisation' or 'long-term economic viability'. For instance, in a special issue on private governance published in 2015, the *Journal of Legal Analysis* published several contributions on the subject, none of which challenged this hypothesis.[35] Similarly, in a recent volume on the local management of the commons, only one contribution (out of 23 in total) explores the possibility of failure.[36]

## B.  The Building Blocks of Private Governance

As noted, the two strands of scholarship on private ordering have developed without any apparent coordination, yet they base their analyses of the various communities at the focus of their studies on a shared theoretical framework. This theoretical framework draws its roots from game theory, and specifically from the most famous game of all – the prisoner's dilemma. Albert Tucker, John Nash's doctoral supervisor, introduced the prisoner's dilemma in order to illustrate the 'Nash equilibrium' in simple terms.[37] According to this illustration, two prisoners who are arrested at a crime scene denounce each other to the police in order to maximise their individual payoffs (by minimising their respective jail time), even though they could have maximised their collective payoff by cooperating (ie by remaining silent). The prisoner's dilemma highlights a discrepancy between individual interest and social good: it suggests that, contrary to a common assumption in economic theory, the interaction between self-interested individuals does not always lead to optimal outcomes.

---

[30] See JM Acheson, *The Lobster Gangs of Maine* (Lebanon, NH, University Press of New England, 1988); JM Acheson, *Capturing the Commons* (Lebanon, NH, University Press of New England, 2003).

[31] See K Clay, 'Trade Without Law: Private-Order Institutions in Mexican California' (1997) 13 *Journal of Law, Economics, and Organization* 202.

[32] See SL Schwarcz, 'Private Ordering of Public Markets: The Rating Agency Paradox' (2002) 1 *University of Illinois Law Review* 1.

[33] CR Drahozal, 'Private Ordering and International Commercial Arbitration' (2008-2009) 113 *Penn State Law Review* 1031.

[34] D Skarbek, 'Governance and Prison Gangs' (2011) 105 *The American Political Science Review* 702; CJ Milhaupt and MD West, 'The Dark Side of Private Ordering: An Institutional and Empirical Analysis of Organized Crime' (2000) 67 *University of Chicago Law Review* 41.

[35] See the contributions in (2015) 7 *Journal of Legal Analysis* 247.

[36] See M De Keyzer, 'Common challenges, different fates. The causal factors of failure or success in the commons: The pre-modern Brecklands (England) and the Campine (Southern Low Countries) compared' in T Haller, T Breu, T de Moor, C Rohr and Z Heinzpeter (eds), *The Commons in a Glocal World: Global Connections and Local Responses* (Abingdon, Routledge, 2019).

[37] See R Leonard, *Von Neumann, Morgenstern, and the Creation of Game Theory* (Cambridge, Cambridge University Press, 2010) 320. See also J Nash, 'Non-cooperative games' (1951) 54 *Annal of Mathematics* 286.

Pioneers of private ordering have explicitly relied on game theory and the prisoner's dilemma in their studies of social norms. Ellickson, for instance, bases his study of Shasta County ranchers on the prisoner's dilemma and the rational-actor model adopted by game theorists, while acknowledging some of its limitations.[38] He praises game theory as 'the main vehicle for the investigation of cooperation',[39] arguing elsewhere that 'the tortoise of game theory may win the race to provide a paradigm that captures the essentials of social life'.[40] Similarly, Ostrom revisits through the lens of the prisoner's dilemma the metaphor famously introduced by Garrett Hardin, in which rational herdsmen increase the number of animals grazing in a given field (the so-called 'tragedy of the commons').[41] Both Bernstein and Richman also rely on the prisoner's dilemma in their respective studies.[42]

An attentive reader might wonder how the prisoner's dilemma, a classic example of non-cooperation, can be invoked in support of scholarship that highlights cooperation based on social norms as an effective tool of governance. In fact, a closer analysis reveals that the pioneers of private ordering rely on a more sophisticated version of the prisoner's dilemma, focused on long-term rather than one-off interactions. Some scholars, most prominently Robert Axelrod, have explored how repeated games favour the emergence of cooperation.[43] In particular, Axelrod tested by means of computer-based tournaments which strategies of repeated games produce the best social outcomes.[44] Axelrod's computer-based tournaments revealed the superiority of a single cooperative strategy called 'tit for tat', summarily defined as the 'strategy of starting with cooperation and thereafter doing what the other player did on the previous move'.[45] Ellickson, Ostrom and Bernstein all rely on Axelrod's analysis of the 'tit-for-tat' strategy in support of their argument that individuals can successfully achieve long-term cooperation, while still pursuing their own interests.[46]

Not only does this conclusion reconcile individual self-interest and social cooperation, it also resolves another issue raised by the prisoner's dilemma, namely that individual interactions lead to sub-optimal social outcomes. I will explain in further detail in section III.A how a theory of repeated interactions

---

[38] Ellickson (n 10) ch 9.

[39] ibid 9.

[40] RC Ellickson, 'Law and Economics Discovers Social Norms' (1998) 27 *The Journal of Legal Studies* 537, 547.

[41] Ostrom (n 24) 3–5; G Hardin, 'The Tragedy of the Commons' (1968) 162 *Science* 1243, 1244. It should be noted that although her initial findings are based on a classic version of rational choice, Ostrom later acknowledged some limitations of rational choice theory. See A Lara, 'Rationality and complexity in the work of Elinor Ostrom' (2015) 9/2 *International Journal of the Commons* 573, 574. See also E Ostrom, 'A Behavioral Approach to the Rational Choice Theory of Collective Action' (1998) 92 *The American Political Science Review* 1; E Ostrom, 'Collective Action and the Evolution of Social Norms' (2000) 14 *The Journal of Economic Perspectives* 137.

[42] See, eg Bernstein (n 14) 142; Richman (n 21) 44.

[43] R Axelrod, *The Evolution of Co-operation* (New York, Penguin Books, 1990) 12.

[44] ibid ch 2.

[45] ibid xii.

[46] Bernstein (n 14) 142; Bernstein (n 17) 1771; Ellickson (n 10), 159–62; Ostrom (n 24) 7, 36, 93.

supports this conclusion. What matters here for the purposes of this introduction is that pioneers of private ordering have followed the lead of game theorists, such as Axelrod, in exploring a new type of governance model, in which individuals establish and maintain cooperation through repeated interactions. Of significance is also the fact that, in line with Axelrod's findings, the pioneers of private ordering argue that this model of governance based on norms is socially efficient or – on a more daring version of the same theory – optimal especially when compared with the law.

Most scholars adopt the first position, according to which private governance is socially *efficient*. Bernstein, for instance, highlights the 'Pareto superior' character of private regimes.[47] Ostrom argues that common-pool resources make efficient use of natural resources, leading to 'long-term economic viability'.[48] She further contends that private orders can offer an 'alternative solution' to the state and the unregulated market.[49] More recently, Stringham provides a similarly nuanced and optimistic account of private orders, arguing that '[p]rivate governance ... brings people to cooperate and to expand the scope of mutually beneficial exchange'.[50] A minority of scholars go further, leaning towards the second position, according to which private governance is socially *optimal*. Ellickson, for instance, speaks of the 'welfare-maximizing' character of the norms implemented in private orders.[51] Richman offers a similar analysis, claiming that 'private ordering is comparatively superior to both firms and public courts' under specific conditions.[52] All of these authors consider that private orders produce and sustain conditions that are beneficial to socio-economic life.[53] This is in fact a key finding of the literature on private governance and a fundamental reason for its success.

## C. Challenges

Scholarship on private governance has enjoyed widespread influence and success, earning Ostrom a Nobel Prize in Economics and spawning a flurry

---

[47] Bernstein (n 14) 117.

[48] Ostrom (n 24). Ostrom 'do[es] not hesitate to call these CPR institutions successful' (ibid 59–60), which she defines as follows: '[b]y "successful," I mean institutions that enable individuals to achieve productive outcomes in situations where temptations to free-ride and shirk are ever present' (ibid 15). She also contrasts the state and the market as being unsuccessful 'in enabling individuals to sustain long-term, productive use of natural resource systems' with CPRs that 'govern some resource systems with reasonable degrees of success over long periods of time'.

[49] Ostrom (n 24) 8–21.

[50] Stringham (n 20) 235.

[51] Ellickson (n 10) ch 10; Ellickson (n 12); Ellickson (n 13) ch 8.

[52] Richman (n 21) 76.

[53] This view is widely shared in the literature. See, eg, A Greif, *Institutions and the Path to the Modern Economy: Lessons from Medieval Trade* (Cambridge, Cambridge University Press, 2006) 87–88; Clay (n 31) 226; JT Landa, 'A Theory of the Ethnically Homogeneous Middleman Group: An Institutional Alternative to Contract Law' (1981) 10 *The Journal of Legal Studies* 349, 362.

of subsequent writings.[54] However, despite this overall success, three broad categories of criticisms have been voiced concerning this approach. In the first category, we find scholars who criticise the methodology used by the existing literature. These scholars specifically accuse this literature of focusing on success stories that unfold over limited time periods. For instance, Granovetter notes a 'selection bias' privileging 'theory-confirming case studies' over 'theory-infirming case studies' that lies at the origins of this theory.[55] Aviram notes the 'static' character of the literature and the need for an 'evolutionary theory' of private orders.[56] In the same vein, Agrawal criticises the 'limited historical scope of most studies of the commons'.[57] In short, these scholars challenge the literature on private governance on the grounds that it focuses exclusively on successful, short-term case studies.[58] A second group of scholars endorse a moral critique of the theory of private governance, pointing out the harmful effects of private orders in terms of discriminations, violence and criminal behaviour.[59] Others argue that private orders often conflict with 'individual freedom and autonomy'[60] and threaten the democratic ideals of 'transparency, predictability, and accountability'.[61] The third category of criticisms reflects a more theoretical outlook, contending that the game theoretic foundations of private governance over-simplify human behaviour by assuming that individuals act rationally.[62] When individuals maximise their self-interest, according

---

[54] The terms 'private order' and 'private ordering' respectively generate 5,330 and 21,100 hits on Google Scholar (last accessed 6 January 2020).

[55] Granovetter (n 9) 39. This critique was specifically addressed at *Order without Law*. It should be noted that Ostrom did consider the possibility of institutional failure. See Ostrom (n 24) ch 5. The notions of 'theory-infirming case studies' and 'theory-confirming case studies' are borrowed from A Lijphart, 'Comparative Politics and the Comparative Method' (1971) 65 *The American Political Science Review* 682.

[56] A Aviram, 'Forces Shaping the Evolution of Private Legal Systems' in P Zumbansen and GP Calliess (eds), *Law, Economics and Evolutionary Theory* (Cheltenham, Edward Elgar Publishing, 2011).

[57] A Agrawal, 'Sustainable Governance of Common Resources: Context, Method, and Politics' (2003) 32 *Annual Review of Anthropology* 253, 259.

[58] See, however, Greif (n 21) 176–78; T de Moor, *The Dilemma of the Commoners: Understanding the Use of Common-Pool Resources in Long-Term Perspectives* (Cambridge, Cambridge University Press, 2015) chs 3 and 4. Greif has been criticised for his selective use of historical records. See, eg, JL Goldberg, *Trade and Institutions in the Medieval Mediterranean: The Geniza Merchants and their Business World* (Cambridge, Cambridge University Press, 2012) (arguing that Greif's theory is 'untenable' on the basis that Geniza merchants trusted individuals outside of their close-knit group and used the 'legal system to circumscribe business relationships and resolve disputes'). Other authors have defended Greif's conclusions. See, eg, L Bernstein, 'Contract Governance in Small-World Networks: The Case of the Maghribi Traders' (2019) 113 *Northwestern University Law Review* 1009. See also A Greif, 'The Maghribi Traders: A Reappraisal?' (2012) 65 *The Economic History Review* 445.

[59] Milhaupt and West (n 34); J McMillan and C Woodruff, 'Private Order under Dysfunctional Public Order' (2000) 98 *Michigan Law Review* 2421.

[60] T Sagy, 'What's So Private about Private Ordering?' (2001) 45 *Law & Society Review* 923.

[61] ED Katz, 'Private Order and Public Institutions' (2000) 98 *Michigan Law Review* 2481, 2491.

[62] S Sassen, *Territory. Authority. Rights: From Medieval to Global Assemblages* (Princeton, NJ, Princeton University Press, 2006) 14. This limitation was noted at the outset of von Neumann's efforts to model games. In 1938, Emile Borel, a prominent mathematician, described von Neumann's attempt to analyse game strategies as 'absolutely insurmountable' owing to the large number of variables involved

to these critics, rational-choice theory says little about their deeper motives.[63] Yet other critics argue that the literature on private governance overlooks the influence of power structures within private orders and the ways in which these structures can influence cooperative behaviour.[64] In fact, few studies of private ordering have examined the influence exercised by community leaders on the functioning of private orders.[65] Most important for the purposes of this book is the fact that the literature usually conflates private orders in which individuals cooperate without formal entities (for instance, the ranchers of Shasta County[66]) with those in which formal entities emerge and govern these systems (for instance, the Diamond Dealers Club in New York[67]). In other words, the theory of private governance does not seem to fully account for the influence of organisations and strategic actors on the management of private orders. The concerns voiced by these critics have not eroded the popularity of the theory, but they do raise important questions that ought to be addressed.

## D. Methodology

The present book seeks to complement the existing scholarship by examining the long-term evolution of the *Prud'homie* on the basis of empirical evidence. The *Prud'homie* provides an ideal case study due to its rich historical records, which allow us to examine its emergence and evolution over the long term. Using the historical past as a source of empirical data presents some serious challenges, not

in these strategies. See Leonard (n 37) 72. Von Neumann and Morgenstern dismiss this objection in *Theory of Game and Economic Behavior*, noting that the 'manifold social influences' are unlikely to affect 'the formal properties of the process of maximizing'. See J von Neumann and O Morgenstern, *Theory of Games and Economic Behavior*, 3rd edn (Princeton, NJ, Princeton University Press, 1953) 9–10. The experiments run by the RAND Corporation in the 1950s further suggested the limited predictive value of game theory due to the 'contextual' nature of rationality. Thomas Schelling, one of the early critics of game theory and Nobel Prize laureate in 2005, wrote *The Strategy of Conflict* while visiting RAND in 1957 and 1958. Scholars of Law and Economics have later tried to supplement the neoclassical model of rational behaviour used by game theorists, see, eg. C Jolls, C Sunstein and R Thaler, 'A Behavioral Approach to Law and Economics' (1998) 50 *Stanford Law Review* 1471; TS Ulen, 'Rational Choice and the Economic Analysis of Law' (1994) 19 *Law & Social Inquiry* 487.

[63] LB Edelman, 'Rivers of Law and Contested Terrain: A Law and Society Approach to Economic Rationality' (2004) 38 *Law & Society Review* 181, 186. See also the response from L Epstein and J Knight, 'Building the Bridge from Both Sides of the River: Law and Society and Rational Choice' (2004) 38 *Law & Society Review* 207.

[64] Sagy (n 60). This critique concerns more generally the Law and Economics scholarship. See Edelman (n 63) 187.

[65] There are a few exceptions in the literature. For instance, Acheson highlights the role played by 'political entrepreneurs' in the management and conservation of lobster fisheries in Maine (Acheson (n 30) 72). Ellickson explores the key role played by individuals endowed with 'superior technical knowledge' in the emergence of social norms (RC Ellickson, 'The Market for Social Norms' (2001) 3/1 *American Law and Economics Review* 1; RC Ellickson, 'The Evolution of Social Norms: A Perspective from the Legal Academy' in M Hechter and KD Hopp (eds), *Social Norms* (New York, Russel Sage Foundation, 2001)).

[66] Ellickson (n 10).

[67] Bernstein (n 14).

least because a given institution constantly adapts to an evolving social context. In this regard, this book is mindful of the criticism of 'excessive ambition' levelled against empirical studies based on historical material.[68] In order to minimise these methodological challenges, this book makes use of empirical data that I have collected from a combination of three main sources: archival documents, interviews and ethnographic research. I have tried to mitigate issues of selective deposit and survival by triangulating over 2,500 archival documents from various sources: the archives of the local administration to which the *Prud'homie* donated its documents (*département des Bouches-du-Rhône*), the French national archives, the city archives of Marseille, the archives of the French navy, the archives of the Chamber of Commerce of Marseille and private archives. I have summarised and listed each of these documents in chronological order in an original table. In addition to examining this archival documentation, I conducted one or more interviews with fishers, individuals who belong to their community (spouses, fishmongers, the local priest, etc), members of the *Prud'homie* and governmental officers. Finally, I supplemented these data by building personal ties with fishers, attending social events in their community (particularly religious ones) and participating in several fishing trips. The data have allowed me to retrace the origins of the *Prud'homie* and to assess its evolution from different standpoints (both within and outside of the *Prud'homie*).

This research is also mindful of the drawbacks of the case-study method, to which the analysis of the *Prud'homie* is not immune. Each case study is unique and exhibits specificities that need to be accounted for in order to support general claims. As a consequence, individual case studies do not easily allow for universal generalisations, and a single case study cannot be used to disprove a general claim without corroboration from a meaningful number of other studies. Taking into account these methodological limits, this book uses the *Prud'homie* as a 'deviant case study' in order to highlight limitations in the general theory of private governance.[69] The goal is not to disprove the general theory, but rather to uncover variables that were not previously considered, to attempt to modify the theory and to open avenues for future research.

## III. The *Prud'homie*: A System of Private Governance?

The scholarship on private ordering is dense and difficult to summarise without falling into oversimplification. However, the main theoretical apparatus used for the analysis of private orders is based on rational choice, namely the utilitarian hypothesis according to which individuals choose institutional settings that

---

[68] J Elster, 'Rational Choice History: A Case of Excessive Ambition' (2000) 94 *American Political Science Review* 685.

[69] For a classification of case studies and a definition of 'deviant case studies', see Lijphart (n 55).

are 'comparatively good at the task'.[70] Building on rational-choice theory, most scholars of private ordering base their explanation of self-regulation on an iterated prisoner's dilemma game in which sub-optimal social outcomes in the first rounds of the game are corrected through repeated interactions.[71] In other words, the negative social outcomes derived from the prisoner's dilemma game are corrected when actors repeat the game in the long term. In this situation, social actors consciously choose to initiate and maintain social cooperation. As seen in section II.B, this argument is consistent with Axelrod's findings concerning the superiority of the 'tit-for-tat' strategy over other social strategies.

The theoretical model relied upon by scholars of private governance is correspondingly based on two broad conditions.[72] The first condition is that individuals have access to adequate information concerning the group to which they belong. Indeed, well-informed individuals can take action against recalcitrant members who refuse to abide by social norms. This condition is central, as private orders usually lack an organisation charged with disciplining recalcitrant members. As Ellickson explains, private orders usually operate through 'first-party' and 'second-party' control: individuals self-discipline themselves ('first-party control') or discipline their immediate counterparts ('second-party control'), but usually do not rely on an external organisation in order to punish group members ('third-party control').[73] The second condition is that social games are repeated indefinitely. Long-term interactions between social actors avoid the so-called 'end-game' problem in which these actors renege on their promise to cooperate when approaching the last round of the game.[74] What matters here is not, strictly speaking, the infinite iteration of the game (given that no social game is truly endless), but a shared belief that the game will be repeated indefinitely. In Ellickson's words, 'the expectation of continued dealings … tends to make participants more willing to invest resources into strengthening their relationship'.[75] Social scientists usually associate this condition with low discount rates: participants in a game that is repeated indefinitely tend to value future gains as much as or even more than immediate gains.[76] This condition is usually fulfilled when individuals expect

---

[70] RC Ellickson, 'When Civil Society Uses an Iron Fist: The Roles of Private Associations in Rulemaking and Adjudication' (2016) 18/2 *American Law and Economics Review* 235.

[71] See, eg, DC North, 'Institutions' (1991) 15 *The Journal of Economic Perspectives* 97; Axelrod (n 43) 130.

[72] Some authors have adopted a broader reading of these conditions. See Sagy (n 60) 928 (identifying five variables: a flat social structure, information networks, the presence of a lock-in situation, the legal culture of the group and the involvement of the public order).

[73] Ellickson (n 10) 131.

[74] Ostrom, 'Collective Action and the Evolution of Social Norms' (n 41) 139; North (n 71); Ellickson (n 13) 92–93.

[75] Ellickson (n 13) 29.

[76] For instance, Acheson notices the importance of low discount rates in the maintenance of cooperative behaviour among lobster fishers on the islands of Maine (Acheson (n 30) 13–14). Ostrom also argues how the clearly defined boundaries found in successful institutions are usually associated with low discount rates (Ostrom (n 24) 91).

their children to be part of the same community, thus guaranteeing an 'intergenerational closure' of social relations that renders collective sanctions and social incentives more tangible.[77]

This theoretical model is widely accepted within the literature on private governance.[78] Although these conditions are described as necessary but not sufficient for the operation and maintenance of private orders, the theory of private governance is predictive in the sense that it anticipates that rational actors will choose the most economically efficient and least costly governance option available to them.[79] One practical limitation on the theory of private governance is that both conditions are rarely met on the empirical level. In fact, very few groups present sufficient unity for their members to be able to sustain a shared belief that interactions will continue in the future.[80] Similarly, information rarely circulates without hindrance within a given social group. According to Ellickson, both conditions are more likely to be fulfilled in 'close-knit groups',[81] defined as 'social network[s] whose members have credible and reciprocal prospects for the application of power against one another and a good supply of information on past and present internal events'.[82] For her part, Bernstein speaks of a 'homogeneous group regime' characterised by 'geographical concentration, ethnic homogeneity, and repeat dealing'.[83] McMillan and Woodruff echo these authors, asserting that 'In close-knit communities, where people interact with each other frequently and information flows freely, people may adhere to social forms of cooperation because it is in their long-term interest to do so.'[84] Ostrom refuses to identify 'necessary conditions' but explains the 'persistence' of successful institutions by their conformance to eight 'design principles',[85] which largely overlap with the features of close-knit groups identified by Ellickson and Bernstein.[86]

In this context, the community of fishers in Marseille seems to fulfil the necessary conditions for the emergence of a private order, namely the existence of long-term interactions and perfect information. It is noteworthy, however, that the fishers of Marseille have not constructed a typical system of private governance. In fact, the emergence of a rather sophisticated organisation like the *Prud'homie*

---

[77] JS Coleman, 'Social Capital in the Creation of Human Capital' (1988) *American Journal of Sociology* S95, S106. On the notion of 'closure', see also JS Coleman, *Foundations of Social Theory* (Cambridge, MA, Harvard University Press, 1990) ch 12.

[78] See, eg, Richman (n 21) 44.

[79] Ellickson (n 10) 270.

[80] See WG Runciman and AK Sen, 'Games, Justice and the General Will' (1965) 74 *Mind* 554, 555, fn 1.

[81] Ellickson (n 10) 177.

[82] ibid 181. Other authors have argued that social norms can also emerge, albeit differently, in 'loose-knit' groups. See LJ Strahilevitz, 'Social Norms from Close-Knit Groups to Loose-Knit Groups' (2003) 70 *The University of Chicago Law Review* 359.

[83] Bernstein (n 14) 140.

[84] McMillan and Woodruff (n 59) 2422.

[85] Ostrom (n 24) 90–91.

[86] ibid 90. Most close-knit groups have clearly defined boundaries, tailor their rules to local conditions, create collective-choice arrangements, with a high level of monitoring, graduated sanctions and mechanisms of conflict resolution.

is unusual, since private orders should – if the predictive aspect of the literature holds – avoid generating formal structures and typically rely on first- and second-party control. I will describe in sections IIII.A and III.B how the community of fishers displays features that seem to fulfil both conditions, before highlighting in section III.C what I call the 'paradox of the *Prud'homie*'.

## A. Long-Term Relations

Pioneers of private governance theory have emphasised how members of close-knit communities expect to sustain their relations in the long term. Ostrom notes, for instance, that '[i]ndividuals have shared a past and expect to share a future' in these communities.[87] Family and intergenerational links are useful indicators in this regard: individuals who have multiple family members within a given group and expect their children to belong to the same group also expect to share a common future.[88]

The community of fishers in Marseille displays features that are entirely consistent with this analysis. In fact, this community has shown strong endogenous features throughout its history. Group members traditionally stem from a small number of families who have created true 'dynasties' of fishers. Consider, for instance, a survey of the community conducted by the *Prud'homie* in 1660.[89] This list of 181 individuals offers a snapshot of the community of fishers in the middle of the seventeenth century. Of these 181 individuals, 119 (almost 66 per cent of the community) had at least one other family member within the community.[90] Some prominent families had six (the Negrel family), seven (the Teissere family) or even nine members (the Lombardon and Fabron families). The data therefore suggest that a significant proportion of the fishers originated from the same families. In addition, the sons of fishers traditionally became fishers, while their daughters were expected to marry other fishers.[91] In the eighteenth century, the fishers of Marseille viewed individuals whom they called 'born fishers' (that is individuals who originated from families of fishers) more favourably.[92] Other historical studies corroborate my findings: Faget mentions the 'social and geographic immobilism' of the fishers of Marseille,[93] and Kaiser reports that almost 70 per cent of fishers' daughters married other fishers at the end of the sixteenth century.[94]

---

[87] ibid 88.

[88] BD Richman, 'How Community Institutions Create Economic Advantage: Jewish Diamond Merchants in New York' (2006) 31 *Law & Social Inquiry* 383, 403.

[89] Minutes of the *Prud'homie*'s Assembly (15 February 1660), in *Livre Rouge*, DA 250E4.

[90] I assumed that fishers sharing the same last names came from the same families.

[91] Outsiders who marry the daughters of fishers are sometime expected to become fishers themselves (as explained by an interviewee).

[92] Description des Pesches, Loix et Ordonnances des Pescheurs de la Ville de Marseille, DA 250E2, 10.

[93] D Faget, *Marseille et la mer: Hommes et environnement marin (XVIIIe-XXe siècle)* (Rennes, Presses universitaires de Rennes, 2011) 23.

[94] W Kaiser, *Marseille au Temps des Troubles: Morphologie sociale et luttes de factions (1559–1596)* (Paris, EHESS, 1991) 102.

The close-knit nature of the fishers' community appears to have persisted up until recently. Most of the fishers I met had succeeded their fathers, who had succeeded their own fathers. For instance, one of my interviewees is the descendant of seven generations of fishers, a lineage that I was able to trace all the way back to the eighteenth century. The intergenerational model remains the one that 'generates most prestige within the community' (in the words of an interviewee), even though the most recent generation tends to embrace other careers.[95] The community of fishers in Marseille therefore seems to have been strongly endogenous throughout its history, and members of this community traditionally consider their mutual relationships over the extreme long term.

## B.  Circulation of Information

In addition to being strongly endogenous, my data suggest that information circulates easily in the community of fishers. This circulation of information results from a combination of factors that makes the community of fishers a prime example of a 'multiplex' community in which different networks overlap.[96] These networks are professional, spatial, religious and familial.[97] The urban space has played a particularly important role in unifying the community of fishers. Most fishers dwell in 'St Jean', a small neighbourhood located on the northern side of the old port of Marseille (see Figure 1.2).

**Figure 1.2** The Old Port of Marseille and the St Jean Quarter

*Source*: Bibliothèque nationale de France (BNF Gallica), *Représentation de la très renommée et admirable ville et port de Marseille* (16th century).

---

[95] Only 38% of the fishers of Provence chose their career because of 'family transmission' in 2014 (CRPMEM PACA, *Etat des lieux et caractérisation de la pêche maritime professionnelle et des élevages marins en PACA*, 2015, 33), a figure that decreased to 32% in 2015 (CRPMEM PACA, *Etat des lieux et caractérisation de la pêche maritime professionnelle et des élevages marins en PACA*, 2016, 33).

[96] M Gluckman, *The Judicial Process among the Barotse of Northern Rhodesia (Zambia)* (Manchester, Manchester University Press, 1955) 19.

[97] F Grisel, 'How Migrations Affect Private Orders: Norms and Practices in the Fishery of Marseille' (2021) 55 *Law & Society Review* 177.

St Jean was composed of a maze of small and narrow streets until it was destroyed and rebuilt, with the *Prud'homie* standing in the centre.[98] Until the mid-twentieth century, this quarter grounded the community in an urban space that its members rarely left. Several streets bore the names of prominent fishers,[99] and one street was even named after the *Prud'homie* (*rue des Prud'hommes*).[100] Word travelled fast in this neighbourhood. In a letter dating from 1830, the *Prud'homie* describes St Jean as a place where 'everyone knows each other' and where 'one can easily gather a meeting in order to discuss an issue that undermines the public interest'.[101] Even today, the fishers know each other well and the use of nicknames among them is widespread.[102] They regularly meet in their own parish, the St Laurent church overlooking the port of Marseille, to observe the multiple religious celebrations that punctuate the life of the community.[103] Fishers are still deeply religious, even 'superstitious' according to the current priest of St Laurent, and they actively participate in these religious celebrations (albeit to a lesser extent in recent times). Their community is essentially male (I have heard of only a single female fisher), but the important role played by women in structuring their network cannot be overlooked. 'When you see a fisher, his wife is never far', one of my interviewees stated. In the familial model that they still perpetuate, fishers heavily rely on their wives to sell the catch. The women fishmongers aggregate each day in the old port of Marseille to sell fish, while chatting among themselves. The scenery of the 'fishmongers of the old port' has become one of the strongest cultural symbols of Marseille and of an ancestral community united by multiplex ties.

## C. The Paradox of the *Prud'homie*

What has been said so far suggests that the conditions for the successful operation of private governance are to be fulfilled in the community of fishers. Because the fishers benefit from a close-knit community, a rational-choice analysis predicts that they should develop a system of private governance based on social norms. In Ellickson's words, 'Under these conditions [perfect information and long-term interactions], members see little advantage in creating a formally structured organization.'[104]

This prediction has partially come true. In fact, my empirical findings point towards the persistence of two overarching norms in the fishery of Marseille.

---

[98] On the destruction of St Jean, see ch 6.
[99] See A Bouyala d'Arnaud, *Evocations du Vieux Marseille* (Paris, Les Editions de Minuit, 1959) 160, 164.
[100] ibid 92.
[101] Lettre de la Prud'homie aux Prud'hommes de St Nazaire (7 December 1830), DA 250E126.
[102] A former *Prud'homme* told me that a former secretary of the *Prud'homie* had consigned all the fishers' nicknames in a small notebook. He added that the same nicknames are often passed from father to son.
[103] See A Sportiello, *Les pêcheurs du Vieux-Port: fêtes et traditions* (Marseille, Jeanne Laffitte, 1981).
[104] Ellickson (n 70) section 4.4.

When reviewing archives, interviewing fishers or simply strolling around the port of Marseille, I was struck by the speed with which the topic of discussion shifts towards the community's 'old principles'.[105] These norms are rarely transcribed or precisely defined, but their importance transpires through the empirical record. Most importantly, the fishers of Marseille cherish the values of equality and fairness. They share a belief that all members of their community are equal and must act in ways that are compatible with the activities of other fishers. In accordance with this norm, they constantly attempt to accommodate their respective practices, as well as to ensure that every single member of the community can earn a living from the fishery. This norm exhibits some similarities with the 'live-and-let-live' norm that Ellickson observed in Shasta County. This norm is intrinsically individualistic and permissive as it aims to accommodate the needs and preferences of individual fishers. The fishers have developed a fierce tradition of egalitarianism in ways that are entirely consistent with Scott's account of 'extrastate' spaces in South East Asia.[106] However, their norm of equality coexists with an essentially communal and prohibitive norm that I call the norm of 'preservation'. According to this norm, fishers in Marseille believe in the necessity to preserve their fishery in the long term. They try to avoid overfishing and minimise the impact of their practices on the fish stocks.

That said, the fishers of Marseille have not only relied on social norms in order to govern their fishery. They have also delegated authority to a formal entity called the *Prud'homie*. Why have they done so, when rational-choice theory teaches us that individuals placed under specified conditions are better off without formal governance structures? This is all the more troubling as the emergence of a hierarchical social formation, such as the *Prud'homie*, stands in tension with the fishers' equalitarian ethos. In fact, the very existence of the *Prud'homie* seems to go against a fundamental principle of the society in which it is embedded. The 'paradox of the *Prud'homie*' can also be captured in terms of Mancur Olson's theory of collective action.[107] Olson explains how freeriding problems are less likely to arise in small communities than in medium-sized or large communities because social control plays out optimally in small groups, thus diminishing the risks of freeriding.[108] The emergence of an organisation (the *Prud'homie*) in a relatively small community of fishers seems to add a twist to Olson's analysis. One can observe a decoupling between the theory of collective action upon which the analysis of private orders is

---

[105] One of the best specialists of the *Prud'homie*, Elisabeth Tempier, makes similar findings concerning the 'principles' of the community of fishers. She identifies two main principles: 'Avoid that a practice supersedes another' and 'Everyone must be able to work.' See E Tempier, *Mode de Régulation de l'Effort de Pêche et le Rôle des Prud'homies: Les Cas de Marseille, Martigues et Le Brusc* (IFREMER, 1985) 34–41.

[106] JC Scott, *The Art of Not Being Governed: An Anarchist History of Upland Southeast Asia* (New Haven, CT, Yale University Press, 2009) 18, 274–77, 329.

[107] M Olson, *The Logic of Collective Action: Public Goods and the Theory of Groups* (Cambridge, MA, Harvard University Press, 1965).

[108] ibid ch 1.

based, and the empirical situation of the fishers' community: if one were to accept the conclusions of the literature on private governance, there would no plausible explanation for the emergence of the *Prud'homie* within the community of fishers. Milgrom, North and Weingast have identified a similar paradox in their article on the Champagne fairs:

> If informal arrangements based on reputations can effectively bond good behavior, then what is the role of formal institutions in helping to support honest exchange? ... [W]hy can't a simple system of reputations motivate honest trade in these various settings?[109]

## IV. Norms and Rules in Systems of Private Governance

In response to these questions, Milgrom, North and Weingast argue that formal entities arise when the reputation mechanisms used for the enforcement of norms grow ineffective.[110] This can happen, for instance, when a system of private governance expands over a large territory or when its population grows beyond a certain size. On their view, institutions emerge in order to centralise information, identify breachers and allow individuals to punish these breachers.[111] In line with this analysis, Dixit distinguishes between a 'relation-based' system, in which individuals enforce social norms by identifying and punishing breachers, and a 'rule-based' system, in which an institution gathers key information concerning breachers.[112] This theory has the merit of identifying the mechanisms through which institutions arise in systems of private governance. It allows us, for instance, to better understand the role played by the Diamond Dealers Club or the International Chamber of Commerce in centralising information concerning cross-border trade.[113] By focusing on the ways in which systems of private governance punish breachers, however, this theory says little about the nature of the obligations that are being enforced and the potential influence that institutions may have on the content of these obligations.

The present section seeks to complement this institutional theory by focusing on the nature of the obligations that are at the core of private orders. In order to do so, this section revisits the distinction between 'norms' and 'rules', and

---

[109] PR Milgrom, DC North and BR Weingast, 'The role of institutions in the revival of trade: the law merchant, private judges and the Champagne fairs' (1990) 2 *Economics and Politics* 1, 2.

[110] ibid.

[111] ibid.

[112] AK Dixit, *Lawlessness and Economics: Alternative Modes of Governance* (Princeton, NJ, Princeton University Press, 2004).

[113] See Bernstein (n 14); F Grisel, 'Arbitration as a Dispute Resolution Process: Historical Developments' in A Björklund, F Ferrari and S Kröll (eds), *Cambridge Compendium of International Commercial and Investment Arbitration* (Cambridge, Cambridge University Press, forthcoming).

analyses how institutions create 'rules' that complement 'norms' in times of social challenges. More specifically, this section argues that the essential features of social norms, namely their open texture and their rigidity, can explain why institutions accrete rule-making functions in systems of private governance.

## A. Norm-Based Order

As seen in section III, scholarship identifies two main conditions for the successful operation of private governance: the sharing of information and the prospect of long-term relations. It is easy to understand why information circulates easily in close-knit communities: individuals with strong ties communicate frequently and intensively. What is less obvious, however, are the reasons why individuals expect or intend to interact in the very long term. The analysis of these reasons is in fact an ideal point of contact between sociology and economics.[114] Consider, for instance, on the side of economics, an interpretation of the theory of private governance formulated by Oliver Williamson, a prominent economist and Nobel laureate. In a famous article, Williamson argues that trust does not matter as much as is usually assumed in systems of private governance, because individuals adapt constantly to a socio-cultural environment that is *exogenous* to their decision. In other words, actors always factor this *exogenous* environment into their decision process through 'calculative assessments'.[115] In Williamson's words, '[r]eference to trust adds nothing [to the analysis]', which should rather focus on 'calculativeness' (a typically individual feature).[116] His analysis reduces the role played by cultural and social factors to virtually nil (Williamson reluctantly recognises the importance of trust only for the 'very special relations between family, friends, and lovers').[117] In a more recent book, Barak Richman extends Williamson's argument, contending that the breakdown of trust in the diamond industry is a consequence, rather than a cause, of the industry's evolution.[118] According to Richman, the progressive integration of the diamond market into firms is a mere substitute for trust rather than an effect of its breakdown.[119] His underlying claim is that economic agents *choose* not to trust each other when the overall context modifies their individual incentives.[120] His analysis

---

[114] On the need to build bridges between sociological and economic studies, see Edelman (n 63) 182; Ellickson (n 40).

[115] OE Williamson, 'Calculativeness, Trust, and Economic Organizations' (1993) 36 *Journal of Law and Economics* 453, 471–73.

[116] ibid 475.

[117] ibid 482–84.

[118] Richman (n 21).

[119] ibid 175.

[120] ibid 173. Richman and Williamson are not alone in their analysis of social norms: Aviram argues that these norms can be 'invented' in order to sustain the activities of private orders. See A Aviram, 'Path Dependence in the Development of Private Ordering' (2014) 1 *Michigan State Law Review* 29.

is consistent with Greif's argument that 'economic interdependence, not inter-nalized norms regarding mutual help or altruism, motivated the parties' in the 'Maghribi traders' coalition'.[121] This strand of scholarship therefore seems to consider individual choices as primarily moved by self-interest, and social norms as a mere tool for individual strategies. Similarly, Posner doubts that 'many people do things because they think they are the right thing to do unless they have first used the plasticity of moral reasoning to align the "right" with their self-interest'.[122] In this view, social norms are mere reflection of practices that are themselves a function of individual interests.[123]

By contrast, most sociologists begin from the standpoint that individuals are culturally and socially 'acted upon' and rarely autonomous 'actors' shaping their own destinies (thus rendering the 'calculative assessment' described by Williamson an arduous task).[124] Fligstein and McAdam write, for instance, that 'much of soci-ology posits that people are enmeshed in social structures that are out of their control and operating at a level that is above or outside of them'.[125] Granovetter similarly emphasises the 'embedded' character of transactions and the fundamen-tal role played by 'trust' in economic relations.[126] Sociologists view social norms as being more than a mere recurring pattern of social practices. In their view, social norms create expectations as to what standards individuals ought to follow.[127] Granovetter illustrates the difference between social patterns and norms by means of the example of chopsticks: the fact that most individuals use chopsticks in certain parts of the world does not elevate this practice to the rank of norm.[128] This is not to deny the fact that a widespread practice might have some signalling effects that *can* slowly transform this practice into a social norm.[129] However, not all recurring practices attain the status of norms, and social norms are not 'always about observed behavior'.[130]

This book adopts a more nuanced approach to this debate. It subscribes to the view that individual choice and social norms are closely intertwined, rather than being separate.[131] Social norms typically constrain the range of individual actions,

---

[121] Greif (n 53) 67.

[122] RA Posner, 'Social Norms, Social Meaning, and Economic Analysis of Law: A Comment' (1998) 27 *The Journal of Legal Studies* 553, 560.

[123] RA Posner, *Law and Social Norms* (Cambridge, MA, Harvard University Press, 2000) 7–8. This conception of norms as a reflection of social behaviour is also apparent in C Sunstein, 'Social Norms and Social Roles' (1996) 96 *Columbia Law Review* 903, 908.

[124] See Greif (n 53) 12–13.

[125] N Fligstein and D McAdam, *A Theory of Social Fields* (Oxford, Oxford University Press, 2012) 6.

[126] M Granovetter, 'Economic Action and Social Structure: The Problem of Embeddedness' (1985) 91 *American Journal of Sociology* 481, 492; Granovetter (n 9) 11–15. See also Coleman (n 77).

[127] See eg, T Parsons, *The Structure of Social Action: A Study in Social Theory with Special Reference to a Group of Recent European Writers* (Glencoe, IL, Free Press, 1949) 75; Coleman. *Foundations of Social Theory* (n 77) 242.

[128] Granovetter (n 9) 27–28.

[129] Posner (n 122) 24–26.

[130] ibid 24.

[131] Granovetter (n 9) 14.

but do not fully or systematically determine outcomes. In fact, these norms fulfil a key role in private governance by providing the social cement on the basis of which an expectation of sustained relations can arise. While individuals can certainly choose to trust (or cease to trust) each other, the claim that social norms play a negligible role in the maintenance of trust seems difficult to sustain in light of empirical evidence.[132] This book further explores the key features of social norms, namely their open texture and rigidity, and the impact of these features on the operation of private governance. Social norms are open-textured because their meaning is vague and subject to multiple interpretations.[133] For instance, the same norm of equality can be interpreted as excluding certain categories of citizens, or as being based on formal property rights rather than on economic rights. In addition to being open-textured, social norms are *rigid* insofar as their formulation is unlikely to evolve in the long term.[134] Group members are often attached to one or several norms, and altering the terms of those norms is unthinkable for them. For instance, Americans proudly proclaim their attachment to 'freedom', while the French insist on their commitment to the *acquis social* (which does not even have a proper translation in English). The rigidity of social norms is sometimes denied by scholars who proclaim their attachment to the law and economics tradition.[135] This denial is unsurprising considering the fact that most of these scholars define these social norms as the statistical recurrence of social behaviour, thus downplaying the subjective dimension of normative beliefs.[136] For instance, Axelrod states that 'a norm exists in a given social setting to the extent that individuals usually act in a certain way and are often punished when seen not to be acting in this way'.[137] From this objective definition of norms based on social behaviour derives the view that 'the standing of a norm can change in a surprisingly short time'.[138] This book introduces the argument that social behaviour is indeed subject to change,

---

[132] See, eg, RM Kramer, 'Trust and Distrust in Organizations: Emerging Perspectives, Enduring Questions' (1999) 50 *Annual Review of Psychology* 569 (providing an overview of the scholarship on trust).

[133] This was noted by RD Cooter, 'Three Effects of Social Norms on Law: Expression, Deterrence, and Internalization' (2000) 79 *Oregon Law Review* 1, 21.

[134] See Sunstein (n 123) 911; H Peyton Young, 'The Evolution of Social Norms' (2015) 7 *Annual Review of Economics* 359. HLA Hart makes a similar argument. See HLA Hart, *The Concept of Law* (Oxford, Oxford University Press, 2012) 92: 'The only mode of change in rules known to such a society will be the slow process of growth, whereby courses of conduct once thought optional become first habitual or usual, and then obligatory, and the converse process of decay, when deviations, once severely dealt with, are first tolerated and then pass unnoticed.'

[135] See, eg, S Qiao, *Chinese Small Property: The Co-Evolution of Law and Social Norms* (Cambridge, Cambridge University Press, 2018) 186 (arguing that property norms are more responsive to social change than property law). It should be noted that a prominent representative of this tradition reluctantly recognises that social norms 'might be sticky' while arguing that 'this is not a particularly interesting implication'. See Posner (n 123) 44.

[136] See ch 6.

[137] R Axelrod, 'An Evolutionary Approach to Norms' (1986) 80 *The American Political Science Review* 1095, 1097.

[138] ibid 1096.

but that social beliefs evolve more slowly and with much greater difficulty. From this perspective, the two faces of social norms can seem contradictory (since the open texture of norms should render them flexible), but they are in fact the two facets of the same reality: the formulation of social norms is unlikely to evolve because these norms are open-textured and able to encompass many different social realities. The analysis of these features helps transcend the debate between the all-normative position advocated by sociologists and the opposing view held by economists: the rigidity of social norms limits the action of individuals, but their open texture allows these individuals to frame their self-interest in accordance with these norms. In other words, social norms empower but also constrain individual action.

## B. Rule-Based Order

Past scholarship has documented the emergence of formal entities in systems of private governance. For instance, Gambetta explains the birth of the *commissione* in the Sicilian mafia by the need to regulate the 'right to kill' at a time when 'families' interpreted the norms of the mafia in ways that accommodated their own interests.[139] Bernstein refers to the multiple steps taken by cotton trade associations in order 'to increase the likelihood that cooperation will endure'.[140] Skarbek shows how gangs developed rules when the 'convict code' broke down in the prison system.[141] However, the ways in which rules emerge and interact with norms have been relatively underexplored. When they do examine the role played by formal entities in systems of private governance, most scholars tend to emphasise the role played by these entities in perfecting information flows.[142] The 'paradox of the *Prud'homie*' provides a backdrop against which one can refocus scholarly attention from the enforcement of obligations to the obligations themselves. In particular, the example of the *Prud'homie* illustrates the ways in which formal entities can complement or even modify existing obligations by producing rules. In contradistinction to norms, rules are *close-ended* and *flexible*. They are *close-ended* because they provide narrow answers to concrete problems. If a rule provides, for instance, that car owners are liable to pay a tax, one can easily identify which individuals fall under this category. In addition, rules are *flexible* because they can be changed again and again. This is not to say that rules always change rapidly. In fact, they

---

[139] D Gambetta, *The Sicilian Mafia: The Business of Private Protection* (Cambridge, MA, Harvard University Press, 1993) 113.

[140] Bernstein (n 14) 1782.

[141] See D Skarbek, *The Social Order of the Underworld: How Prison Gangs Govern the American Penal System*, (Oxford, Oxford University Press, 2014), ch 3. On the governance functions of criminal networks, see also Gambetta (n 139) ch 5; F Varese, *The Russian Mafia: Private Protection in a New Market Economy* (Oxford, Oxford University Press, 2001).

[142] See eg, Dixit (n 112).

can be constrained by social norms or overarching principles that prevent them from evolving rapidly.[143] The distinction between norms and rules is reminiscent of another distinction famously drawn by Ronald Dworkin between 'principles' and 'rules'.[144] Dworkin argues that a 'principle' is a 'requirement of justice or fairness', whose 'weight' is always 'relative' due to its open-endedness.[145] A 'rule', on the other hand, is 'applicable in an all-or-nothing fashion'.[146] It can only be valid or invalid on the basis of a given set of facts.[147]

Because of their open texture, social norms are often used as political tools in community debates: for instance, the same practices can be deemed to comply with a social norm or to violate the same norm, and disputing parties will rely on the same norm to defend their respective positions. At the same time, social norms are difficult to evolve due to their rigidity. The most practical issues can therefore place social norms under significant strain. Let me borrow an example from Walter Runciman and Amartya Sen in order to contextualise this argument. Runciman and Sen describe a situation in which individuals feel entitled to drive on either the left-hand side or the right-hand side of the road, and two classes of drivers compete in order to impose their own preferences.[148] I further assume, for the sake of argument, that these drivers broadly accept a social norm of collective safety.[149] It is then hard to say which class of drivers is complying with this social norm, since both practices are equally safe in themselves, but their combination increases the risk of accidents. According to Runciman and Sen, the only workable solution is to establish a 'game of fair division' in order to accommodate each practice with the overall norm of safety.[150] This 'game of fair division' requires the creation of rules that provide clear answers to the concrete question that most drivers face: when, and where, am I allowed to drive on the left or on the right without risking an accident?

The distinction between norms and rules can help us to re-examine some of the case studies and debates found in the literature on private governance. For instance, Ellickson's Shasta County seems like a prime example of norm-based order, while Bernstein's diamond community appears closer to a rule-based order. In addition, this typology transcends the distinction between 'social' and 'legal'

---

[143] See, eg, GN Rosenberg, *The Hollow Hope: Can Courts Bring About Social Change?*, 2nd edn (Chicago, IL, The University of Chicago Press, 2008) 96–97. An important question is that of the ways in which rules arise from an existing normative structure. A key article on this question is A Stone Sweet, 'Judicialization and the Construction of Governance' (1999) 32 *Comparative Political Studies* 147.

[144] R Dworkin, *Taking Rights Seriously* (Cambridge, MA, Harvard University Press, 1977), ch 3.

[145] ibid 22.

[146] ibid 24.

[147] ibid 27.

[148] Runciman and Sen (n 80) 558.

[149] It could be argued that if these drivers recognised a broader norm of collective safety, they would never develop these conflicting practices. But it is precisely because norms are open-textured that each class of drivers feel like 'they are the ones' complying with the social norm of collective safety.

[150] Runciman and Sen (n 80) 559–60.

that obscures rather than illuminates our understanding of societies.[151] Consider, for instance, Feldman's famous study of the 'tuna court' of Tokyo, which explores the mechanisms through which tuna merchants have turned towards a formal system of governance in order to settle disputes arising from the sale of tuna on the Tsukiji market.[152] In a ground-breaking study, Feldman suggests that 'members of close-knit groups may turn to law rather than norms because legal rules and institutions can be breathtakingly fast and inexpensive.[153] It is not clear, however, whether the tuna court actually does qualify as a 'specialized public court.[154] Feldman places particular emphasis on the fact that an ordinance of the Tokyo Metropolitan Government codified the powers of the tuna court in 1971 and that it operates on government-owned land.[155] Other organisations, such as arbitral tribunals, display comparable features and are usually not considered to be 'public courts'. The Tokyo tuna court certainly generates rules, but are these rules social or legal? No one knows for certain, and in any case, the sharp division between the 'social' and the 'legal' seems artificial. What might matter, however, are the reasons underlying the tuna merchants' decision to create a formal entity to regulate the sales of tuna. Feldman briefly mentions how the tuna court emerged in the mid-1950s when 'unwanted tension' created a situation of 'stalemate' between two groups within the community of tuna merchants.[156] These circumstances might be key in understanding the reasons why the merchants chose to create a formal entity with its own set of rules that complement their norms.

## V. Conclusion

In this chapter, I have laid down some of the theoretical background that will be used in what follows. I have raised what I call the 'paradox of the *Prud'homie*' and the difficulty of reconciling the emergence of a formal entity such as the *Prud'homie* with the tenets of the literature on private governance. I have also outlined the distinction between 'norm-based' and 'rule-based' orders, which will

---

[151] The distinction between the 'legal' and the 'social' is based on the contestable view that law is autonomous from the 'social'. See B Latour, *The Making of Law: An Ethnography of the Conseil d'Etat* (Cambridge, Polity Press, 2010) 262.

[152] EA Feldman, 'The Tuna Court: Law and Norms in the World's Premier Fish Market' (2006) 94 *California Law Review* 313.

[153] ibid 318.

[154] ibid 354.

[155] ibid 353.

[156] ibid 331. Feldman does not identify the reasons lying behind the tuna traders' shift away from an informal system towards a public court. See ibid 360: 'In effect, they turned their backs on informal norms (perhaps because they were inadequate, or contested, or for some other reason; the historical record is insufficient to say), and moved away from what some scholars suggest is a particularly efficient way of handling conflict.'

be used to interpret the empirical material presented in the subsequent chapters. Although this structure suggests a deductive approach, the methodology used in this book is clearly and intentionally inductive. In fact, the theory presented in chapter 1 results from the exhaustive analysis of the empirical material gathered through archival research, interviews and ethnographic work. It is this empirical material that has guided my efforts to frame the data in the ways that are suggested in chapter 1. Chapters 2 to 5 are descriptive in the sense that they offer a thick account of the empirical reality of the *Prud'homie* throughout its history.[157] These chapters derive explanations from the framework presented in chapter 1, which they try to refine in light of the empirical data.

Chapter 2 ('From Norms to Rules') presents an overview of the social norms in the community of fishers in Marseille. This chapter identifies the issues raised by the implementation of the community's norms, and explains why the *Prud'homie* emerged in the early fifteenth century in order to resolve the conflicts that arose among fishers over the concrete application of these norms. It then illustrates the constant challenges faced by the *Prud'homie* in accommodating new fishing practices while limiting their scope.

Chapter 3 ('Along Came Globalisation') highlights how the *Prud'homie* coped with the social changes incurred in the early stages of globalisation (seventeenth and eighteenth centuries). It shows how the fishers' social norms framed the regulatory response that the *Prud'homie* articulated to these changes by focusing on two case studies: the emergence of a new fishing technique called *madragues* in the seventeenth century and the arrival of Catalan fishers in the eighteenth century. In both cases, the fishers' social norms shaped the *Prud'homie*'s rule-making capacities and created a constitutional frame that constrained its capacity to respond to social changes.

Chapter 4 ('A Battle of Norms') shows how the inherent tension between the norms of the fishers increased when they were confronted with the emergence of major technologies such as the engine, electricity and dynamite. In this context, the *Prud'homie* experienced difficulties in striking a balance between its norms, ultimately privileging its commitment to equality over the preservation of the fishery.

Chapter 5 ('Law and (Private) Order') explores the widely held view that the *Prud'homie* collapsed because the French state ceased lending support to its system of private governance. This explanation is consistent with scholarly views that emphasise the importance of public support for the maintenance of private governance. The case of the *Prud'homie* shows that this explanation might need to be modified. In fact, the data suggest that the French state deferred to the *Prud'homie* because of the benefits that it could draw from the latter, and

---

[157] On the importance of descriptive work, see B Latour, *Reassembling the Social: An Introduction to Actor-Network-Theory* (Oxford, Oxford University Press, 2006) 136.

that it stopped lending its support to the *Prud'homie* when these benefits faded. In other words, the account of the causal relationship might need to be reversed: the *Prud'homie* did not decline when the state stopped lending its support, but rather the state progressively stopped supporting the *Prud'homie* when the latter was in decline.

Chapter 6 ('Between Facts and Beliefs') brings the analysis back to the theoretical framework presented in chapter 1. It retraces the steps that have led to the progressive decline of the *Prud'homie*. On the basis of the empirical material presented in this book, this chapter argues that the fragility of private governance resides in the strength of its social norms. Strong norms prevent systems of private governance from evolving as quickly as they should in order to accommodate social changes. This discrepancy generates institutional schizophrenia, with rules stretched to the breaking point between evolving practices and existing norms. In short, chapter 6 presents the central argument of this book that social norms are the great strength, but also the main weakness of private orders.

><((((°>

# 2

## From Norms to Rules

## I. Introduction

Marseille is the second largest city in France, as well as its oldest, having been founded around 600 BC as a Greek colony known as 'Massilia'.[1] Marseille is tucked away in the 'Gulf of the Lion' between the estuary of the Rhône to the West and a series of vertical cliffs to the East (*les calanques*). This location has endowed Marseille with one of the greatest fisheries in the Mediterranean. The Rhône carries with it a vast quantity of nutrients that contribute to the development of Posidania meadows (a natural habitat for the reproduction of fish), while the *calanques* harbour a wide variety of rockfish that are used to make *bouillabaisse*, the signature dish of Marseille.

The history of Marseille is closely bound with that of its fishery.[2] According to legend, the city takes its name from the moment when Greek colonisers threw a line to a local fisher and asked him to bind it to a pole.[3] The ancient name 'Massilia' is, on this account, a compound of *mastos* (fishing knot and, by extension, bind) and *alieus* (fisher).[4] Figure 2.1 reproduces one of the oldest depictions of the port of Marseille, drawn by Matteo Florimi, an Italian artist from Sienna, on the basis of a print engraved around 1580.[5]

In this drawing, Florimi shows the population concentrated in the northern part of the port and depicts numerous boats, as well as the chain that protected the port from being attacked by sea. Most importantly for the purposes of this chapter, the upper left-hand corner of the drawing contains one of the first known representations of the fishery of Marseille.[6] The drawing is telling in several respects. First, the artist increased the scale of the fishing scenes relative to the city and the port. He probably did so in order to make the details visible, but he may also have

---

[1] See O Abulafia, *The Great Sea: A Human History of the Mediterranean* (London, Penguin Books, 2014) 123, 124.

[2] See B Fagan, *Fishing: How the Sea Fed Civilization* (New Haven, CT, Yale University Press, 2017) 141 et seq (arguing that early civilisations and urban centres often grew alongside sophisticated fisheries).

[3] See A de Ruffi, *Histoire de la ville de Marseille* (Marseille, Claude Garcin, 1642) 5.

[4] ibid.

[5] Some of Matteo Florimi's prints can be viewed at the British Museum, at www.britishmuseum.org/collection/term/BIOG27422 (last checked 9 February 2021).

[6] See J Mille, *Les calanques et massifs voisins: Histoire d'une cartographie (1290–XXe siècle)* (Turriers, Transfaire, 2015).

**Figure 2.1** The Port of Marseille by Matteo Florimi (ca 1580)
*Source*: Bibliothèque nationale de France (BNF Gallica).

been trying to highlight the importance of fishing for the city of Marseille. In fact, in the period when Florimi made his drawing, the fishery of Marseille was particularly rich and endowed with a wide variety of species.[7] Various texts mention the 'miraculous' fishery of Marseille and refer to the capture of 8,000 tuna in a single day in the sixteenth century.[8] Second, this scene portrays one of the oldest fishing techniques in Provence, called *eyssaugue*. *Eyssaugue* is a type of net (and by extension a fishing technique) that is deployed from the shore as a beach seine. The term *eyssaugue*, which comes from the Ancient Greek *eis* (within) and *ago* (to lead), indicates how much this technique depends on the closely coordinated efforts of fishers.[9] In Florimi's drawing, five fishers remain on shore holding one end of the seine net, while four other fishers circle the net back to the shore in a small boat.[10] The scene evokes a sense of great coordination among the fishers;

[7] de Ruffi (n 3) 441.

[8] See P Quiberan de Beaujeu, *Louée soit la Provence* (Arles, Actes Sud, 1999) 135; *Rapport de M Jules Guibert au Conseil municipal de Marseille* (22 June 1870), DA 6S10/3.

[9] See *Eléments relatifs à l'intérêt historique de la pêche à l'eyssaugue dans le Golfe de Marseille* (February 1994), DA 2331W281.

[10] For a description of *eyssaugue*, see also JJ Baudrillart, *Traité général des eaux et forêts, chasses et pêches*, vol IX (Paris, Librairie d'Arthus Bertrand, 1827) 148; *Description des Pesches, Loix et Ordonnances des Pescheurs de la Ville de Marseille*, DA 250E2, 71.

in fact, *eyssaugue* requires a high level of cooperation not only within individual fishing crews, but also among the different crews who compete over the limited number of areas where it can be practised.

This chapter explores the ways in which the fishers of Marseille have developed and maintained cooperative mechanisms for the operation of their fishery. It highlights the ways in which the birth of the *Prud'homie* resulted from a long evolutionary process that crystallised in 1431, when the fishers of Marseille decided to elect their representatives to a formal body. It examines how the fishers of Marseille developed their guild in the Middle Ages, and how the communal system of Marseille fostered the emergence of social norms. It also studies the emergence of the *Prud'homie* at a time when conflicts arose among fishers over the concrete application of these norms. Finally, it highlights the ongoing tensions between the social norms of the fishers and the need to accommodate new practices in the fishery of Marseille.

## II. The Fishers of Marseille and their Social Norms

This section examines the ancient roots of the community of fishers and their ancestral use of fishing techniques that required a high level of cooperation, before exploring the cooperative mechanisms put in place by the fishers in the context of the commune – a defining moment of self-determination in medieval Marseille.

## A. Cooperation Among Fishers in Ancient Marseille

We do not know much about ancient Marseille, and even less about how fishers operated at this time. What is generally accepted, however, is that the founders of Marseille were skilled sailors who quickly exploited their fishery's rich stocks and that fishing played a central role in ancient Marseille.[11] In fact, the oldest traces of human presence in Marseille are the remains of a fishing boat dating back to the end of the sixth century BC.[12] The importance of fishing in ancient Marseille is also indicated by an engraved plaque exhibited in the History Museum of Marseille, which portrays a fishing scenery of the Hellenistic period. Archaeological evidence also suggests that fishers collaborated closely in order to ply their trade. For instance, fishers set up a camp dedicated to tuna fishing on the island of Riou off the coast of Marseille in the first century BC.[13]

---

[11] de Ruffi (n 3) 2.

[12] See P Pomey, 'Les épaves grecques et romaines de la place Jules-Verne à Marseille' (1995) 2 *Comptes rendus des séances de l'Académie des Inscriptions et Belles-Lettres* 459, 471–75.

[13] Fragments of amphora used to store brine and tuna bones are exhibited at the History Museum of Marseille.

Contemporary observers also indicate that local fishers were highly organised and cooperated very extensively. For instance, Oppian (a poet of the second century AD) gives a vivid account of the techniques used to capture swordfish in Marseille, highlighting the considerable level of coordination required for the deployment of these fishing techniques:

> The fishermen fashion boats in the likeness of the Swordfishes themselves, with fishlike body and swords, and steer to meet the fish. The Swordfish shrinks not from the chase, believing that what he sees are not benched ships but other Swordfishes, the same race as himself, until the men encircle him on every side. ... Moreover, when encircled in the crooked arms of the net the greatly stupid Swordfish perishes by his own folly.[14]

Oppian describes how fishers in Marseille built gigantic set traps likened to 'cities', resorting to watchmen in order to spot the arrival of schools of tuna:

> There first a skilful Tunny-watcher ascends a steep high hill, who remarks the various shoals, their kind and size, and informs his comrades. Then, straightway all the nets are set forth in the waves like a city, and the net has its gate-warders and gates withal and inner courts. And swiftly the Tunnies speed on in line, like ranks of men marching tribe by tribe – these younger, those older, those in the mid-season of their age. Without end they pour within the nets, so long as they desire and as the net can receive the throng of them; and rich and excellent is the spoil.[15]

In Oppian's account, the fishing techniques used in ancient Marseille involved numerous participants who coordinated their actions to catch their prey. A contemporary of Oppian named Aelian corroborates his account of tuna fishing in the ancient Mediterranean. Aelian, a historian and zoologist, describes in detail the elaborate techniques used by tuna fishers in this region. These fishers built 'lookout places' that mobilised no fewer than 30 individuals, five boats and nets of 'considerable length' in order to track the migrations of tuna:

> Now the inhabitants of the whole of that country know exactly of the coming of the Tunny, and at that season of the year the fish arrive and much gear has been got ready to deal with them, boats and nets and a high lookout-place. This lookout-place is fixed on some beach and stands where there is a wide, uninterrupted view. It is no trouble to me to explain, and you who listen should be pleased to hear, how it is constructed. Two high pine-trunks held apart by wide balks of timber, are set up; the latter are interwoven in the structure at short intervals and are of great assistance to the watchman in mounting to the top. Each of the boats has six young men, strong rowers, on either side. The nets are of considerable length; they are not too light and so far from being kept floating by corks are actually weighted with lead, and these fish swim into them in shoals.
>
> ...
>
> When the company of Tunnies makes for the open sea the man in the lookout who has an accurate knowledge of their ways shouts at the top of his voice telling the men to give chase in that direction and to row straight for the open sea. And the men after fastening

---

[14] Oppian, *Halieutica* or *Fishing* (Cambridge, MA, Harvard University Press, 1928) 393.
[15] ibid 399, 401.

to one of the pines supporting the lookout a very long rope attached to the nets, then proceed to row their boats in close order and in column, keeping near to one another, because, you see, the net is distributed between each boat. And the first boat drops its portion of the net and turns back; then the second does the same, then the third, and the fourth has to let go its portion. But the rowers in the fifth boat delay, for they must not let go yet. Then the others row in different directions and haul their part of the net, and then pause. Now the Tunny are sluggish and incapable of any action that involves daring, and they remain huddled together and quite still.[16]

According to both authors, the fishers captured tuna and swordfish by encircling them, using a combination of net traps.[17] This operation involved a large number of fishers operating on several boats, a complex system of nets and the assistance of watchmen who guided the fishers towards their prey. In Fagan's words, 'The teamwork between the shore-based watchers, the helmsmen and oarsmen, and those who maneuvered the nets had to be exquisitely precise.'[18]

The evidence is too thin to draw much in the way of conclusions about the community of fishers in ancient Marseille. What does emerge from these testimonies, however, is the high level of cooperation that prevailed among fishers from the earliest stages of Marseille's history. This cooperation is pervasively attested in the later archival record, which is replete with references to two overarching norms: one relating to equality, the other to the preservation of the fishery. Before examining these norms in more detail, a detour through the political history of Marseille will provide the context that is needed to understand the emergence of the *Prud'homie* in the late Middle Ages.

## B. The Guild of Fishers in the Commune of Marseille

The empirical record does not contain any further reference to the fishers of Marseille until the early thirteenth century, a time when the city of Marseille experienced a fascinating yet strangely overlooked episode of democratic governance. This democratic experiment was part of a wider movement toward local autonomy spanning Southern Europe in the Middle Ages.[19] At that time, the feudal city of Marseille was made up of three separate entities: the 'upper city' controlled by the Bishop of Marseille; the 'lower city' controlled by the viscounts of Provence; and the 'abbey city' controlled by clerics gathered in

---

[16] Aelian, *On the Characteristics of Animals*, vol III (Cambridge, MA, Harvard University Press, 1959) X, 5–6, 213–15.

[17] Aelian also reports the use of hooks to capture tuna in Ancient Marseille. See ibid XIII, 16, 107: 'I learn that the Celts and the people of Massalia and all those in Liguria catch Tunny with hooks; but these must be made of iron and of great size and stout'.

[18] Fagan (n 2) 169.

[19] M Weber, *Economy and Society: An Outline of Interpretive Sociology* (Berkeley, CA, University of California Press, 1978) 1253.

the Abbey of St Victor.[20] Fishers dwelled in the upper and lower cities, and were subject to different rules depending on the part of the city in which they lived. For instance, fishers in the upper city were not allowed to fish on Sundays and holidays (a rule with obvious religious ramifications), unlike those based in the lower city.[21] In the early thirteenth century, the residents of the lower city created a 'commune' and progressively asserted a wide variety of rights from the viscounts of Provence in exchange for cash payment. The oldest document in the *Prud'homie*'s archives is in fact an arbitral award dated 1225, pursuant to which the commune of Marseille paid 25,000 guilders to the Count of Provence (Raymond Bérenger) in exchange for the latter's confirmation of various rights (including fishing rights) that the viscounts of Provence had previously granted to the commune.[22] This document is one of the many devolutions pursuant to which the commune of Marseille gained wide autonomy from feudal lords. In order to give voice to the people of the lower city, the commune of Marseille implemented a political structure based on three main entities: an executive branch called the *Podestat*, a Great Council (or General Council) composed of 89 members and a General Assembly (or Parliament) comprising the whole population of the city. The Great Council comprised three categories of members: 80 burghers, three lawyers and six representatives elected by local guilds. Figuring among these guilds were the fishers, who routinely elected representatives to take part in the affairs of the commune. This experience had long-lasting consequences for the community of fishers. In fact, long after the Count of Provence had regained control over the commune,[23] fishers kept electing so-called 'consuls' who were involved in public affairs.[24] The fishers' guild also persisted and operated its own system of charity in the fourteenth century.[25] The commune of Marseille therefore encouraged self-awareness and political autonomy among fishers, deeply moulding the values of this community.

---

[20] See D Lord Smail, *The Consumption of Justice: Emotions, Publicity, and Legal Culture in Marseille, 1264–1423* (Ithaca, NY, Cornell University Press, 2003) 29–30. The 'upper city' was itself divided into two parts (the 'episcopal city', which submitted to the jurisdiction of the bishop, and a smaller jurisdiction known as the *Praepositura*).

[21] The Count of Provence decided to unify these rules in 1327. See Patent Letters of Robert, Count of Provence (2 September 1327), MA AA25/1. See also de Ruffi (n 3) 142.

[22] *Sentence arbitrale entre le seigneur comte de Provence et la communauté de Marseille, par laquelle ladite communauté acquiert toute la juridiction qu'avait ledit compte sur la mer jusqu'au Port-de-Bouc* (22 January 1225), DA 250E1.

[23] The structure of the commune of Marseille persisted after the Count of Provence regained some of its powers in 1257, but the guilds lost the authority to appoint members of the Great Council. See AD Crémieux, *Le VIme Livre des Statuts de Marseille* (Aix-en-Provence, F Chauvet, 1917) xxiii, 15.

[24] See, eg, Minutes of the Council of Marseille (15 February 1339), MA BB19; Minutes of the Council of Marseille (12 December 1368), MA BB20.

[25] See L Méry and F Guindon, *Histoire analytique et chronologique des actes et des délibérations du corps et du conseil de la municipalité de Marseille depuis le Xème siècle jusqu'à nos jours*, vol 5 (Marseille, Feissat Aîné et Demonchy, 1847) 412 (reporting the existence of a '*Bureau de l'aumône des pêcheurs*' in 1385).

## C. Norms and Conflict Resolution in the Middle Ages

The communal experience of Marseille not only nurtured democratic feelings among fishers and prompted them to elect their own representatives, it also influenced the ways in which they resolved their disputes in the Middle Ages. The archives of the city of Marseille provide details on two disputes that emerged within the community of fishers. The mechanisms employed to solve these disputes show the accretion of institutional mechanisms that anticipate the features of the *Prud'homie*.[26]

The first dispute opposed two groups of fishers in the late thirteenth century: on the one hand, fishers using a technique called *bregin* (*bregin* is a variation of *eyssaugue* practised in shallower waters); on the other hand, fishers using a more aggressive technique called *sardinau* (because it is used primarily to capture sardines).[27] An incredibly well-preserved parchment from 1291 provides a rich account of the resolution of this dispute.[28] In what would become a well-rehearsed argument in the fishery of Marseille, the first category of fishers (the proponents of *bregin*) complained that the proponents of the other technique (*sardinau*) were preventing them from practising their own trade and depleting the fish stocks.[29] In short, the *bregin* fishers accused their competitors of violating the two fundamental norms of the fishery: the norm of equality, which guaranteed the coexistence of various categories of fishers using different techniques, and the norm of preservation, which aimed to guarantee the long-term viability of the fishery. Raynaud Porcellet (a high-ranking city official) and the Great Council appointed four fishers (two representing each side) charged with delimiting a zone in which *bregin* could be used during the day and *sardinau* could be used at night.[30] Two of the four representatives were asked to agree on the boundaries of this zone, while the two others remained available to intervene in case of deadlock.[31] This process entailed a high level of sophistication and democratic maturity: only a group with fairly strong cooperative norms could possibly reach an agreement.

The second dispute arose a few decades later, in the mid-fourteenth century, between *bregin* fishers and *eyssaugue* fishers.[32] As seen above, the two techniques are essentially the same, but the *bregin* can be used in shallower waters and involves smaller nets than *eyssaugue*. The archival record mentions the complaints

---

[26] This observation is consistent with that of Cheyette showing how legalistic mechanisms superseded social norms for the settlement of disputes in 13th-century France. See FL Cheyette, 'Suum cuique tribuere' (1970) 6 *French Historical Studies* 287.

[27] Declaration of Raynaud Porcellet (chevalier vicaire of Marseille) (10 August 1291), MA HH369. For an account of *sardinau*, see *Description des Pesches, Loix et Ordonnances des Pescheurs de la Ville de Marseille*, DA 250E2, 171–72.

[28] Declaration of Raynaud Porcellet (n 27).

[29] ibid.

[30] ibid.

[31] ibid.

[32] Minutes of the Council of Marseille (21 January 1350), MA BB21.

of *eyssaugue* fishers against 'three hundred dishonest men' practising *bregin*, who 'insulted' them and 'prevented' them from fishing.[33] Once again, the dispute was framed in relation to the norm of equality that appears to have been prevalent in the community of fishers. Just as in 1291, a high-ranking city official (the *vicaire* of Marseille) picked four 'virtuous' (*probi*) individuals from the Great Council to settle the dispute.[34] Although the outcome of the dispute remains unknown, this example confirms that the fishers were an integral part of the communal project of Marseille, which entrusted them with the management of their own affairs. In fact, the city authorities actively encouraged self-organisation among fishers. In an ordinance from 1255, the Countess of Provence gave the fishers of Marseille licence to exploit the coral resources in Bosa (a port city in Sardinia) and explicitly referred to the 'council of the coral fishers'.[35] This council appears to have been a representative body, perhaps a forerunner of the *Prud'homie*.[36] In 1337, the city council of Marseille advised that two coral fishers who had requested permission to fish sardines should determine 'on their own behalf and on behalf of all the other fishers of the city' their right do so.[37] This political independence also came with some level of financial autonomy. For instance, fishers were exempted from the payment of taxes on 'fish and coral' several times between 1295 and 1430.[38] These political developments are crucial to fully understand the birth of the *Prud'homie* in the early fourteenth century. This emergence does not appear to have occurred in a vacuum but was deeply rooted in the democratic experience of medieval Marseille.

## III. The Birth of the *Prud'homie* and its Rule-Making Functions

As previously explained, the fishers of Marseille took an active part in the management of the commune of Marseille throughout the Middle Ages. It is

---

[33] ibid.

[34] ibid.

[35] Ordinance of the Countess of Provence (2 April 1255), MA AA-63.

[36] ibid.

[37] Minutes of the Council of Marseille (15 April 1337), MA BB18. Coral fishers were much more mobile than their peers in Marseille; they not only operated along the coast of Provence, but also migrated to Alghero (Sardinia) to collect red coral. Their mobility may explain the need to generate some type of organisation when operating overseas. The operation of coral fishers from Marseille in Sardinia came to a temporary halt in the late 14th century owing to an upsurge in kidnappings at sea. In 1381, the city of Marseille ordered the return of fishers from Sardinia in order to prevent kidnappings for ransom by the 'Moors' (Minutes of the Council of Marseille (16 September 1381), MA BB28; Minutes of the Council of Marseille (14 November 1381), MA BB28). For the same reasons, the city of Marseille forbade coral fishers from operating in Sardinia in 1403 (Minutes of the Council of Marseille (27 April 1403), MA BB 32).

[38] These tax exemptions are mentioned and confirmed in a Patent Letter of the Count of Provence (6 October 1355), MA AA44/2. See also Patent Letter of King Louis II (31 August 1402), AD 250E15-B; Ordinance of Queen Jeanne II (30 June 1430), MA AA44-6.

therefore not surprising that the city of Marseille actively supported the formal establishment of the *Prud'homie* in 1431. Before examining the birth of the *Prud'homie* and the emergence of its rule-making functions, I will first introduce the notion of *Prud'homie* and trace the roots of this notion back to the life of the medieval city.

## A. The Medieval Notion of *Prud'homie*

In modern French, the term *Prud'homie* designates a special jurisdiction in charge of deciding labour law disputes[39] and, for those interested in fishing, the institutions that have spread on the Mediterranean coast following the institutional example studied in this book.[40] However, most French-language speakers are not aware that this term is rooted in the life of the medieval city, and that one cannot fully understand the idea of the *Prud'homie* without examining its medieval origins.

In fact, the use of this term is pervasive and variegated in medieval Europe.[41] Literally speaking, the *Prud'hommes* – or *probi homines* in Latin – are 'good' or 'virtuous' (*probi*) 'men' (*homines*). The Magna Carta, for instance, uses the same term to refer to those trusted with the task of guarding castles.[42] But the *probi homines* are more than 'virtuous men'. The term also bears a connotation of freedom, autonomy and success that the translation 'virtuous men' does not fully capture. The arbitral award of 1225 pursuant to which the Count of Provence recognised the rights of the commune of Marseille used the term *probi homines* to refer to the vassals of the Count of Provence and the fact that they were bound to enforce this award.[43] In the feudal context, the term denotes a sense of respect towards vassals and a recognition of their ability to comply with their duties.

References to *probi homines* are pervasive in the medieval archives of Marseille. For instance, the term appears in a devolution pursuant to which the Count of Provence granted grazing rights to the citizens of Marseille over a large tract of land in 1200.[44] In this act, the term *probi homines* designates the free

---

[39] See P Cam, *Les Prud'hommes: Juges ou Arbitres? Les fonctions sociales de la justice du travail* (Paris, Presses de la Fondation Nationale des Sciences Politiques, 1981).

[40] The *Prud'homie* of Marseille was replicated in several places. There are currently about 33 *Prud'homies de Pêche* on the French Mediterranean coast. See ch 5.

[41] See, eg, JL Lefebvre, 'Prud'hommes et bonnes gens dans les sources flamandes et wallonnes du Moyen Age tardif ou l'éligibilité dans la fonction publique médiévale' (2002) 2 *Le Moyen Age* 253.

[42] *Magna Carta* (1215), Art 29.

[43] *Sentence arbitrale entre le seigneur comte de Provence et la communauté de Marseille, par laquelle ladite communauté acquiert toute la juridiction qu'avait ledit compte sur la mer jusqu'au Port-de-Bouc* (22 January 1225), DA 250E1.

[44] A copy of this document can be found in L Méry and F Guindon, *Histoire analytique et chronologique des actes et des délibérations du corps et du conseil de la municipalité de Marseille depuis le Xème siècle jusqu'à nos jours*, vol 1 (Marseille, Feissat Aîné et Demonchy, 1841) 197 et seq. It is also mentioned in F Portal, *La République Marseillaise du XIIIe siècle (1200–1263)* (Marseille, Librairie Paul Ruat, 1907) 16d.

citizens of Marseille and implies a level of independence and autonomy that these individuals did, in fact, progressively acquire. Various references are made to *probi homines* in charge of drafting the statutes of Marseille,[45] controlling the quality of bread,[46] verifying the weight of coins,[47] solving disputes among masons[48] and organising religious pilgrimages.[49] Whatever these individuals did, they were considered trustworthy members of the community, who performed important tasks on its behalf. The term '*Prud'homie*' is, in and of itself, a token of autonomy and freedom, which the fishers adamantly sought to preserve in the late Middle Ages.

## B. The Birth of the *Prud'homie*

The birth of the *Prud'homie* can be dated with precision. It was created on 13 October 1431, when city officials gathered the fishers of Marseille to 'make peace concerning some disagreements and disputes' that arose between them.[50] These disputes primarily concerned a tuna-fishing technique called *senche*, which is used to encircle a school of tuna by means of an elaborate system of boats and nets.[51] This technique is capital- and labour-intensive: it mobilises several boats, numerous fishers who have to display strong resolve and cooperative skills, and a significant number of expensive nets.[52] *Senche* is strikingly similar to the ancient techniques described by Oppian and Aelian in antiquity.

The founding document of the *Prud'homie* states that, in order to resolve the disputes arising from the operation of *senches*, 'all the fishers of the city, or their major part' agreed to elect every year four members of the community – the 'best they could find' – to regulate their fishery and settle disputes.[53] Why did fishers create a formal organisation (the *Prud'homie*) in order to regulate tuna fishing in the fifteenth century, when they had managed to do without such an organisation in antiquity? A closer look at the founding document of the *Prud'homie* may provide an answer to this apparent conundrum. The *Prud'homie* was created to control some abuses arising from the fishers' taste for equality. Because the fishers could reap large benefits from the *senches* and because these benefits were divided equally among them, there was great temptation to participate in the *senches* even when they were ill-equipped for this type of fishing. The first rule that the

---

[45] Crémieux (n 23) xxxii.
[46] ibid li.
[47] ibid 2.
[48] ibid 2.
[49] ibid 48.
[50] Agreement concerning the organisation of fishing (13 October 1431), DA 250E6.
[51] This technique is described in *Description des Pesches, Loix et Ordonnances des Pescheurs de la Ville de Marseille*, DA 250E2, 127. See also P Gourret, *Les Pêcheries et les Poissons de la Méditerranée (Provence)* (Paris, Librairie J-B Baillère et Fils, 1894) 277–79.
[52] *Description des Pesches, Loix et Ordonnances des Pescheurs de la Ville de Marseille*, DA 250E2, p 127.
[53] ibid.

*Prud'homie* was called to enforce was the requirement that fishing crews contain a minimum of four men. If a crew included only three fishers, the *Prud'homie* could determine whether these fishers were sufficiently 'competent' to offset the fact that they were working shorthanded.[54] The goal was to avoid a situation in which a group of fishers could claim an equal share of the catch without having invested the same labour resources as other groups. The second rule compelled all boats involved in the *senches* to be equipped with 'tight and well-repaired' nets of a certain dimension.[55] If fishers used damaged or undersized nets, the *Prud'homie* could reduce their individual share of the global profits generated by the *senches*.[56] In fact, members of the *Prud'homie* directly intervened in the enforcement of these rules by heading the 'companies' that tuna fishers created for the purposes of *senche*.[57] Again, the goal was to avoid the losses that would arise *globally* from the *individual* use of a damaged or undersized net (a piece of equipment that required a significant capital investment), since *senche* was based on the combination of numerous nets of a large size.[58]

The *Prud'homie* was officially in charge of preventing freeriding problems, in which individuals chose not to cooperate in order to accrue personal profit. But again, why did fishers need the support of an organisation to avoid freeriding problems when the theory of private governance teaches us that social norms should be sufficient to maintain cooperation in close-knit communities? The answer seems to lie in the level of social complexity involved in tuna fishing and the fact that the social norms of the community were too open-ended to provide concrete answers to the questions raised by the *senche*.

In fact, *senche* generated a myriad of complex questions that could lead to conflicts. How many fishers and boats are needed for *senche*? If a fishing crew falls short of the requirements, can one take into account the special skills of the crew-members to compensate for their reduced number? How large should the nets be? Can the use of defective nets justify a cut in individual profits? How should different 'companies' of fishers interact at a fishing site? These questions could be interpreted in many different ways, and the fishers needed an organisation such as the *Prud'homie* to provide answers. Without the *Prud'homie*, these questions generated endless conflicts undermining the sense of community among the fishers. Each side in community debates could in fact argue that its own practices complied with the community's social norms.

---

[54] Agreement concerning the organisation of fishing (13 October 1431), DA 250E6.

[55] ibid.

[56] ibid.

[57] The *Prud'homme* who headed a 'company' was called a 'captain'. The captain was authorised to settle disputes within the company. See *Description des Pesches, Loix et Ordonnances des Pescheurs de la Ville de Marseille*, AD 250E2, 129–31.

[58] The founding document of 1431 contains additional rules concerning the possibility of fishing on Sundays and holidays (a question that had divided the community since the 14th century), the creation of fishing zones and the regulation of fishing techniques other than *senches*.

Quite remarkably, the technique of *senche* continued to be used in Marseille until the 1960s, and the *Prud'homie* was actively involved in its regulation throughout. For instance, the *Prud'homie* promulgated a set of rules regulating, in exquisite detail, the interactions between several 'companies' of *senche* in 1958.[59] One of these rules considered a scenario in which a fishing site (called a 'post') is situated between two posts occupied by separate 'companies' of fishers but is left vacant.[60] In this scenario, each 'company' of fishers benefits indirectly from this neighbouring post, but the extent to which the catch of each group benefits from this post is unclear, thus raising potential conflicts. In order to avoid these conflicts, the *Prud'homie* decided that both companies should equally share their catch of tuna.[61] This rule answered a question the norm of equality could not clearly address due to its open texture. Less than a year later, the *Prud'homie* applied this rule in a dispute between two 'companies' practising *senche*.[62] The first 'company' complained that the second 'company' failed to share its catch of tuna in accordance with the *Prud'homie*'s rule. The *Prud'homie* ultimately decided to dismiss the first company's claim (perhaps because the rule was so new), but still levied a fine of 500,000 francs (approximately £700) from the second company for violating the rule.

These observations shed new light on Ellickson's analysis of a particular cooperative strategy at play in private orders, which he calls the 'even-up' strategy.[63] In this strategy, according to Ellickson, each individual keeps a 'running mental account of how he st[ands] with each other member of the group.'[64] By contrast with Axelrod's tit-for-tat strategy, a breach results in the creation of a debit line in the mental account of the individual who has suffered harm, rather than an immediate sanction against the breacher. Ellickson argues that because it is smoother than tit-for-tat, 'Even-Up is a strategy more suited ... to the variegated, transaction-cost laden, mistake-filled world in which we live.'[65] The evidence presented above suggests that the even-up strategy might be unsuitable for the regulation of complex social relations, in which the occurrence of a breach can be subject to endless debate. In the case of tuna fishing, individuals were often at a loss to determine whether there had been a breach of social norms and how much of a 'debit' this breach deserved in their mental account. As pointed out in chapter 1, social norms are rigid but open-ended. They do not provide ready-made answers to concrete problems. In these circumstances, the fishers found it necessary to set up a formal organisation that could determine their specific rights and obligations.

---

[59] Règlement Prud'homal de la Seinche aux Thons, dated 27 April 1958, NA 20160293/112.

[60] ibid Rule 6.

[61] ibid.

[62] Decision of the *Prud'homie*, dated 22 February 1959, PA.

[63] RC Ellickson, *Order without Law: How Neighbors Settle Disputes* (Cambridge, MA, Harvard University Press, 1991) 225.

[64] ibid 226.

[65] ibid 227.

The institutional structure described in the *Prud'homie*'s founding document was given some teeth: the *Prud'homie* could apply fines of 100 livres when there was a breach, half to be paid to state courts and the remaining half to the 'commons of the fishers'.[66] By sharing the proceeds of their fines, the *Prud'homie* initiated a skilful policy of siding with the nascent French state. This policy later extended to the Catholic Church and was instrumental in preserving the autonomy of the community from outside interference. Public authorities and the *Prud'homie* supported each other in *quid pro quos* that served their respective interests. One historical episode illustrates the nature of these *quid pro quos*. In the late 1440s, René of Anjou, Count of Provence, decided to build fortifications in order to protect the port of Marseille against external invasions. His goal was to prevent incursions by Catalonian troops, who had plundered the city in 1423. He decided to build the Tower of St Jean, which still overlooks the entrance to the port.[67] However, the construction of this fortification placed considerable strain on the city budget, and Count René decided to levy a payment of 1,200 florins from the fishers of Marseille to fund construction of the tower.[68] What is usually presented as the expression of Count René's discretionary power was, in fact, leveraged by the fishers with a view to securing significant benefits that would increase their long-term autonomy and power. For instance, the *Prud'homie* obtained a concession in perpetuity over the creek (*calanque*) of Morgiou (the very place to which they later invited King Louis XIII for a fishing party) in exchange for the payment of 1,200 florins.[69] Control over Morgiou was of particular interest to the *Prud'homie* because it extended its jurisdiction to the far east of Marseille over particularly rich waters. The *Prud'homie* obtained several other advantages, including a tax exemption over six years and the possibility to levy a tax on foreign fishers who sold their fish in Marseille during the same time period.[70] These reciprocal transfers of resources between the *Prud'homie* and public authorities are consistent with the conclusion of the scholarship on trade guilds, which highlights the interdependence between public and private authorities in medieval cities.[71] However, contrary to what has been suggested by this scholarship,[72] these ties of interdependence have not prevented the *Prud'homie* from actively promoting and maintaining collaborative mechanisms within its community. The scope of this interdependence will be further explored in chapter 5.

---

[66] ibid.

[67] See F Pizzorni-Itié, *L'Histoire du fort Saint-Jean* (Marseille, MUCEM, 2014).

[68] ibid 49.

[69] *Acte du port de Morgiou, par le roi René et son conseil, en faveur de Messieurs les Prud'hommes pour la somme de mil deux cent florins* (11 April 1452), AD 250E1.

[70] Patent Letter of King René (4 May 1452), AD 250E6.

[71] See S Ogilvie, *The European Guilds: An Economic Analysis* (Princeton, NJ, Princeton University Press, 2019) ch 2.

[72] ibid.

## C. The Rule-Making Functions of the *Prud'homie*

From the outset of its existence, the *Prud'homie* regulated the fishery of Marseille by actively generating rules. The following sections shed light on the rule-making functions of the *Prud'homie*, namely the creation, collection and application of rules.

### i. Creating Rules

As discussed in section III.B, the *Prud'homie* formally emerged in 1431, when the fishers of Marseille agreed to create specific rules in order to regulate a technique for tuna fishing called *senche*.[73] Since then, every year after Christmas, the community has elected four fishers for a yearly mandate as members of the *Prud'homie* (the elections have taken place every three years since 1926 and the *Prud'homie* now comprises up to seven members). The *Prud'homie* submits resolutions proposing specific rules to a vote by the other fishers and it adjudicates disputes in accordance with these rules on a weekly basis (each Sunday after mass). I will return later to the second function, focusing here on the first. The *Prud'homie* typically exercises this legislative function when the community needs to resolve internal conflicts generated by the use of competing techniques or skirmishes at the borders of fishing zones. Although the fishers had the power to turn down the *Prud'homie's* resolutions by a majority vote, the archival records show that they rarely did so. The legislative activities of the *Prud'homie* have led to a very rich regulatory corpus over the centuries. The rules created by the *Prud'homie* address the wide variety of techniques (hooks, dragnets and set nets) used in the fishery of Marseille and are highly consistent with the social norms of the community.

For instance, the *Prud'homie* regulated the size of the hooks in order to prevent the catching of smaller fish and to preserve the regeneration of the fish stocks.[74] Another example concerns *eyssaugue*, the fishing technique portrayed by Florimi in Figure 2.1. *Eyssaugue* could only be practised in specific locations (called 'posts') located close to the shores and endowed with sufficient depth and with sandy beds (so that the nets would not be torn apart by rocks).[75] Because the number of these posts was limited and because fishers would naturally target the posts endowed with the richest fish stock, the community constantly faced potential 'tragedies of the commons'. In response to this collective action problem, the *Prud'homie* devised a sophisticated system comprising a certain number of rules. Each team would work at each post following a sequence that had been agreed upon the previous evening. The ship's boys would circulate from house to house throughout

---

[73] Agreement concerning the organisation of fishing (13 October 1431), DA 250E6.

[74] *Description des Pesches, Loix et Ordonnances des Pescheurs de la Ville de Marseille*, DA 250E2, 46.

[75] ibid 88–89. Fishers usually keep the location of these posts secret.

**Figure 2.2** The Regulation of *Eyssaugue* in Marseille

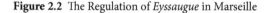

SEA

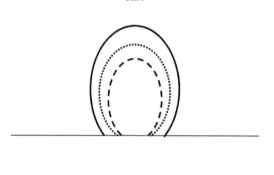

LAND

Nets of the first crew:   – – –     Nets of the second crew:   ........     Nets of the third crew: ──

the neighbourhood of St Jean every evening in order to make sure that each crew knew its 'rank'.[76] The first fishing crew was allowed to unfold a net of a certain size, while the second fishing crew could deploy a larger net covering a larger area, and so on (see Figure 2.2).[77] As a result of this 'sequential system', each crew had an opportunity to fish at the best location and to exploit resources that had been left untapped by the previous crew. This ingenious system is entirely consistent with the egalitarian and conservationist ethos of the fishers. The *Prud'homie* effectively gave all fishers an equal right over the posts of the fishery, while making sure that the best posts were not over-exploited. The level of regulatory detail provided by the *Prud'homie* is staggering. It even determined the size of the nets that could be used at each fishing site (depending on the spatial configuration of the location in question).[78] Figure 2.3 shows an extract from a table in which the *Prud'homie* recorded the size of the nets for each post in the early eighteenth century.

## ii.  Collecting Rules

The *Prud'homie* not only generates rules, but also collects them. The *Prud'homie* carefully preserves the numerous documents that contains its deliberations and the rules of the fishery. For instance, the *Prud'homie* compiled its deliberations from 1489 until 1759 in a manuscript called the 'Red Book' (*Livre Rouge*).[79]

---

[76] ibid.

[77] ibid 6, 75.

[78] *Description des Pesches, Loix et Ordonnances des Pescheurs de la Ville de Marseille*, DA 250E2, 73.

[79] See *Livre Rouge*, DA 250E4.

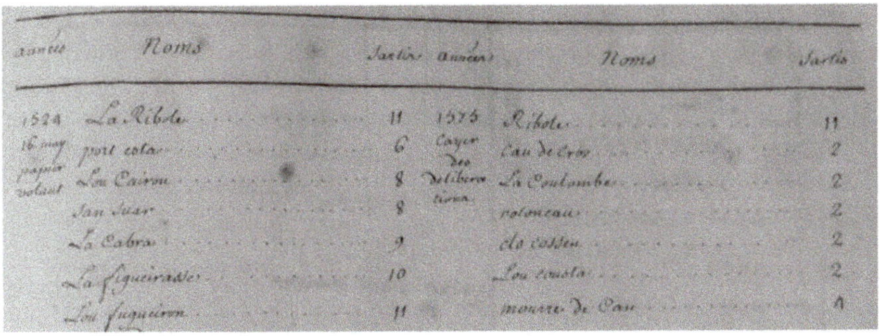

**Figure 2.3** The Regulation of *Eyssaugue*: Fishing Posts and Net Size (1727)
*Source: Description des Pesches, Loix et Ordonnances des Pescheurs de la Ville de Marseille*, AD 250E2, 73.

This compilation was a crucial development as it testified to and guaranteed the autonomy of the *Prud'homie* in relation to other institutions. It also retraced the genealogy of the rules that the *Prud'homie* was often called upon to apply. In addition, the preference for oral communication within the community made these archives crucial for the *Prud'homie*. They were, in fact, the only formal traces of activity that the community maintained. Even today, a shroud of secrecy surrounds the existence of the *Prud'homie*'s regulations (*les règlements prud'homaux*), thus reinforcing their mythic stature. Several governmental officials told me, usually with a kind of irritated disbelief, that these regulations are a mere figment of the imagination that do not actually exist. My review of archival records shows, however, that the *Prud'homie* actively codified its rules and that the *règlements prud'homaux* did exist for a very long time. The *Prud'homie* used its written textual history as a reference point when claims were made challenging its autonomy.[80] Paradoxically, it cherished orality for the very same reason. For instance, the *Prud'homie* rendered its judgments orally until the mid-nineteenth century in order to prevent state courts from scrutinising its judgments.

The problem of access to the *Prud'homie*'s archives gave rise to numerous conflicts, for instance when its members refused to hand over these documents to their successors. Correspondingly, the history of the *Prud'homie* is punctuated by efforts to retain or retrieve its archives. For instance, the *Prud'homie* initiated court proceedings in 1512 after losing part of its archives, notably documents containing proof of its recognition by feudal authorities.[81] The goal of the proceedings was to obtain a judicial declaration of the *Prud'homie*'s autonomous powers. During the proceedings, the *Prud'homie* gathered 19 fishers

---

[80] On the political role of written genealogies, see JC Scott, *The Art of Not Being Governed: An Anarchist History of Upland Southeast Asia* (New Haven, CT, Yale University Press, 2009) 276.

[81] *Enquête des Prud'hommes sur les anciens privilèges qui leur ont été dérobés* (8 January 1512), DA 250E1.

(including former *Prud'hommes*) to testify in court. All of the witnesses insisted on the impossibility of appealing the *Prud'homie*'s decisions and the high rate of compliance with its judgments. In another incident in 1644, the *Prud'homie* ordered its former members to return all of its papers and documents.[82] The *Prud'homie* subsequently created a system to prevent its files from disappearing: the fourth member of the *Prud'homie* would lock them in a box, to which only the first member of the *Prud'homie* had the key.[83] The archives were later stored on premises owned by the *Prud'homie*, and the organisation's secretary was entrusted with the key. In 1761, the widow of a secretary (Eloi Aubert) returned this key to a member of the *Prud'homie* upon her husband's death, and this *Prud'homme* then refused to hand it over to the newly appointed secretary.[84] The other members of the *Prud'homie* harshly criticised his conduct, emphasising that 'the archives are necessary at all times for the members of the *Prud'homie* to exercise their duties and decide the disputes submitted to their jurisdiction'.[85] The *Prud'homie*'s archives are extremely important for a community that is adamant about preserving its independence. The community is still fiercely protective of its rules and heritage and, as a matter of principle, the *Prud'homie* does not disclose its most recent archives to outsiders. Fortunately for researchers, the *Prud'homie* (for unknown reasons) turned over a large portion of its older documents to the local archives in 1933.[86]

In order to preserve secrecy, the *Prud'homie* has traditionally been reluctant to provide a full codification of its rules. It preferred keeping a sparse paper trail that only insiders could follow. The only significant deviation from this practice occurred in 1727, when the *Prud'homie* entrusted a local doctor and scientist called Jean-André Peyssonnel with the task of codifying the rules in a manuscript book.[87] Peyssonnel was a community outsider who had gained the trust of the *Prud'homie* by living in St Jean and building numerous ties with local fishers through his research on red corals.[88] When Peyssonnel suggested that his manuscript could be made public, however, the *Prud'homie*'s response was decisive: members of the *Prud'homie* told Peyssonnel that the rules were strictly confidential and that they could only be transmitted 'from father to son' in order

---

[82] Ordinance of the *Prud'homie* (March 1644), DA 250E35.

[83] Ordinance of the *Prud'homie* (7 January 1688) in *Livre Rouge*, DA 250E4.

[84] Notary act concerning the transmission of archives from the widow of the first secretary of the *Prud'homie* (9 September 1761), DA 250E35.

[85] ibid.

[86] Minutes of the *Prud'homie*'s Assembly (28 May 1933), PA. This decision turned out to be providential, as the German army destroyed the *Prud'homie*'s building 10 years later in 1943 (see ch 6).

[87] See *Description des Pesches, Loix et Ordonnances des Pescheurs de la Ville de Marseille*, DA 250E2; D Faget, *Marseille et la mer: Hommes et environnement marin (XVIIIe–XXe siècle)* (Rennes, Presses universitaires de Rennes, 2011) 28–29.

[88] See J Vandersmissen, 'Experiments and Evolving Frameworks of Scientific Exploration: Jean-André Peyssonnel's Work on Coral' in M Klemun and U Spring (eds), *Expeditions as Experiments* (London, Palgrave Macmillan, 2016) 51, 56.

to prevent 'chicanery' from entering its doors.[89] Peyssonnel's manuscript can still be found in the archives and provides a unique window into past regulations of the *Prud'homie*.[90] It also provides useful information concerning the species targeted by the fishers and their fishing techniques up until the early eighteenth century.

### iii.  Applying Rules

In addition to producing and collecting rules, the *Prud'homie* actively applied them by adjudicating disputes and policing the community in various ways. The *Prud'homie* performed the first task every Sunday after mass, with its jurisdiction extending to any fishing dispute that arose on its territory.[91] The procedure was as follows: the plaintiff placed two coins in a special box in order to summon the defendant to appear before the *Prud'homie* the following Sunday. Both parties then presented their arguments before the *Prud'homie*, which rendered its decision immediately after the hearing. The losing party could not appeal the *Prud'homie*'s decision. The procedure was oral, the judgment was swift and its enforcement was immediate. Most defendants complied voluntarily with the *Prud'homie*'s judgments. In the proceedings initiated by the *Prud'homie* after the loss of its archives in 1512, most of the witnesses testified that they had never seen a defendant try to appeal or refuse to comply.[92] Some witnesses reported a case where a fisher appealed the *Prud'homie*'s judgment, but subsequently withdrew his motion after being shown a record of the rights and privileges of the *Prud'homie*.[93]

The *Prud'homie* seems (at least initially) to have used relational devices based on the social benefits that fishers could derive from the group in order to enforce its judgments and rules. Fishers who lost a case before the *Prud'homie* usually complied voluntarily with its judgments in order to avoid ostracism and loss of status. Ultimately, a non-compliant member could be expelled from the community, stripped of his voting rights or exposed to public criticism. For instance, in 1632, the *Prud'homie* expelled several fishers who were involved with a competing fishery.[94] In 1647, the *Prud'homie* expelled a fisher called Jacques Clappier for having insulted one of its members.[95] In 1677, the *Prud'homie* stripped the four previous members of the *Prud'homie* (as well as their treasurer) of their voting rights due to allegations of financial fraud,

---

[89] *Mémoire pour les Prud'hommes de la Communauté des Patrons-Pêcheurs de la Ville de Marseille* (1787), DA 250E8, 12.

[90] *Description des Pesches, Loix et Ordonnances des Pescheurs de la Ville de Marseille*, DA 250E2.

[91] The *Prud'homie*'s territory was broadly defined until the 20th century. See F Grisel, 'Miles and Norms in the Fishery of Marseille: On the Interface between Social Norms and Legal Rules' (on file with the author).

[92] *Enquête des Prud'hommes sur les anciens privilèges qui leur ont été dérobés* (8 January 1512), DA 250E1.

[93] ibid.

[94] Minutes of the *Prud'homie*'s Assembly (4 January 1632), in *Livre Rouge*, DA 250E4.

[95] Minutes of the *Prud'homie*'s Assembly (20 October 1647), in *Livre Rouge*, DA 250E4.

until they returned 'what they wrongly retained from the community'.[96] The *Prud'homie* also resorted to 'naming and shaming' to enforce its rules. For instance, in 1653, the *Prud'homie* publicly summoned some of its members to attend the weekly assembly on Sundays, emphasising the 'great prejudice' that their absence caused for the community.[97]

The *Prud'homie* also exercised police powers by fining non-compliant fishers starting in the fifteenth century,[98] but it does not appear to have actually resorted to that power until later in its history. The *Prud'homie* was entitled to issue a fine of 100 livres if a fisher disobeyed its rules. The proceeds of the fine were initially divided between the King of France and the 'commons of the fishers',[99] and a third share was subsequently created for the Catholic Church.[100] The *Prud'homie* built alliances with the state and the Catholic, Church by giving them a direct financial interest in its own jurisdiction. The *Prud'homie* did not initially fine non-compliant members, arguably because most individuals voluntarily complied with its judgments and rules. However, the *Prud'homie* used fines as a means of disciplining non-compliant members during the seventeenth century. For instance, a fisher from a neighbouring city, called Vincent Icard, was condemned to pay 100 livres in fines in 1629 after damaging the nets of local fishers.[101] Peyssonnel's manuscript from 1727 contains data on 55 fines pronounced by the *Prud'homie* between 1688 and 1714. These data provide a good window on the breaches that occurred most frequently in the community and the types of rules that the *Prud'homie* actively enforced. I coded for the types of social conduct sanctioned by the *Prud'homie* and classified them into four categories: breach of religious rules, lack of respect for the *Prud'homie*, lack of respect for the king and breach of fishing rules. The data are presented in Figure 2.4.

Figure 2.4 shows that 42 per cent of the fines sanctioned a breach of a religious rule (mostly linked with the prohibition to fish on Sundays and religious holidays), 40 per cent sanctioned a breach of fishing rules, 16 per cent sanctioned a lack of respect for the *Prud'homie* and 2 per cent sanctioned a lack of respect for the king. Therefore, a non-trivial number of the fines (16 per cent) were imposed on fishers who had challenged the authority of the *Prud'homie*. Even more significantly, the *Prud'homie* actively supported external polities such as the king and the Catholic Church, a position that will be explored further in chapter 5.

As a last resort, the *Prud'homie* could immobilise the boats and seize the nets of non-compliant fishers, but this measure was used rarely, if at all. I noted only

---

[96] Minutes of the *Prud'homie's* Assembly (21 March 1677), in *Livre Rouge*, DA 250E4. The same sentence was pronounced in 1689 against 16 fishers who organised a protest during the election of the *Prud'homie* (Minutes of the *Prud'homie's* Assembly (23 January 1689), in *Livre Rouge*, DA 250E4).

[97] Minutes of the *Prud'homie's* Assembly (19/20 January 1653), in *Livre Rouge*, DA 250E4.

[98] Agreement concerning the organisation of fishing (13 October 1431), DA 250E6; Renewal of the *Prud'homie's* privileges (7 April 1489), DA 250E3.

[99] Agreement concerning the organisation of fishing (13 October 1431), DA 250E6.

[100] Renewal of the *Prud'homie's* privileges (7 April 1489), DA 250E3.

[101] Appeal before the Parliament of Provence against Vincent Icard (29 May 1629), DA 250E195.

**Figure 2.4** The Fines Imposed by the *Prud'homie* (1688–1717)

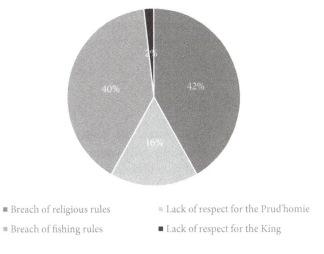

- Breach of religious rules
- Lack of respect for the Prud'homie
- Breach of fishing rules
- Lack of respect for the King

one use of this measure, when the *Prud'homie* seized the sails and lines of foreign fishers in 1774.[102] The fact that these fishers were community outsiders suggests that the *Prud'homie* might have been reluctant to immobilise the production means of its own members, but felt more comfortable doing so against outsiders.

## IV.  Accommodating New Practices: The Case of the Floating Nets

This section illustrates the regulatory methods used by the *Prud'homie* with a case study. Until the fifteenth century, fishers in Marseille predominantly relied on 'set nets' anchored with plumbs in the seabed in order to catch species such as tuna or sardines. Beginning in the second half of the fifteenth century, however, the fishers increasingly used nets that are said to be 'floating' because they are not anchored in the seabed. The emergence of these 'floating nets' generated debates between incumbents (the users of set nets) and their challengers (the proponents of floating nets), with each side summoning the social norms of the community in support of its own position. Incumbents typically argued that the new techniques undermined the norm of preservation by damaging the fish stock, while their challengers claimed their right to practise the new techniques pursuant to

---

[102] Notary act concerning the seizure by the *Prud'homie* of sails and *palangres* belonging to three Calatan fishers (15 May 1774), DA 250E41. This event led to court proceedings that are further described in ch 3. The *Prud'homie* also tried to seize the rudder of a boat in 1717, but this attempt was unsuccessful (DA 250E255).

the norm of equality. The *Prud'homie* intervened in these debates by creating rules that accommodated the social norms of the community with emerging practices in the fishery of Marseille. In all the disputes that are analysed below, the *Prud'homie* allowed the use of floating nets while trying to regulate their potential impact on the fish stock.

## A. Floating Nets and Tuna Fishing

In the field of tuna fishing, fishers traditionally relied on fixed nets that were anchored in the seabed (in addition to the *senche* described earlier in this chapter). The use of these fixed nets, called *tonnaires de poste*, was organised through a system of cooperation that bore a strong resemblance to the sequence rules used in *eyssaugue*. In this system, fishers placed their nets at specific locations called *postes*.[103] Because these posts were limited in number, fishing crews took turns, following a predetermined order. The crew that first arrived at a post had priority over other crews, provided the latter crews could place their own nets at the same location in the following days.[104] To signal its interest in the post, the second crew could inform the first crew directly or, alternatively, they could leave a mark on the piece of cork that indicated the location of the first crew's nets.[105] If the first crew did not comply and failed to haul in its net, the second crew would then be entitled to its catch.[106] The emergence of floating nets (called *tonnaires de corre* or *correntilles*) in the late fifteenth century represented a challenge to this cooperative system. The *tonnaire de corre* involved a large net secured to a boat via a system of ropes, floating in mid-water and dragged by the currents (see Figure 2.5).

These floating nets are more aggressive for fish stocks than fixed nets because they cover a larger territory and result in a higher yield. Fishers placed their nets wherever they wanted and the currents carried the nets randomly throughout the sea, including to the posts where fixed nets were located. A document from 1477 sheds light on the disputes generated by the use of these new nets.[107] Fishers who practised the traditional technique of *tonnaire de poste* complained that floating nets threatened the long-term maintenance of the fishery in contravention of the norm of preservation.[108] At the same time, advocates of the new technique defended their right to use the *tonnaire de corre* as a matter of equality. They argued

---

[103] This system is described in *Description des Pesches, Loix et Ordonnances des Pescheurs de la Ville de Marseille*, DA 250E2, 104.

[104] ibid.

[105] ibid.

[106] ibid.

[107] Ordinance of the King incorporating the arbitral award of the bishop of Marseille (16 November 1477), DA 250E6. This document is discussed in de Ruffi (n 3) 233. De Ruffi confuses *tonnaires de poste* with *madragues*, as noted elsewhere by J Billioud, 'La pêche au thon et les madragues de Marseille' (1955) 26 *Marseille – Revue municipale* 3, 4.

[108] Ordinance of the King incorporating the arbitral award of the bishop of Marseille (n 107).

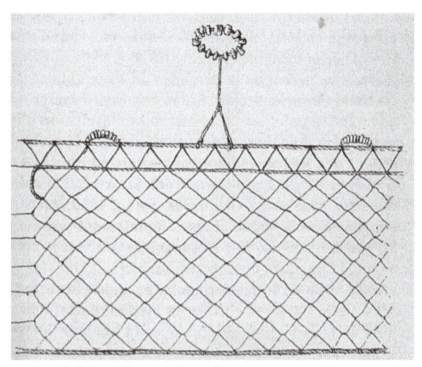

**Figure 2.5** The *Tonnaire de Corre* or *Correntille*

*Source*: P Gourret, *Les Pêcheries et Les Poissons de la Méditerranée (Provence)* (Paris, Librairie JB Baillière et Fils, 1894) 209; *Bibliothèque nationale de France* (BNF Gallica).

that they were entitled to exploit the fishery just as much as their counterparts who used *tonnaire de poste*.

The dispute became so heated that the Count of Provence stepped in 'to bring the fishers back to peace' by delegating authority to two prominent members of the Catholic Church to resolve the dispute. The clerics gathered the fishers of Marseille and struck an agreement that was incorporated into an ordinance. It should be noted that although the Catholic Church played a key role in the settlement of this dispute, the rules that resulted from its involvement are entirely consistent with the regulating techniques of the *Prud'homie*. The ordinance of 1477 laid out a geographical and temporal division between the two forms of fishing. Floating nets were allowed within a limited fishing zone between 24 June and the following Easter. During the remaining period (between Easter and 24 June), only fixed nets were allowed in another fishing zone. The ordinance also mentions the need 'not to challenge the other nets and fishing positions assigned by the *Prud'homie*'.[109] The obvious goal was to alternate each type of fishing practice at different locations, in order to allow different groups to

---

[109] ibid.

practise their preferred technique while permitting the regeneration of fish stocks. The rules drawn up by the Catholic Church (and endorsed by the *Prud'homie*) played a mediating role between the norms of the community and a new practice that had emerged in the fishery. In particular, these rules sought to maintain a balance between the norm of equality and that of conservation, by striking a compromise between the use of a new technique on the one hand and the preservation of the fishery on the other. The second example further illustrates how much this mediating exercise was needed to preserve social peace among the fishers.

## B. Floating Nets and Sardine Fishing

Fishers traditionally caught sardines using set nets. Because these set nets rest on the seabed, the fishers called this technique *sardinau de fond* (literally 'seabed sardinau'). The fishers practising *sardinau de fond* place their nets in specific posts and follow the sequence system designed by the *Prud'homie*. According to these rules, the first fisher to arrive at a fishing post has priority over the others, but must yield his place to any other fisher who wishes to use the same post.[110]

In the fifteenth century, a new technique for the fishing of sardines emerged in Marseille. Instead of grounding their nets in the seabed, fishers started placing these nets in mid-water by means of a system of ropes and cork. For this reason, this technique was called *sardinau entre deux eaux* (or 'sardinau between waters'). This new technique was criticised for wasting resources and for scaring the fish away from the fishery. Ironically, the proponents of *sardinau de fond* voiced the same criticisms that they themselves had faced in 1291.[111] The archives illuminate the debates between traditionalists who strongly opposed *sardinau entre deux eaux* and modernists who embraced the new technique. The modernists argued that this new technique did not significantly affect the overall stock of sardines.[112] They also blamed the traditionalists for depleting resources by using nets that damaged the seabed and caught smaller and younger subjects than their own technique.[113] Each side therefore framed its position in accordance with the preservation norm and accused the other side of threatening the fish stocks. Although the traditionalists were a minority, the *Prud'homie* sided with them and prohibited the use of floating nets in 1554.[114]

---

[110] *Description des Pesches, Loix et Ordonnances des Pescheurs de la Ville de Marseille*, DA 250E2, 175.
[111] See section II.C.
[112] Fishers commonly justify their use of new technologies by placing emphasis on the 'inexhaustible supply' of fish. See SJ Kennelly and MK Broadhurst, 'By-catch begone: changes in the philosophy of fishing technology' (2002) 3 *Fish and Fisheries* 340; TJ Pitcher, 'Fisheries managed to rebuild ecosystems? Reconstructing the past to salvage the future' (2001) 11 *Ecological Applications* 601, 603.
[113] These arguments can be found in DA 250E168.
[114] These debates are documented in DA 250E169.

From there, the dispute spiralled out of control. Because the traditionalists with whom it had sided constituted a minority, the *Prud'homie* decided to change the voting procedure from a direct to an indirect method in 1554. Instead of being elected by the whole community, the *Prud'homie* decided to create an electoral college composed of 24 former members of the *Prud'homie*. Although it is not entirely clear that this procedural change was aimed at buttressing the *Prud'homie*'s decision to prohibit floating nets, the archives suggest that the coming together of the two decisions was not coincidental. The apparent goal of filtering the election through its former members was to favour the more traditional position.[115] This strategy appears to have been successful at least until 1564, when the *Prud'homie* reversed its decision and allowed the practice of floating nets for sardine fishing. The response from former members of the *Prud'homie* (1554) was unprecedented. They sued the newly elected members of the *Prud'homie* (1564 and 1565) before the royal courts (*Parlement de Provence*).[116] After hearing arguments on both sides, the courts decided to allow the new technique in 1567.[117] Because its decision did not assuage tensions within the community, however, the royal court empowered 10 experts with the task of finding a compromise between the two groups.[118] Although the outcome of this expertise is unknown, it appears that fixed nets almost entirely disappeared from the fishery and were replaced by floating nets within decades.[119] This episode therefore suggests that the *Prud'homie*'s mission of reconciling fishing practices and social norms was particularly complex. Fishers broadly recognised these social norms, as shown by the fact they framed their claims in terms of these norms. However, the norms seem to have been rather inadequate for regulating the fishery, because although they were broad enough to justify conflicting practices, they lacked sufficient detail to effectively regulate these practices.

# V. Conclusion

This chapter highlights the origins of *Prud'homie* and traces its roots back to the communal experience of medieval Marseille. Archival documentation suggests that the democratic experience of the commune of Marseille encouraged fishers to elect their own representatives and to take an active part in the public affairs of the city. The archival record also highlights the temporal continuity of two norms in the community of fishers: the norm of equality (all fishers are equal and must act in ways that do not impede the activities of other fishers) and the norm of preservation (fishers shall not damage the resources of the fishery when practising their trade).

---

[115] See, eg, Minutes of the *Prud'homie*'s Assembly (22 December 1554), DA 250E169.
[116] This court case is reported in DA 250E168.
[117] Decision of the Parliament of Provence (1 March 1567), DA 250E168.
[118] Decision of the Parliament of Provence (14 January 1569), DA 250E168.
[119] *Description des Pesches, Loix et Ordonnances des Pescheurs de la Ville de Marseille*, DA 250E2, 171.

The fishers created the *Prud'homie* in 1431 in order to resolve disputes arising from the concrete application of these norms. The *Prud'homie* was given a mandate to decide these disputes by creating, collecting and enforcing specific rules. However, this mandate quickly generated formidable challenges. For instance, the emergence of floating nets in the late fifteenth century stirred longstanding debates and divisions within the community of fishers, with each side claiming to be the true proponent of the community's norms. The most effective response was to accommodate the new practices while limiting their scope, a balancing exercise that the *Prud'homie* engaged in constantly throughout its history.

><((((°>

# PART II

## Resistance

# 3

## Along Came Globalisation

About a hundred paces from the spot where the two friends were ..., was the small village of the Catalans. One day a mysterious colony quitted Spain, and settled on the tongue of land on which it is to this day. ... This village, constructed in a singular and picturesque manner, half Moorish, half Spanish, is that we behold at the present day inhabited by the descendants of those men who speak the language of their fathers. ... [T]hey remained faithful to this small promontory, on which they had settled like a light of sea-birds, without mixing with the Marseillaise population, intermarrying, and preserving their original customs and the costume of their mother-country, as they have preserved its language.

Alexandre Dumas, *The Count of Monte Cristo*[1]

## I. Introduction

The first scenes of *The Count of Monte Cristo* take place in the immediate vicinity of the port of Marseille, at a location now called Catalan Beach. This tract of land owes its name to the Catalan fishers who migrated to Marseille in the early 1730s and created the small settlement described by Alexandre Dumas. The Catalan fishers refrained from mingling with the French population, did not share the social norms of the local fishers and refused to recognise their *Prud'homie*. The migrations of Catalan fishers to Marseille are just one example of a broader process that resulted from decades, perhaps centuries, of human development. This process, which is universally known by the name 'globalisation', was in its early stages in the Mediterranean of the early seventeenth century.[2] At this time, an itinerant labour force swarmed across the Mediterranean, a 'saturated space' where the maritime republics of Italy, the Ottomans and newcomers, such as

---

[1] A Dumas, *The Count of Monte Cristo*, vol 1 [1844–46] (London, George Routledge & Sons, 1910) 11.
[2] Historians have termed 'proto-globalisation' the historical period covering the 17th and 18th centuries. See AG Hopkins, *Globalisation in World History* (London, Random House, 2002). This 'proto-globalisation' was a key stage of the globalisation process, characterised by the progressive growth of trade levels across nations, the migration of techniques and workers, and technological changes. The contemporary reader might find this process too restricted to be considered part of globalisation as we currently understand it. However, one should consider that the 'scalings' of globalisation have evolved over time, and that what might seem 'local' or 'regional' in our eyes was already part of the globalisation process several centuries ago. See S Sassen, *Territory. Authority. Rights: From Medieval to Global Assemblages* (Princeton, NJ, Princeton University Press, 2006) 10–11.

English and Dutch merchants, competed for control of the trade routes.[3] Marseille participated actively in this burgeoning globalisation as a major port from which 'barques and galleons ... were sailing over the entire Mediterranean'.[4] In fact, the 'global expansion' of Marseille occurred during the seventeenth and eighteenth centuries, with its port becoming an entryway into Europe for primary goods imported from North Africa and the Near East.[5]

Because of its location in Marseille and its rich archival records, the *Prud'homie* offers empirical material enabling us to explore the ways in which a system of private governance responds to changes prompted by globalisation. Past scholarship has identified potential difficulties that these systems might face. For instance, Ostrom points out how 'having larger number of participants' in a system of private governance 'increases the difficulty of organising, agreeing on rules, and enforcing rules'.[6] Ellickson notes how the global competition between close-knit groups of whale hunters may have aggravated overfishing.[7] Greif highlights the 'commitment problem' that arises when a close-knit group, such as 'Maghribi traders', conducts business overseas.[8] While these scholars suggest, from several different angles, that private orders might be ill-equipped to tackle the challenges of globalisation,[9] it is not entirely clear how these systems evolve (or fail to evolve) when the close-knit communities in which they are embedded are confronted with the early stages of globalisation.

This chapter focuses on two socially significant events that emerged directly out of the early stages of globalisation and explores how these events impacted the life of the *Prud'homie*: the first is the importation of a new fishing technique called the *madrague* in the early seventeenth century; the second is the arrival of migrant fishers from Catalonia throughout the eighteenth century. The archival records concerning both events are incredibly rich and contain multiple traces of the heated debates that they triggered within the community of fishers. On the basis of this empirical evidence, this chapter argues that the *Prud'homie* had difficulties in addressing the challenges arising from early globalisation, because its

---

[3] G Calafat, *Une Mer Jalousée: Contribution à l'histoire de la souveraineté (Méditerranée, XVIIe siècle)* (Paris, Seuil, 2019) 13; F Braudel, *The Mediterranean and the Mediterranean World in the Age of Philip II*, vol 1 (Berkeley, CA, University of California Press, 1972) 433.

[4] F Braudel, *The Mediterranean and the Mediterranean World in the Age of Philip II*, vol 2 (Berkeley, CA, University of California Press, 1973) 220.

[5] P Echinard and E Témime, 'La Préhistoire De la Migration (1482–1830)' in E Temime (ed), *Histoire des Migrations à Marseille*, vol 1 (Saint-Rémy-de-Provence, Edisud, 1989) 81–94.

[6] E Ostrom et al, 'Revisiting the Commons: Local Lessons, Global Challenges' (1999) *Science* 278, 281; PC Stern, 'Design principles for global commons: natural resources and emerging technologies' (2001) 5/2 *International Journal of the Commons* 213 (adapting Ostrom's approach to the 'global commons').

[7] RC Ellickson, 'A Hypothesis of Wealth-Maximizing Norms: Evidence from the Whaling Industry' (1989) 5/1 *Journal of Law, Economics, and Organization* 83, 95–96.

[8] A Greif, *Institutions and the Path to the Modern Economy: Lessons from Medieval Trade* (Cambridge, Cambridge University Press, 2006) ch 3.

[9] Greif argues that the Maghribi traders tackled some of these challenges by appointing 'overseas agents' whom they were able to control. See Greif, ibid.

scope for action was deeply constrained by the social norms of its community. These norms created a constitutional framework that guided, but also constrained, the *Prud'homie*'s rule-making functions. In other words, the *Prud'homie* combined norms and rules in a path-dependent process: it constantly tried to accommodate social changes with the norms of the community, but its rules remained heavily constrained by these norms.

# II. The *Madragues* in the Fishery of Marseille

The first example concerns the emergence of a fishing technique called *madrague* that was used to fish tuna in various parts of the Mediterranean in the early seventeenth century.[10] *Madragues* emerged in Tunisia, before spreading to Spain, France and Italy.[11] The term *madrague*, which comes from a Spanish word (*almadraba*) that is itself derived from Arabic, bears traces of this cosmopolitan origin.[12]

A *madrague* is a gigantic fish trap that can spread over a length of 250 metres and which is placed relatively close to the coast (300 to 500 metres away from the shore), to which it is connected with a single net.[13] *Madragues* are placed strategically in the current so that they can direct tuna toward a succession of net compartments. When the tuna are trapped in the last compartment of the *madrague* (also called the 'chamber of death'), fishers use a system of nets to haul them up to the surface. Figure 3.1 depicts one of the *madragues* used in Marseille in the early eighteenth century.

Prior to the seventeenth century, the fishers mainly used the techniques of *senche* and *tonnaire* in order to fish tuna.[14] The *senche* consisted of circling groups of tuna with an elaborate system of nets, while the *tonnaire* used a single net placed in a fixed position or dragged by the current. *Madragues* borrowed features from both techniques: like *senche*, a *madrague* was based on a complex system of nets used to encircle the tuna, but these nets were placed at fixed locations like the *tonnaires*. *Madragues* allowed a large number of fish to be caught, while sparing fishers the need to pursue them. For this reason, *madragues* seemed like a financial boon to the fishers of Marseille. A single *madrague* could capture up to 1,000 tuna during their migration periods (over the spring and summer)[15] and keep them

---

[10] Braudel (n 3) 258.

[11] F de Cormis, *Recueil de consultations sur diverses matières*, vol 2 (Paris, Montalant, 1735) 1199; D Faget, *L'écaille et le banc: Ressources de la mer dans la Méditerranée moderne XVIe–XVIIIe siècle* (Aix-en-Provence, Presses universitaires de Provence, 2017) 127.

[12] Faget (n 11) 126.

[13] ibid 143; JJ Baudrillart, *Traité général des eaux et forêts, chasses et pêches*, vol IX (Paris, Librairie d'Arthus Bertrand, 1827) 75.

[14] See ch 2.

[15] M Duhamel du Monceau, *Traité Général des Pêches*, vol 1 (Paris, Saillant & Nyon, 1769) 170; *Description des Pesches, Loix et Ordonnances des Pescheurs de la Ville de Marseille* (1725), AD 250E2, 144.

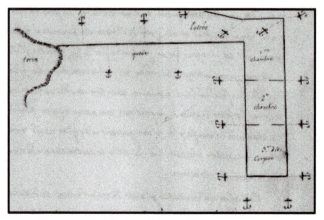

**Figure 3.1** A *Madrague* in Marseille (around 1725)

Source: *Description des Pesches, Loix et Ordonnances des Pescheurs de la Ville de Marseille* (1725), AD 250E2, 143. The various crosses on each side of the *madrague* are anchors. As one can see from the image, the *madrague* is connected by a net to the coast and is composed of three net compartments.

alive for some time, thus allowing fishers to sell the stock progressively.[16] For all these reasons, the *madragues* became extremely popular throughout the course of the seventeenth century and the *Prud'homie* decided to set up a first *madrague* in Morgiou (south of Marseille) in 1619 and a second one in l'Estaque (north of Marseille) in 1623.[17]

However, the organisation of the *madragues* quickly gave rise to collective-action problems. The main challenge was financial: although the operation of the *madragues* was potentially rewarding, their construction and maintenance required significant liquidity.[18] Their construction necessitated a large number of nets, anchors and cork. The storage of this material also required considerable space.[19] These significant costs, combined with high potential benefits, made the prospect of freeriding more attractive in a community that was particularly attached to the idea of equal access to the fishery. The *Prud'homie* tried to mitigate these risks by implementing two successive systems of rules. Initially, it created rules that were shaped by the norm of equality. This 'equal shareholding' system quickly turned out to be inadequate for the management of a capital-intensive

---

[16] See P Gourret, *Les pêcheries et les poissons de la Méditerranée (Provence)* (Paris, Librairie J-B Baillère et Fils,1894) 266–27; Duhamel du Monceau (n 15) 173: 'Il y a des propriétaires de madragues qui font de ce corpou un réservoir de poisons où ils ne prennent les Thons qu'à mesure qu'à mesure qu'ils savent en avoir un débit avantageux.'

[17] Minutes of the *Prud'homie*'s Assembly (28 July 1619), DA 250E4, 31; Minutes of the *Prud'homie*'s Assembly (6 January 1623), DA 250E4, 64.

[18] Duhamel du Monceau (n 15) 173: 'Cette pêche, qui exige de grands frais, est très lucrative quand les Thons donnent abondamment à la côte.'

[19] Minutes of the *Prud'homie*'s Assembly (30 November 1637), DA 250E4.

technique such as the *madragues*. Despite the clear inadequacy of its rules, the *Prud'homie* was very slow in responding and creating a new system of rules. When it finally managed to do so by implementing a system based on tenancy rights, the *Prud'homie* then tried to limit the knock-on effects of what was deemed to be a problematic adjustment to one of its overarching norms.

## A. The Equal-Shareholding System

When the *Prud'homie* set up its first *madrague* in Morgiou in 1619, it decided that each fisher who owned a boat was allowed to hold a single share in the *madrague*.[20] This system was consistent with the horizontal ethos of the *Prud'homie* and the norm of equality that prevailed in its community.[21] However, the fishers could not contribute equally to the *madragues*, because they simply did not have the same financial means. As a result, the question quickly arose as to whether this shareholding system was appropriate for the operation of the *madragues*. In 1620, the community discussed whether fishers should hold only a single share in the *madragues*, or if they should be able to obtain additional shares on the basis of their personal wealth and their ability to contribute to the *madragues* (as measured by the number of boats they owned).[22] Although the second institutional design was probably best suited to addressing the significant costs generated by the *madragues*, the community opted for the equal-shareholding system by an overwhelming majority (78 votes in favour to one vote against).[23] As a result, 172 fishers (arguably the entire community) held individual shares in the *madragues* in 1625.[24]

This rigidity proved to be an impediment to the development of the *madragues*, because fishers were unable to contribute equally to their operation. In 1625, the *Prud'homie* reported the 'great losses' incurred by the *madragues* and a cumulative debt of 2,250 ecus.[25] The community was in dire need of cash, as demonstrated by an attempt to force a rich fisher (Jean-Antoine Bauduf) to make a financial contribution to the *madragues* in 1629.[26] In 1635, the community allowed the *Prud'homie* to resort to outside borrowing to finance the costs of the *madragues*.[27] In each subsequent year of the next decades, the *Prud'homie* sought express authorisation from the community to solicit loans. Until 1640, the *Prud'homie* maintained this model based on an equal-shareholding structure, notwithstanding the grave

---

[20] Ordinance of the *Prud'homie* (5 January 1620), DA 250E4.
[21] See ch 2.
[22] Minutes of the *Prud'homie*'s Assembly (5 January 1620), DA 250E4, 33.
[23] ibid.
[24] Minutes of the *Prud'homie*'s Assembly (19 January 1625), DA 250E4, 81.
[25] ibid.
[26] Minutes of the *Prud'homie*'s Assembly (14 June 1639), DA 250E4, 106.
[27] Minutes of the *Prud'homie*'s Assembly (22 April 1635), DA 250E4, 149.

financial consequences generated by this model.[28] In 1636, the debt grew to 8,300 ecus (24,900 livres),[29] causing an acute financial crisis. In response to this crisis, King Louis XIII temporarily placed the *Prud'homie* under the Crown's direct control and intervened in the election process in order to install new members of the *Prud'homie* responsible for clearing the community's debts.[30] For a very long time, the *Prud'homie* stubbornly refused to amend a rule that reflected an essential norm of its community. It took 20 years, enormous debt and the direct involvement of the royal state to overcome the *Prud'homie*'s resistance. Even after the *Prud'homie* agreed to amend its rules, its reluctance to challenge the social norms of its community remained intact, as will be shown in further detail in section II.B.

## B. The Tenancy System

After many years of efforts to reconcile the management of the *madragues* with its norm of equality, the *Prud'homie* abandoned the shareholding system and explored a second system based on the tenancy of the *madragues* around 1640. By that time, the debts of the *Prud'homie* had reached unprecedented levels and it was vital to create a new system that could displace some of these costs externally. The tenancy system presented such an advantage: it allowed the *Prud'homie* to lease its *madragues*, which could generate rental income and externalise operation costs. However, the tenancy model also undermined the norm of equality, insofar as it allowed a single tenant to benefit from the financial income generated by the *madragues* and prevented fishers from benefiting from this technique. The data that I have collected concerning the leasing of the *madragues* between 1640 and 1688 (Table 3.1) also suggest that the tenancy model enabled the involvement of community outsiders in the operation of the *madragues*.

**Table 3.1** The Tenancy System (1641–88)

| Period | 1641–45 | 1659–63 | 1664–70 | 1670–76 | 1676–82 | 1682–88 |
|---|---|---|---|---|---|---|
| Tenant | Jean Broulhard | Jean Maïousse | Jean Bauduf | JB Jourdan | Pierre Giboin | Pierre Alleman |
| Insider/ Outsider | Outsider | Insider | Insider | Outsider | Outsider | Outsider |
| Price (per year) | 2,964 livres | 4,200 livres | 7,200 livres | 12,000 livres | 8,625 livres | 6,035 livres |

---

[28] Minutes of the *Prud'homie*'s Assembly (5 February 1640), DA 250E4, 170.
[29] Minutes of the *Prud'homie*'s Assembly (9 March 1636), DA 250E4, 157.
[30] ibid.

In fact, the *Prud'homie* first leased the *madragues* to an outsider named Jean Broulhard in 1640 (for a period of 14 years).[31] However, Broulhard quickly transferred his tenancy rights to three other outsiders (De Gastines, Martin and Durand). For reasons that are not made clear in the archival records, the *Prud'homie* did not maintain this first tenancy for very long, and it recovered the rights to exploit the *madragues* in 1645, less than five years later.[32] It seems likely that the *Prud'homie* did this in order to re-assert the community's rights over the exploitation of the *madragues* (another sign of the resilience of its norms). However, the community then found itself in the same situation it had been in prior to 1640, as it once again needed to subsidise the financial costs of the *madragues*. In 1657, for instance, a document from the *Prud'homie* reports 'important charges and expenses' incurred by the *madragues*.[33]

In 1659, the *Prud'homie* turned once again to the tenancy system, entering into a second contract with a community insider named Jean Maïousse for a five-year period (1659–63).[34] Maïousse was a prominent fisher whose family counted no fewer than six *Prud'hommes* throughout the seventeenth century (Jean Maïousse himself was elected at the *Prud'homie* in 1678). The Maïousse family was so deeply entrenched within the community that a street in the St Jean neighbourhood bore its name. Shortly after signing the tenancy contract with the *Prud'homie* in 1659, Maïousse signed a counter-letter with 31 other fishers in order to share the benefits of the *madragues* with them.[35] Maïousse's efforts to open the *madragues* to his fellow fishers may indicate that these *madragues* were too costly to operate for a single fisher, but this interpretation seems rather unlikely considering the prominence and wealth of the Maïousse family at the time. A more plausible interpretation is that Maïousse was attempting to share the proceeds of the *madragues* with fellow fishers in ways that are consistent with the equality norm.

After the *Prud'homie* sued Maïousse for what was, in effect, an attempt to bypass the tenancy system, the *Prud'homie* leased the *madragues* to Jean Bauduf from 1664 until 1670.[36] Bauduf was the son of Jean-Antoine Bauduf, the rich fisher whom the *Prud'homie* had solicited to replenish its funds in 1629 (and a member of the *Prud'homie* in 1644). Clearly, the *madragues* could only be managed by the richest and most prominent fishers or, alternatively, by community outsiders. The *Prud'homie* was, by that point, prepared to lease its *madragues* to outsiders, as

---

[31] Minutes of the Auction of the *Madragues* (9 November 1640), DA 250E30.

[32] Settlement Agreement between the *Prud'homie* and Messrs De Gastines, Martin & Durand (9 May 1645), DA 250E31.

[33] Minutes of the *Prud'homie*'s Assembly (7 January 1657), DA 250E4, 205.

[34] Rental Agreement of the *madragues* to Jean Maïousse (7 January 1659), DA 250E31.

[35] ibid.

[36] The *Prud'homie* sued Maïousse in 1663, arguing that he conspired to divert the profits of the *madragues* (40,000 livres according to the complaint) and channel them back to those who granted him the tenancy (Inventory of the documents produced during the trial between Jean Maïousse and the *Prud'homie* (1663), DA 250E213). In 1663, the royal court of Aix ordered that the tenancy be placed back to auction (Decision of the Parliament of Provence (14 March 1663), DA 250E213).

indicated in Table 3.1. However, as will be shown, the *Prud'homie* was ill at ease with the prospect of sharing its *madragues* with rich outsiders, as evidenced by the multiple lawsuits it filed against them. Trusting rich outsiders with the operation of its *madragues* was contrary to the egalitarian ethos of the *Prud'homie*, which seemed determined to aggressively assert its rights against the outsiders to whom it had leased its two *madragues*.

## C.  Growing Debt and Social Conflicts

After the implementation of the tenancy system and the externalisation of maintenance costs after 1676, one would expect to see a decrease in the community's debt. However, the *Prud'homie*'s debts continued to grow at a rapid pace (see Graph 3.1), reaching 75,000 livres in 1666, 140,000 livres in 1710 and 230,000 livres in 1740. The financial situation of the *Prud'homie* only stabilised and improved around the mid-eighteenth century, after the royal administration placed it under its direct control.[37]

One possible explanation for this growing debt is that the community of fishers progressively ceased benefiting from the *madragues* after 1676. The *Prud'homie* externalised its costs and collected rents from its tenants, but, at the same time,

**Graph 3.1** The Debts of the *Prud'homie de pêche* (1625–1789)

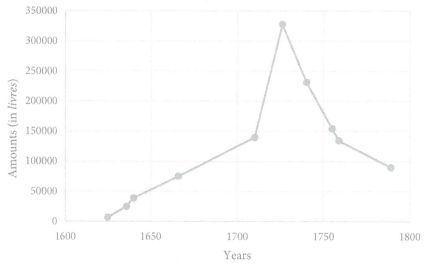

---

[37] This control began in 1727. See Decision of the Council of State (27 August 1727), DA 250E75 (ordering that the *Prud'homie* be accountable to the royal administration in Provence). Inflation rates were negligible during this period.

members of its community no longer benefited from the substantial income generated by the *madragues*. Another possible explanation seems to be even more pertinent, which is closely associated with the demise of the equal-shareholding system and the growing involvement of outsiders in the management of the *madragues*.

In fact, the involvement of outsiders generated disputes that the *Prud'homie* was unable to handle internally. In order to resolve these disputes, the *Prud'homie* initiated a long string of cases in the royal courts, which were extremely costly for the community and increased its debt.[38] I have identified nine cases litigated between 1624 and 1678 in state courts in connection with the *madragues* that involved the *Prud'homie*. What were these cases about? And why were there so many? The cases fall into two categories: the first category concerned the efforts of outsiders to participate in and reap the benefits of the *madragues* (and the corresponding efforts of the *Prud'homie* to keep them out of the fishery), while the second category concerned disputes arising out of the tenancy agreements themselves.

Court cases falling within the first category resulted from the attraction exerted by the *madragues* on community outsiders and the corresponding efforts of the *Prud'homie* to maintain a monopoly over their exploitation. Some outsiders sought to benefit from the shareholding system put in place between 1623 and 1640, while others solicited the royal authority in order to set up their own *madragues*. In all of the cases, the *Prud'homie* aggressively asserted its rights over the *madragues* by suing the outsiders. However, it was unable to do so via its own court system (which was reserved for the settlement of disputes arising between fishers) and had to turn to the royal courts. For instance, the *Prud'homie* sued four outsiders who had pretended to be fishers in order to obtain shares in the *madragues* in 1623 and 1624.[39] The case was brought before the administrative authority in Marseille (*Lieutenant de l'Amirauté*) and then before the royal courts in Aix-en-Provence (*Parlement de Provence*). Even more challenging for the *Prud'homie* were the efforts of wealthy outsiders (often members of the aristocracy) to set up additional *madragues* in Marseille.[40] The *Prud'homie* reacted internally by expelling any fisher who assisted these outsiders with the construction and maintenance of new *madragues*.[41] However, these measures were insufficient to prevent outsiders from establishing a foothold in the fishery of Marseille, arguably because these outsiders were insensitive to the pressure exerted by the *Prud'homie*. As a consequence, the *Prud'homie* initiated lengthy and costly proceedings before the royal courts

---

[38] For instance, the *Prud'homie* took out a loan in 1635 to cover its litigation costs. See Minutes of the *Prud'homie*'s Assembly (22 April 1635), DA 250E4, 149.

[39] The record of this lawsuit can be found in DA 250E191.

[40] See, eg, Letter from the King granting to François de Seystres the right to establish a *madrague* in Carry (29 June 1643), DA 250E32, 96. A list of these privileges can be found in J Billioud, 'La pêche au thon et les madragues de Marseille' (1955) 26 *Marseille: Revue municipale* 3.

[41] Minutes of the *Prud'homie*'s Assembly (4 January 1632), DA 250E4, 125.

(*Parlements*) in Aix and Grenoble to prohibit the construction of the *madragues* by rich outsiders. The proceedings were largely unsuccessful for the *Prud'homie*: for instance, the royal court of Aix enjoined the *Prud'homie* from preventing the setting up of a new *madrague* north of Marseille in 1646.[42] The *Prud'homie* similarly failed in its court claims against the Count of Luc, to whom Louis XIV granted the right to set up several *madragues*.[43] Even when the courts sided with the *Prud'homie* (as was the case in 1673, when the courts denied Dominique de la Crosse, a favourite of Queen Maria Theresa, the possibility to set up *madragues* at Sormiou and Montredon),[44] additional *madragues* would nonetheless appear after a few decades (as was the case in Montredon).

The second category of cases highlights the concrete difficulties raised by the tenancy model. The *Prud'homie* brought court cases against almost all of its tenants. These cases show the weaknesses of the tenancy system: the price of tenancy appeared to be too high (or the duration of the tenancy too limited) for the tenants to break even. Three tenants requested a price reduction on the basis that they could not generate sufficient profits to recoup their costs. One of these tenants (Pierre Giboin) produced data showing his revenues and expenses between 1676 and 1678 during his trial.[45]

Table 3.2 indicates that Giboin operated the *madragues* at a substantial loss between 1676 and 1678, resulting in a shortfall of 22,910 livres. The income generated by the *madragues* (31,419 livres) was sufficient to cover the operating costs (and generate a profit), but insufficient when rent was also taken into account.[46]

**Table 3.2** Financial Statement of the *Madragues* (1676–78)

| Year | Revenues | Expenses | | TOTAL |
| --- | --- | --- | --- | --- |
| | | Operational costs | Rent | |
| 1676 | 13,698 | 10,130 | 8,625 | −5,057 |
| 1677 | 12,945 | 8,828 | 8,625 | −4,508 |
| 1678 | 4,776 | 9,496 | 8,625 | −13,345 |
| TOTAL | 31,419 | 28,454 | 25,875 | −22,910 |

[42] Decision from the Parliament of Provence (30 April 1646), DA 250E32, 108.

[43] Judicial proceedings initiated by the *Prud'homie* against the Count of Luc (17 September 1705), DA 250E40. After the Count of Luc installed several *madragues* on the *Prud'homie*'s territory (the archival records are unclear on their number, mentioning two, three or five *madragues*), the *Prud'homie* unsuccessfully tried to buy these *madragues* back from the Count of Luc, with the intention of destroying them (Letter to Admiral Poncet (30 September 1727), NA C5/1).

[44] Decision from the Parliament of Provence (29 May 1673), DA 250E227.

[45] Summary of the revenues and expenses of the *madragues*, DA 250E235, 9.

[46] Another tenant (Jean Bauduf) sought to increase the profitability of the *madragues* by raising the price of tuna. However, he faced another lawsuit initiated by the city of Marseille to maintain tuna prices at constant levels. See Records of trial between the city of Marseille and Jean Bauduf, forbidding him to sell tuna for more than 3 sols per livre (30 September 1664), MA HH372.

The attractiveness of the *madragues* declined as lessees appeared unable to maintain sufficient profitability to operate them. The situation ended in a stalemate, because the fishers were unable to operate the *madragues* themselves, while the tenants could not generate sufficient profits because of the high rent levels. In 1688, the *Prud'homie* reported that for the last year and a half, no one had made a bid to lease the *madragues*.[47] The solution came in the form of a decrease in rent levels in order to increase the profitability of the *madragues*. For instance, the rent for the *madragues* decreased to 1,674 livres in 1717.[48] In 1735, only a single individual presented a bid at a steep discount (150 livres/year).[49] As a consequence, the tenancy model continued to persist until the nineteenth century, but it generated decreased rental income for the *Prud'homie*.

In sum, the experimentation with the *madragues* was rather unsuccessful. It divided the community, threatened its independence vis-à-vis the royal authority and posed a serious challenge to its budget. The *Prud'homie* proved unable to handle disputes within the bounds of its own system, particularly since these disputes involved wealthy outsiders who did not recognise the authority of the *Prud'homie*. More importantly, the *Prud'homie* experienced great difficulties in creating rules that were consistent with the social norm of equality while offering clear responses to the concrete challenges raised by the *madragues*. These difficulties illustrate one of the main themes explored in this book: norms are a powerful tool of governance, but also a significant force of social inertia. An unintended consequence of the *Prud'homie's* passion for equality was the loss of its monopoly over the *madragues* and their subsequent proliferation.

## D. The Proliferation of the *Madragues* and the Decline of Tuna Stocks

As we have seen, the *Prud'homie* failed to maintain a monopoly over the operation of the *madragues*. It was unable to preserve its equal-shareholding system, thus resulting in the leasing of the *madragues* to rich outsiders and the multiplication of *madragues* directly controlled by these outsiders. In fact, no fewer than 10 *madragues* appeared in the fishery of Marseille during this time period.[50] Only two of these *madragues* (*l'Estaque* and *Morgiou*) belonged to the *Prud'homie*, while community outsiders controlled all the rest. I have indicated on the first map, reproduced as Figure 3.2, the location of the *madragues*, with black arrows in order to assist the reader. On the second map (Figure 3.3), the reader

---

[47] Minutes of the *Prud'homie's* Assembly (18 January 1688), DA 250E4, 369.
[48] Request from the *Prud'homie* to the Lieutenant Général de l'Amirauté (17 July 1719), DA 250E256.
[49] Minutes of the *Prud'homie's* Assembly (6 February 1735), DA 250E4, 392.
[50] See *Mémoire adressé à l'Assemblée nationale pour la colonie des pêcheurs catalans* (1790), CCI YC/2209, 21. These *madragues* bore the following names, from West to East: *Madragues de Sainte Croix, Sausset, Gignac, l'Estaque, la Ville, Pointe Rouge, Montredon, Podestat* and *Morgiou*.

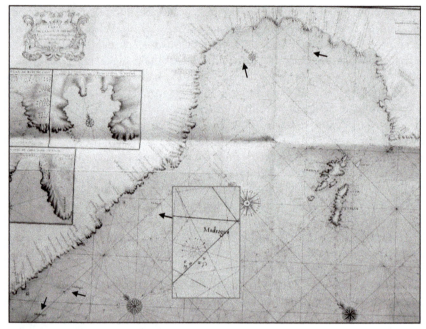

**Figure 3.2** The West Coast of Marseille and its *Madragues* in 1694

*Source: Carte de la Baie de Marseille avec les plans particuliers des endroits où on peut mouiller* (1694), Archives Nationales (France), Cartes et Plans.

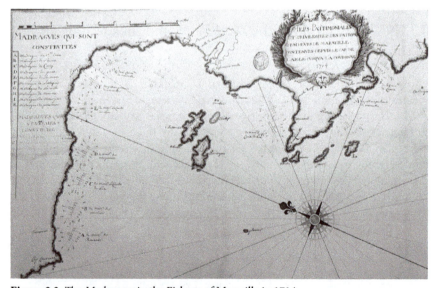

**Figure 3.3** The *Madragues* in the Fishery of Marseille in 1714

*Source: Mers Patrimoniales et Privilèges des Patrons Pêcheurs de Marseille contenues depuis le Cap de l'Aigle jusqu'à la Couronne* (1714), AM 78Fi36.

can identify the rectangular shape of *madragues* surrounded by anchors along the coast of Marseille. This map shows that, along with the 10 existing *madragues*, plans were made to build four more (as explained on the original legend on the left side of the map). *Madragues* clearly were the new bonanza in the fishery of Marseille, and they escaped the purview of a *Prud'homie* that remained deeply entrenched in the defence of its norms.

This bonanza came at a price, however, since the proliferation of *madragues* along the coast of Marseille seems to have negatively impacted the stock of tuna. There are several reasons for this outcome. Bluefin tuna are a migratory species that are present throughout the Atlantic Ocean and the Mediterranean region. Fishing practices in a specific area should therefore have only a limited impact on a stock of fish circulating throughout a large geographic area. This was, in fact, one of the arguments raised by the *Prud'homie* to justify the installation of the *madragues* in the early seventeenth century.[51] However, tuna reproduce in warm waters during the spring and summer seasons.[52] This period coincides with the tuna-fishing season in Marseille, and *madragues* were typically set up in areas close to the coast.[53] The *madragues* therefore captured tuna at a key stage and in key areas in their reproduction cycle, thus having a maximal impact on their stock. And in fact there are several reports of a collapse in tuna stocks starting in the second half of the seventeenth century.[54] A contemporary observer reports in 1769 that the *Prud'homie* abandoned one of its *madragues* because tuna had deserted the coast of Marseille.[55] In the 1850s, seven of the 10 *madragues* were discontinued.[56] An internal report commissioned by the city of Marseille emphasised the 'discontinuation and demise' of the *madragues* because of the collapse of tuna stocks in 1870.[57] In the early twentieth century, another report stated that tuna had disappeared from the coast of Marseille and highlighted the need to discontinue the remaining *madragues*.[58] The last *madrague* of the fishery of Marseille was dismantled in 1913.[59]

[51] *Description des Pesches, Loix et Ordonnances des Pescheurs de la Ville de Marseille* (1725), DA 250E2, 146.

[52] Ifremer, *Le thon rouge Atlantique* (4 September 2019) available at https://wwz.ifremer.fr/content/download/41835/file/DP%20thon%20rouge%202019_MiseAjour.pdf.

[53] Braudel (n 3) 258.

[54] See Faget (n 11) 138. There are also reports of a collapse of the overall fish stock. Fishers were so desperate that they turned to the Bishop of Marseille, asking him to pray for the return of fish (see A Fabre, *Les Rues de Marseille*, vol 2 (Marseille, E Camoin, 1867) 357–58.

[55] *Quelles sont les causes de la diminution de la pêche sur les côtes de Provence? Et quels sont les moyens de la rendre plus abondante? Discours du Père Menc à l'Académie de Marseille* (7 April 1769), BNF Gallica, 9.

[56] See Gourret (n 16) 249.

[57] *Rapport de M Jules Guibert au Conseil municipal de Marseille pour l'interdiction des filets traînants* (22 June 1870), DA 6S10/3.

[58] *Rapport final de l'ingénieur des Ponts et Chaussées rejetant la demande d'indemnisation de M Fremin du Sartel* (22 February 1905), DA 6S52/1.

[59] Billioud (n 40) 16.

It is, of course, challenging to identify the causes shaping the evolution of fish stocks, which is influenced by myriad factors other than fishing. Indeed, the archival records suggest the potential role played by other matters, such as the expansion of the port of Marseille, in the decline of tuna stocks and the disappearance of the *madragues*. The map following (Figure 3.4), drawn in 1904, shows the effects that the construction of a new pier had on the migratory flows of tuna and on the operation of the very last *madrague* of Marseille.

That said, it remains highly likely that the proliferation of *madragues* contributed to the decline in tuna stocks, and that this proliferation was an indirect outcome of the *Prud'homie*'s policy. The difficulty faced by the *Prud'homie* in governing the *madragues* in accordance with its equality norm encouraged rich outsiders to reap the benefits of its fishery, resulting in their proliferation and the over-exploitation of tuna stocks. Even more striking is the fact that the fishers of Marseille remained strongly attached to their norm of equality during this time period and that they favoured a narrow interpretation of this norm, despite the fact that this interpretation seemed incompatible with the exploitation of the *madragues*. The open-ended character of norms would have easily allowed the *Prud'homie* to promote a more flexible interpretation of the norm of equality. When the *Prud'homie* tried to do so by implementing a new system of rules based on tenancy rights, the fishers tried to bypass these rules (as evidenced by Maïousse's seeking to involve other fishers in the tenancy of the *madragues*) and the *madragues* fell into the hands of

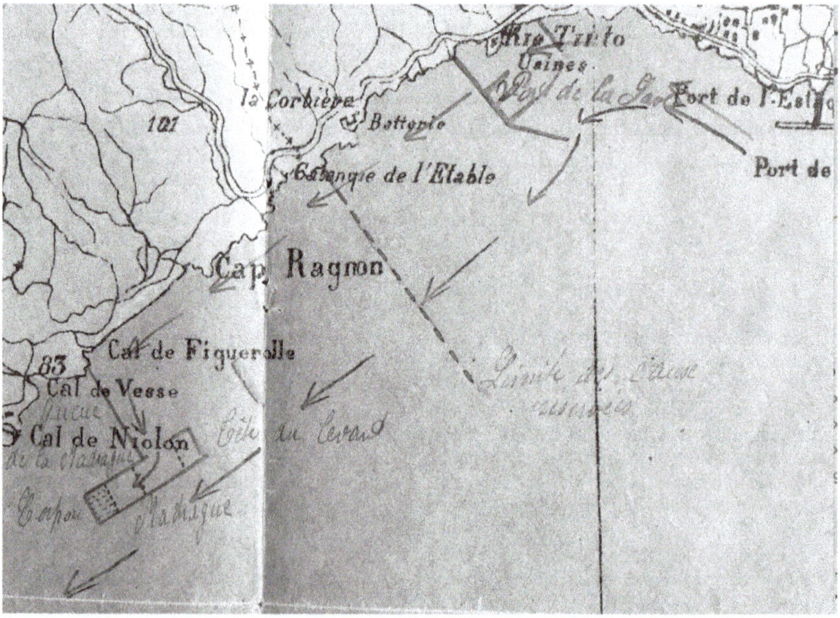

**Figure 3.4** The Last *Madrague* of Marseille (1904)

*Source*: Letter from Mr Fremin du Sartel to the Préfet des Bouches-du-Rhône (18 January 1905), DA 6S52/1.

rich outsiders. The community's dedication to its norms, as well as the unintended consequences of this dedication, became even more apparent when it faced the arrival of foreign fishers in the early eighteenth century.

## III. Labour Migrations and the Arrival of the Catalans

Starting in the 1720s, the *Prud'homie* faced yet another challenge, when Catalan fishers progressively began to settle in Marseille. These Catalan fishers left Spain for France for reasons that remain unclear.[60] What is fairly certain is that their settlement in Marseille was part of successive streams of labour migrations that unfolded beginning in the late sixteenth century in overpopulated Mediterranean Europe.[61] In other words, the arrival of Catalan fishers in Marseille is another manifestation of the early globalisation that had already made itself felt with the apparition of *madragues*. Their arrival deeply affected the life of the *Prud'homie*, in a historical context that was already challenging for local fishers: their finances had been gravely affected by the *madragues* and, to make matters worse, they had suffered heavily from the Great Plague that hit the port of Marseille in the early 1720s. As Dumas vividly describes it, the Spanish fishers created their own separate enclave and refused to submit to the jurisdiction of the *Prud'homie*. The following section thus describes the arrival of the Catalan fishers in Marseille throughout the eighteenth century, their failure to abide by the norms of the community and their repeated violations of the *Prud'homie*'s rules. In response to these violations, the *Prud'homie* displayed a stubborn attachment to its norms and a reluctance to adapt its rules. This section confirms the view that social norms are a factor not only of resistance, but also of social inertia in the operation of private orders.

### A. The Arrival of the Catalans

Catalan fishers arrived in Marseille in successive streams of migration starting in the 1720s. They settled in the southern part of the port of Marseille, while local fishers lived in the St Jean quarter located in the northern part of the port. Faget reports the arrival of 39 Catalan fishers (presumably with their children and wives) between 1722 and 1792 on the basis of notary records.[62] The *Prud'homie* reported the presence of 102 Catalan boats with 812 crew members in 1787 (clearly a politically motivated exaggeration).[63]

---

[60] See D Faget, 'Maîtres de l'onde, maîtres des marchés et des techniques: les migrants catalans à Marseille au XVIIIe siècle (1720–1793)' (2012) 84 *Cahiers de la Méditerranée* 159, 160.

[61] See eg, Braudel (n 3) 415–18; Echinard and Témime (n 5) 93–94.

[62] D Faget, *Marseille et la mer: Hommes et environnement marin (XVIIIe–XXe siècle)* (Rennes, Presses universitaires de Rennes, 2011) 357.

[63] *Mémoire pour les Prud'hommes de la Communauté des Patrons-Pêcheurs de la Ville de Marseille* (1787), DA 250E8, 89.

The records of the police department of Marseille provide a more precise and dispassionate accounting of the population of Catalan fishers in 1826,[64] identifying 117 fishers, the majority of whom (83) were born in Marseille.[65] The estimate given by the police is consistent with my own accounting of the community based on an exhaustive review of the number of fishing boats in the port of Marseille between 1816 and 1818.[66] My data show 22 Catalan boats with 115 crew members (112 of whom were described as 'Spanish'). This empirical evidence enables a comparison between the size of the Catalan community and the overall community of local fishers: the local fishers operated 141 boats with 683 crew members. Therefore, the Catalan fishers represented 14 per cent or 16 per cent of the entire community (depending on whether this proportion is calculated in terms of the number of crew members or boats) approximately 100 years after their first arrival. These figures, although they do not allow us to track the demographic evolution throughout the eighteenth century, provide a snapshot of the community and of its size immediately after the relevant time period (the eighteenth century). They show that the Catalan fishers represented a non-trivial proportion of the entire population of fishers in Marseille.[67]

## B. Tit-for-Tat in the Fishery of Marseille

As noted in previous chapters, the fishers of Marseille have been particularly adamant about preserving the resources of their fishery, if only to enable their children to exploit it in the long term. Accordingly, the *Prud'homie* created rules to ensure that fishing practices would not impact fish stocks. When settling in Marseille, the Catalans seemed indifferent to this norm. They seemed to have no interest in preserving fish stocks, perhaps because they did not expect to stay in Marseille for long: in particular, they repeatedly violated the rules of the *Prud'homie* governing a fishing technique called *palangre*. A *palangre* is a long line to which multiple smaller lines and hundreds of hooks are attached. Figure 3.5 offers an illustration of this technique – which is still used in the fishery of Marseille – based on the detail of an original map. *Palangre* fishers are very proud of their chosen technique. There are only a few of them left in Marseille, and they describe the *palangre* as a 'beautiful' fishing technique that (unlike the use of nets) preserves the bodily integrity of the fish.

The *Prud'homie* regulated the size of hooks used for *palangres* in order to prevent the capture of juvenile fish. The ultimate goal of this practice was to preserve the reproduction cycle of the fish by sparing juvenile subjects.

---

[64] Letter from the Préfet to the Mayor of Marseille requesting an account of the Catalans (31 March 1826), MA 18F6.

[65] Letter from the Police Commissioner to the Mayor of Marseille transmitting an account of the Catalans (April 1826), MA 18F6.

[66] Inventory of the boats in Marseille (1819), AA 13 P10 3.

[67] R Axelrod, *The Evolution of Cooperation* (New York, NY, Penguin Books, 1990) 66–67.

*Filet dit PALANGRE composé de 500 Hameçons qui sert a prendre. touttes Sortes de Poissons il y en a quantité.*

**Figure 3.5** A *Palangre* around 1660

Source: Extract from a map entitled *Carte d'une partie des costes maritimes de Provence, 1660*, *Bibliothèque nationale de France* (BNF Gallica).

However, in utter disregard of this rule, the Catalans used smaller hooks than those allowed by the *Prud'homie*, resulting in the capture of younger subjects (and impacting the fish stocks more aggressively). The Catalans also deployed their *palangres* further out from the shore, thanks to their use of narrower and faster boats than those used by local fishers. Additionally, the Catalan fishers refused to comply with the *Prud'homie*'s prohibition of fishing on Sundays and the obligation to submit to its court on that day.[68] In sum, the Catalan fishers showed little regard for the *Prud'homie*'s rules, which they constantly flouted.

The local fishers reacted strongly to these violations. The *Prud'homie* expressed its own concerns shortly after the arrival of the first Catalans in the 1720s and initially touted the merits of its jurisdiction to the Catalans, probably in the hope of winning them over to its rules:

> In the last few years, since 1722, [the prud'hommes] have been appalled to see foreigners from Catalonia coming to Marseille with palangres equipped with small hooks. The prud'hommes, seeing the harm done to the seas through the use of small hooks, reiterated the prohibition and rules, according to which only hooks numbered 13 or 14, which are harmless for [the fish stocks], can be used with palangre.[69]

The *Prud'homie* also tried to convince the Catalans to pay the 'half-share', its special tax on the sale of fish.[70] However, this strategy did not bear fruit and the *Prud'homie* then tried more forcefully to make the Catalans submit to its jurisdiction. For instance, in a letter from 1735, the Minister of the Navy mentions the *Prud'homie*'s efforts to 'force' the Catalans to comply with its rules:

> by forcing the Catalans to fish with boats and nets similar to those used by the fishers in Marseille and to have the same number of crew members, [the Catalans] are expected

---

[68] Faget (n 62) 45–48.

[69] *Description des Pesches, Loix et Ordonnances des Pescheurs de la Ville de Marseille* (1725), DA 250E2, 45.

[70] See, eg, Letter of the *Prud'homie* to the First President of the Parliament of Provence (17 November 1736), DA 250E5.

to stop fishing with palangres in the fishery of Marseille in order to avoid the additional expenses associated with these new boats and nets ...[71]

The *Prud'homie* mobilised a wide array of retaliatory measures to bring the Catalans back in line. For instance, the *Prud'homie* prevented the Catalans from drying their nets on its docks.[72] It even confiscated the sails and lines of three Catalan fishers who refused to comply with its rules in 1774.[73] However, it soon became evident that the Catalan fishers were impervious to the *Prud'homie*'s measures and that they intended to keep fishing as they wished.

The situation became even more complicated for the *Prud'homie* as the Catalan fishers became a valuable source for the supply of fish in Marseille. By catching more (and arguably better-quality) fish through the aggressive use of *palangres*, the Catalan fishers gained the sympathy of local stakeholders, such as city officials. On 7 November 1790, for instance, the municipal council of Marseille credited the Catalan fishers with the 'affluence of better fish' in the previous 50 years.[74] The *Prud'homie* reacted to the new-found influence of the Catalans by actively seeking the support of the French state. In order to drive the Catalans away from its fishery, the *Prud'homie* built an alliance with the royal authority that will be examined further in chapter 5. As a result of this alliance, the Council of State rendered no fewer than five decisions between 1738 and 1786 clarifying the powers of the *Prud'homie* over the Catalans. The king even sent a special envoy to Marseille, Daniel-Marc-Antoine Chardon, in order to regulate the *palangre* and resolve the disputes between the French and Catalan fishers. These efforts resulted in a statute of 1790, which made clear that the *Prud'homie* had jurisdiction over the Catalans and that the Catalans had the same rights and obligation as local fishers (for instance, the obligation to pay the half-share and the right to be candidates in the *Prud'homie*'s elections).[75] However, these measures did not yield significant results. In particular, they did not put an end to the conflicts between the fishers of Marseille and their Catalan counterparts. The Catalans still formed their own community and continued to pay little or no heed to the *Prud'homie*'s rules long after their first arrival.[76]

---

[71] Letter from the Count of Maurepas to Mr De Langerie (15 November 1735), DA 250E5.

[72] Request from the *Prud'homie* to the Intendance de Marseille in order to prohibit the *Catalans* from drying their fishing nets on the lands owned by the *Prud'homie* (19 September 1777), DA 250E276.

[73] Notarised declaration of the *Prud'homie* (15 May 1774), DA 250E41. The royal court of Aix overturned the *Prud'homie*'s decision to confiscate these sails and lines in two judgments that were later reversed by the Council of State and even prompted an official complaint by the Ambassador of Spain to the French Government. See Minutes of the General Assembly of the *Prud'homie* (30 April 1775), DA C4028; Letter from the Count of Aranda, Spanish Ambassador to France, to Mr de Vergennes, Secretary of Foreign Affairs of France (22 May 1775), DA C4028.

[74] Observations from the City Council of Marseille on the disputes between French fishers and Catalan fishers (7 November 1790), MA 18F6.

[75] *Loi Relative aux Pêcheurs des différents Ports du Royaume, et notamment à ceux de la ville de Marseille* (12 December 1790), CCI E/159, Arts 1, 2, 3 and 4.

[76] See, eg, Letter from the Préfet des Bouches-du-Rhône to the mayor of Marseille concerning a complaint from a Spanish consul as to the way in which the *Prud'hommes* have treated the Catalans (11 January 1817), MA 18F6.

## C. Increased Tensions

As already suggested, the *Prud'homie* was overwhelmed by the arrival of outsiders. Archival documents depict the utter desolation of the *Prud'homie* when faced with the repeated violations of its rules by the Catalan fishers:

> All those breaches are frequent, as are the violations of rules. They [the Catalans] practice pit-lamping at night, despite its being prohibited under the laws of the fishery. They never pay the 'half-share' [the tax imposed by the Prud'homie], even though they recognise that this tax is owed by them. The prohibition against fishing on Sundays and holidays does not stop them. In particular, they avoid leaving [the port] with local fishers on Sunday night in order to reach their fishing site …, and are always one step ahead of them: they are where they choose to be, occupy the fishing sites as they wish against the laws of cooperation and equality, which they breach without hesitation. The negative consequences are significant. The flight of fish and their near destruction are the least of these. What is even more noteworthy is the reduced equality, the insubordination and the disorder and disastrous consequences brought about by this insubordination.[77]

The emergence of a rival group of outsiders who successfully competed with the *Prud'homie* relegated the local fishers to a secondary role and generated tensions within their community. Because the Catalans excelled at practising *palangre*, some local fishers started selling sardines (the bait used by the Catalans for their *palangres*) to them. When the *Prud'homie* tried to prohibit the sale of sardines to the Catalans, it quickly faced opposition from within its own ranks because of the profits generated through these sales.[78] The superiority of the fishing techniques used by the Catalans also encouraged the local fishers to emulate the foreigners rather than to stick with their traditional techniques. In a decision of 20 March 1786, the Council of the King implemented a series of measures aimed at encouraging the local fishers to practise *palangre*. Local fishers who expressed a wish to fish with *palangres* were given a boat, an exemption from the half-share tax for three years and an exemption from military service.[79] The royal authority therefore intervened directly, in order to encourage the local fishers to address the competitive pressure exerted by the Catalans. The *Prud'homie* also supported this policy by allocating 8,000 livres for the purchase of lines by local fishers who wished to practise *palangre*.[80] These efforts were of little or no avail. The Catalans were the masters of the *palangre*, and the local fishers simply could not match their skill.[81] The *Prud'homie* proved unwilling to modify its rules in ways that would allow local fishers to compete with the foreigners. As with the *madragues*, it would

---

[77] Memorial of the *Prud'homie* sent to Mr Chardon against the foreigners (1786), DA 250E36, 6.

[78] Faget (n 62) 61.

[79] Decision of the Council of the King on the regulation between French and foreign fishers in Marseille (20 March 1786), CCI E/159.

[80] Memorial for the *Prud'homie* (1787), DA 250E8, 52.

[81] This failure is mentioned by Faget (n 61) 78–79.

have been easy for the *Prud'homie* to do so. In fact, the *Prud'homie* could have interpreted its norms in ways more conducive to regulatory compromise and to the creation of new rules that would be more strictly compliant with its norms. The *Prud'homie*'s failure to do so confirms the fact, already observed in chapter 2, that social norms create a path that constrains regulatory activities in systems of private governance. This path can be more or less narrow depending on the willingness of community members to compromise. The ambivalent character of social norms, both open-ended and rigid, seems to be a key aspect that will be explored further in subsequent chapters.

# IV. Conclusion

This chapter has examined the functioning of the *Prud'homie* when it was confronted with the early stages of globalisation. In particular, two categories of social events arising from this 'proto-globalisation' have been examined: the emergence of a new fishing technique called *madragues* in the seventeenth century and the arrival of Catalan fishers in the eighteenth century. The rich empirical record of the *Prud'homie* provides evidence of the ways in which it responded to these social events. In both cases, the *Prud'homie* remained strongly attached to the norms of its community and – especially when faced with the arrival of the Catalans – was extremely reluctant to adapt its rules. Moreover, even when, under great financial and political strain, it adjusted its rules, the fishers typically ignored these new rules in favour of the social norms in which they believed (as in the case of the management of the *madragues*). In other words, the fishers' social norms created a constitutional frame for the *Prud'homie*'s regulatory functions by steering the shape and content of the rules that it generated over the centuries.

The fishers' social norms thus resemble a doughnut, with a hole at the centre leaving room for interpretation, while placing constraints on the rules conceived by the *Prud'homie* to address concrete challenges. The *Prud'homie*'s rules are surrounded by the outer layer of the doughnut, which frames their scope and interpretation. The next chapter will add another twist to this analysis, by exploring how the *Prud'homie* reacted when conflict arose between different communal norms.

><((((°>

# 4

## A Battle of Norms

## I. Introduction

Fishing is an arduous venture. It requires special skills, patience and luck. The fishers of Marseille often compare themselves to hunters who incessantly track their prey in the Mediterranean Sea. They are envious and actively compete with one another. In the apt words of one old fisher, 'a good fisher is always jealous of other fishers'. The temptation is therefore great for fishers to use larger nets, more powerful boats and gear that can help them catch more fish, more rapidly than their competitors. A major downside of this tendency to gear up for fishing is the overexploitation of fish stocks and, ultimately, the dreaded prospect of a Mediterranean emptied of its fish.

The *Prud'homie* has always been well aware of the tension between the hunting instinct of the fishers and the need to preserve the fishery from the disastrous consequences of overfishing. The previous chapters have shown how the *Prud'homie* tried to limit the impact of new, presumably aggressive techniques on the resources of the fishery. When accommodating new techniques, the *Prud'homie* balanced out the permissive norm of equality with the restrictive norm of conservation. This fine-tuning exercise often resulted in the combination of welcoming new techniques, while limiting their potential impact on the fishery. As shown in previous chapters, the *Prud'homie* established numerous rules concerning the size of nets, the type of hooks, the geographical areas and times in which fishers could use specific techniques, and so on.[1]

The present chapter shifts the focus to the ways in which the emergence of major technologies, such as electricity or the combustion engine, rendered this fine-tuning exercise more challenging. The inherent tension between the norms of equality and conservation increased as fishers learned how to use these technologies. The archival records of the nineteenth and twentieth centuries offer numerous examples of this 'battle of norms'. I will focus in this chapter on three technological developments that the fishers of Marseille embraced with a view to facilitating their work and increasing their productivity: the engine, electricity and dynamite. Each of these technologies operates in different ways at various stages of the fishing process. The engine is a prime mover that outperforms wind

---

[1] See ch 2, section IV (on the introduction of floating nets in Marseille).

or muscle power when it comes to operating boats and nets. The light produced by electricity provides compelling bait that attracts fish into the nets. Dynamite can be used to kill very large quantities of fish instantly. Drawing on these examples, this chapter examines how the *Prud'homie* accommodated new technologies through political compromise, with the unintended consequence that harmful techniques had a ratcheting effect with respect to future ones. The *Prud'homie* had difficulties balancing its norms, with the commitment to equality ultimately prevailing over the long-term preservation of fish stocks. The *Prud'homie's* inclination towards equality encouraged a race to the bottom that it was unable or unwilling to curtail, even though this evolution was detrimental to the maintenance of its norm of conservation.

# II.  Engines and Dragnets

The engine progressively emerged as a prime mover between the seventeenth and the late nineteenth centuries, and significantly bolstered the productivity of fishers in Marseille. The arrival of engines in Marseille was not entirely unprecedented, however, as ancient fishing practices based on dragnets provided fertile ground for their introduction. Notwithstanding the enormous impact of engines on fish stocks, the *Prud'homie's* response was weak, and engines quickly replaced sailing and muscle power as the prime mover in Marseille. As a preliminary matter, this section briefly summarises the progressive development of the engine and shows how fishing progressively benefited from this prime mover. It then describes the introduction of the engine into the fishery of Marseille and examines the *Prud'homie's* response to this development.

## A.  The Rise of the Engine as a Prime Mover

The history of the engine is a process of trial and error, in which scientists and engineers attempted to replace muscular strength with mechanically generated power. That this was even possible was less than evident in the seventeenth century, when scientific pioneers started laying the ground for the so-called 'Machine Age'.[2] More than four centuries later, history has vindicated these pioneers, whose research was instrumental in the emergence of the engine. One of these pioneers, a scientist named Denis Papin (1647–1713), was the first to consider steam as a means to drive a piston in a cylinder in the late seventeenth century.[3] He even constructed the first ship powered by a steam engine connected to paddle-wheels

---

[2] C Singer, EJ Holmyard, AR Hall and TI Williams, *A History of Technology*, vol IV (Oxford, Clarendon Press, 1958) 148.
[3] ibid 173.

in 1705.[4] Legend has it that Papin experimented with his paddle-steamer on the Weser River in Germany and that local boatsmen wrecked his invention out of fear for their livelihood.[5] The reader might be more familiar with other pioneers of this technology, such as Thomas Newcomen (1663–1729), who designed the first sophisticated steam engine based on a piston and cylinder, and James Watt (1736–1819), who further improved this 'Newcomen machine'. Watt minimised the loss of energy in the Newcomen machine by maintaining the cylinder at the same temperature as the steam. He also optimised mechanical movements by converting the single-acting piston (which generates power moving downward in the cylinder) into a double-acting piston (which operates downward and upward in the cylinder).[6] By the end of the eighteenth century, the stationary steam engine was already well established, but it took several more years to successfully adapt the steam-propulsion system designed by Watt to ships. Papin's unfortunate experience on the Weser in the early seventeenth century was the first in a long line of experiments that eventually led to the adoption of steam-propelled paddles in the first half of the nineteenth century.[7] At that time, paddle-steamers ensured passenger service on the Hudson River (1807), crossed the Atlantic Ocean (1819) and were even used by privateers (1821). It took several more decades for the first steamships to make their appearance in the port of Marseille, in the early 1870s.[8]

The technology improved again when Francis Pettit Smith (1808–74) applied screw-propulsion to a steamboat. Although the screw designed by Pettit Smith ultimately broke off under the pressure of the water, his idea stimulated further research. In a subsequent trial aimed at testing the efficiency of screw-propulsion, the Royal Navy organised a tug-of-war contest in 1845 between HMS *Rattler*, a screw-propelled warship, and HMS *Alecto*, a paddle-wheeler.[9] The contest ended conclusively when the *Rattler* towed the *Alecto* backwards, thus establishing the superiority of screw-propulsion over paddle-wheels.[10] The invention of the turbine and its application to marine propulsion in the late nineteenth century were also significant leaps forward in the mechanical design of engines. In 1897, the aptly-named *Turbinia*, the first vessel to be propelled by a steam turbine, made a spectacular appearance at the navy review held in 1897 for Queen Victoria's Diamond Jubilee, where it easily outran a navy boat in hot pursuit.[11] From that time onwards, screw-propulsion became the dominant technology for motor boats.

---

[4] R Woodman, *The History of the Ship* (London, Conway Maritime Press, 1997) 134.

[5] ibid.

[6] Singer et al (n 2) 182–86.

[7] C Singer, EJ Holmyard, AR Hall and TI Williams, *A History of Technology*, vol V (Oxford, Clarendon Press, 1958) 142–46.

[8] Statistics of the Port of Marseille, DA PHI529/1.

[9] Woodman (n 4) 142.

[10] ibid.

[11] Singer et al (n 7) 151.

became the dominant fishing practice in subsequent centuries. Like *bregin* and *eyssaugue*, *gangui* fundamentally involves nets equipped with sinkers that drag the sea-bottom. Some *gangui* are even equipped with a dredger made of wood or iron. Unlike *bregin* and *eyssaugue*, however, the *gangui* net is not dragged by muscular force, but by the boat itself. The *gangui* is, in fact, an early precursor of modern trawlers. Consequently, it can be used away from the shore, and its dredging power is much more significant than that of *bregin* and *eyssaugue*. In particular, the *gangui* destroys the algae that provide a reproduction ground and a natural habitat for juvenile fish. In 1362, some fishers already complained that *gangui* could cause the destruction of fish stocks.[15] The archival records of the fifteenth century contain various references to the conflicts that arose among fishers due to the use of *gangui*. When the *Prud'homie* was created in 1431, the fishers of Marseille agreed to allow the *gangui* within a limited zone, but prohibited it outside of this zone 'under a penalty fine of 100 livres'.[16] A document from April 1462 contains a summary of the *Prud'homie*'s efforts to reconcile fishers practising *gangui* with the other fishers by defining separate fishing grounds for each of them.[17] The same document mentions that the 'limits for *gangui*' should be 'announced publicly every year so that everyone knows them and no one dares breaching them'.[18] The tension between the norms of equality and conservation appears clearly in the historical records. The *Prud'homie* tried to resolve this conflict by accommodating the practices of the *gangui* fishers in the name of equality, while restricting their impact on the fish stocks in the name of conservation. However, the *Prud'homie* progressively relaxed the restrictions attached to *gangui* and extended the fishing zone that had originally been defined in the fifteenth century.[19] Quite remarkably, criticisms never ceased to be levelled against *gangui* in subsequent centuries. They appear, for instance, in a pamphlet from 1754, which criticises the 'abuses' related to *gangui* and the need to burn the nets used for this type of fishing.[20] They are found yet again in an internal note of the French administration, which points out the dangers of this fishing technique for the environment in 1999.[21] The *Prud'homie* played an ambiguous role in these debates by constantly moving

---

[15] ibid

[16] See Agreement concerning the organisation of fishing (13 October 1431), DA 250E6. The fishing zone that was specifically created for *gangui* is mentioned again in 1454. See Ordinance from the viguier of Marseille (23 February 1454), PA.

[17] See Arbitral award (12 April 1462), DA 250E6.

[18] ibid.

[19] In his codification of the *Prud'homie*'s rules, Peyssonnel noted this expansion of the fishing zone and added that the *gangui* catches very small fish, destroys the sea-bottom and has a negative impact on fish stocks. See *Description des Pesches, Loix et Ordonnances des Pescheurs de la Ville de Marseille*, DA 250E2, 101.

[20] *Mémoire servant à faire connaître les abus du filet appelé gangui qui s'emploie également au boeuf et les moyens propres pour y remédier* (June 1754), NA MAR/C/4/179.

[21] *Note d'information rapide sur la senne tournante, senne de plage et gangui en Méditerranée* (1 February 1999), NA 20160293/180.

on a continuum between prohibition and acceptance of the *gangui*. In a remarkable letter sent to the Government in 1803, the *Prud'homie* criticises the prohibition of *gangui*, arguing that the *gangui* 'bends' the algae, that it can 'only' be practised nine months a year and that 'the majority of us' use it.[22] In 1835, the *Prud'homie* voted by a large majority to maintain *gangui* (87 votes for, 16 votes against).[23] Starting in the mid-twentieth century, the *Prud'homie* took a more active stance against the *gangui*, and agreed with state authorities in the late 1940s that it should be prohibited.[24] Although the *Prud'homie* occasionally enforced this prohibition (for instance, when condemning a fisher, François Ruggiero, to pay a fine of 50 francs for using *gangui* in 1961[25]), it never managed to suppress the use of *gangui* in Marseille. It was reported in 1974 that fishers 'seem to have forgotten' the prohibition against *gangui*.[26] In the 1980s and 1990s, the *Prud'homie* tolerated the use of *gangui*, at least until the European Union prohibited its use in the mid-1990s.[27] The example of the *gangui* illustrates the doubts of the *Prud'homie* when confronted with a harmful technique that was used by a non-trivial proportion of its members. It seems that the *Prud'homie* favoured the individual right to use a fishing technique over the need to preserve the fish stocks in the long term.

As a further step in this evolution, fishers began using larger nets dragged by larger sail boats in the early eighteenth century. These boats, named *tartanes*, usually carried up to 10 crew members and could be used far from the coast in strong winds. The name *tartane* refers not only to these boats, but also to the larger nets (sometimes called 'great *gangui*' or *grand gangui*) these boats dragged behind them.[28] Figure 4.3 shows a *tartane*, which is recognisable from its large sails and crew. As an additional step in this arms race, fishers combined two *tartanes* to pull a single net, thus considerably expanding the dragging power of the net. This fishing technique is called *pêche au boeuf*, which can be literally translated by 'ox fishing'. The exact origins of the term are unknown: it may refer to the triangular shape of two sail boats dragging a net (which resembles the head of an ox), or to the fact that both *tartanes* are 'ploughing' the sea-bottom like a pair of oxen. Figure 4.4 shows an example of *pêche au boeuf*.

A comparison between Figures 4.1, 4.2, 4.3 and 4.4 confirms what should now be apparent: the fishers of Marseille used increasingly powerful gear to drag

---

[22] Letter from the *Prud'homie* to the Ministre de la Marine et des Colonies (10 June 1803), AA CC5/374.

[23] Letter from the *Prud'homie* to the Commissaire des Classes (13 June 1835), DA 250E126.

[24] See, eg, *Arrêté réglementant l'emploi du gangui à poissons dans les eaux de la Prud'homie de Marseille* (1 October 1949), MA 100ii264.

[25] Minutes of the *Prud'homie* (5 July 1961), PA.

[26] See Minutes of the *Comité Local des Pêches* (30 January 1974), PA; Minutes of the *Comité de Liaison Méditerranéen* (9 June 2000), NA 20160293/180.

[27] The prohibition of *gangui* ultimately resulted from an EU regulation (Regulation no 1626/94), as explained in ch 5. See also F Gauthiez, *Point sur les mesures techniques en Méditerranée* (5 March 2001), NA 20160293/180.

[28] JJ Baudrillart, *Traité général des eaux et forêts, chasses et pêches*, vol 4 (Paris, Arthus Bertrand, 1827) 526–30.

**Figure 4.3** The Boats Used for *Tartane*

Source: *Bibliothèque nationale de France* (BNF Gallica) (PJ Guéroult du Pas, *Recueil de vues de tous les différents bâtiments de la mer Méditerranée et de l'Océan avec leurs noms et usages* (Paris, Pierre Giffart, 1710) 3).

**Figure 4.4** The *Pêche au Boeuf*

Source: *Bibliothèque nationale de France* (BNF Gallica) (VF Garau, *Traité de pêche maritime pratique illustré et des industries secondaires en Algérie* (Algiers, Imp P Crescenzo, 1909) 70).

larger nets further away from shore. The dragnets used in Marseille affected the sea-bottom in ways that provoked strong criticism. However, the *Prud'homie* offered only mild responses, if any, to this. For instance, Daniel-Marc-Antoine Chardon, the king's special envoy to Marseille in the late eighteenth century, criticised *bregin* and *gangui* for being 'very harmful' to the fishery.[29] In 1883, Antoine-Fortuné Marion, a professor of biology at the University of Marseille, noted the 'disastrous' effects of *gangui* on the seabed's fish and the near destruction of molluscs such as *Umbrella mediterranea* because of this technique.[30] Paul Gourret (another biologist and a student of Marion) criticised *bregin, tartanes* and *pêche au boeuf* for capturing an important proportion of juvenile fish, destroying their natural habitat and generating 'considerable damage' to the fishery.[31] Another protagonist in this debate was Paul-Antoine Menc, a Dominican father who, in a speech to the Academy of Science of Marseille, vigorously denounced all types of dragnets (*bregin, eyssaugues, gangui* and *tartanes*) in 1769.[32] Although the scientific basis for his speech seemed rather tenuous, Menc was sufficiently convincing to prompt a response from the *Prud'homie*. In a memorandum, the *Prud'homie* evoked the fact that fish 'devour each other' as an explanation for their disappearance from the fishery, a vague and slightly ridiculous argument to make in this important debate.[33]

In fact, the *Prud'homie*'s position was so weak that it prompted a response from a group of dissenting fishers. These fishers enlisted the services of an attorney, Laget de Podio, who relayed their concerns in writing to the mayor and the public prosecutor of Marseille in 1835.[34] Laget de Podio denounced the attitude of the *Prud'homie* and criticised it for failing to prohibit dragnets, despite their harmful effects on the fishery.[35] Laget de Podio even accused the four members of the *Prud'homie* of using dragnets and practising the *pêche au boeuf*, thus implying that they were refraining from prohibiting an activity that they themselves were engaged in.[36] This does not mean that every fisher in Marseille used dragnets. The fact that some of them enlisted the services of an attorney to take action against the *Prud'homie* shows that dragnets were not used by the entire community and that they created significant controversies among the fishers. However, the use of dragnets seemed sufficiently widespread to encourage the *Prud'homie* to allow them, even though they caused potential harm to the fish stocks in the long term. This is not to say that dragnets were left unregulated over the centuries; in fact, they

---

[29] Chardon was sent to Marseille to solve the dispute between the local fishers and the Catalans (see ch 3, section III.B). See *Note de Chardon sur les différentes pêches qui se font dans les ports de Toulon, Marseille et ses environs* (8 July 1784), NA MAR/C/4/179.

[30] AF Marion, *Esquisse d'une topographie zoologique du Golfe de Marseille* (Marseille, Cayer & Cie, 1883) 66–67.

[31] P Gourret, *Les pêcheries et les poissons de la Méditerranée* (Paris, Librairie JB Baillière et Fils, 1894) 147–50, 179–80.

[32] *Quelles sont les causes de la diminution de la pêche sur les côtes de la Provence? Et quels sont les moyens de la rendre plus abondante?* (5 April 1769), BNF Gallica.

[33] *Mémoire des Prud'hommes pêcheurs de la ville de Marseille sur le Code des Pêches* (10 March 1806), CCI YC/22/09, 12.

[34] See *Les pêcheurs de la ville de Marseille et autres pêcheurs de sa banlieue, côtes et villes voisines à M le Maire de la Ville de Marseille* (Marseille, Marius Olive, 1835); *Mémoire de M Laget de Podio, avocat, au nom des pêcheurs de la ville de Marseille adressé au Procureur du Roi auprès du Tribunal civil de Marseille* (11 June 1835), MA 18F6.

[35] ibid.

[36] ibid.

were the object of regulations that are too numerous to list and summarise here.[37] Nevertheless, the vast majority of these regulations were issued by the French state and the *Prud'homie* did not consider itself bound by them, at least until the mid-nineteenth century.[38] Laget de Podio's complaint found an echo several decades later, when a city councillor denounced the 'complicit' attitude of the *Prud'homie* towards dragnet fishing, which, according to him, led to the 'ruin' of other fishers and the 'desertion' of the fish.[39] Gourret, a famous zoologist of the late nineteenth century and author of a reference book on fishing in the Mediterranean, reported that members of the *Prud'homie* were 'influenced by breachers and close[d] their eyes on violations' arising from the use of dragnets.[40] At the end of the nineteenth century, dragnets were destroying the fishery, and members of the *Prud'homie* seemed complicit in this process. In fact, they seemed constantly drawn to favour the individual right to exploit the fishery over its preservation.

The picture that I have drawn thus far of the regulation of dragnets might seem gloomy, but the situation worsened further when steam and internal-combustion engines made their appearance in Marseille in the early twentieth century. Until then, the use of muscle power or wind energy had placed intrinsic limits on the techniques that could be used by fishers, even if these techniques grew increasingly powerful over time.[41] In fact, the type of nets and their size directly depend on the power of the boat that drags them. The brute strength and virtually unlimited power of the internal-combustion engine unleashed the power of dragnets, which then made their full impact on the fishery.

## C. Modernity Meets History: The Race Towards Engine Power

In an interview given to a local newspaper in 1911, the secretary of the *Prud'homie* praised the *gangui* for being 'less destructive than is usually assumed' when deployed from sail boats.[42] In uttering these words, however, the secretary could not possibly have been unaware of the recent arrival of fishing boats equipped with steam engines (1903) and internal-combustion engines (1909) in Marseille.[43] A few years after this interview, a Marseille-based company named

---

[37] The first prohibition against the *pêche au boeuf* was issued by the Council of State. See Decision of the Council of State (25 September 1725), DA 250E5.

[38] This argument is further developed in ch 5.

[39] *Rapport de M Jules Guibert au Conseil municipal de Marseille pour l'interdiction des filets traînants* (22 June 1870), DA 6S/10/3.

[40] Gourret (n 31) 322.

[41] *Bregin, eyssaugue, gangui* and *tartanes* can all be placed on a continuum from less to more powerful techniques.

[42] *A propos des arts traînants* (14 August 1911), DA 6S/10/3.

[43] *A Marseille, la pêche avant les chalutiers à vapeur* (May 1975), CCI MR/45221; 'La Pêche maritime en France: Sur le littoral méditerranéen' *Le Petit Journal* (23 May 1912) (referring to two steam-propelled trawlers measuring 32 m and 37 m respectively operating in Marseille).

**Graph 4.1**   The Number of Fishing Boats in Marseille, per Year and Type (1909–2014)

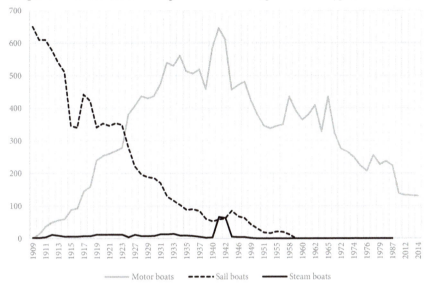

```
—————— Motor boats      ▪▪▪▪▪ Sail boats      ——— Steam boats
```

Beaudouin designed a small gasoline engine of 5 horsepower (HP) and manu-
factured its first diesel engine.[44] The Beaudouin engines went on to equip many
fishing boats in Marseille and became a symbol of the city's fishing industry.
Motorboats opened a new chapter in the history of fishing on the southern coast
of France. Fishers quickly realised the formidable power of engines and their
potential benefits for the operation of dragnets. Engines can pull larger nets and
haul them over much longer distances than sail boats using muscle power. It
soon appeared that the formidable power of engines caused a manifold increase
in the impact of dragnets on the seabed. In the late 1920s, fishers organised
protests against the steam-propelled trawlers that operated close to the shores.
For instance, in February 1927, hundreds of fishers demonstrated in the streets
of Marseille against trawler fishing.[45]

One would assume that, following these protests, the *Prud'homie* would seek
a compromise, by allowing the use of engines while curtailing their effects on the
fishery (for instance, by limiting the size of nets and/or the power of engines).
While the *Prud'homie* did engage, albeit timidly, in an exercise of this sort, its
ability to limit the impact of powerful engines seems to have been impaired by
the appeal these engines held for the fishers. It is clear that sail boats did not fare
well after motor boats appeared and spread rapidly in the fishery of Marseille.
Graph 4.1 shows that the use of motor boats progressed rapidly and inexorably

---

[44] See www.baudouin.com/fr/historique.html (last checked on 10 September 2020).
[45] See Letter from the Police Commissioner of Marseille to the Préfet des Bouches-du-Rhône
(7 February 1927), AD 4M2333.

until the 1940s, and that sail boats completely disappeared from the fishery of Marseille by the end of the 1950s.

The *Prud'homie* could have tried to curtail this evolution by limiting the number of motor boats, the horsepower or the size of nets that could be used in the fishery. However, the *Prud'homie* was particularly hesitant in its efforts to regulate the effects of engines for reasons that seem directly linked with the permissive nature of the egalitarian norm. I will illustrate my argument by focusing on three fishing techniques that are commonly associated with motorboats: set-net fishing, purse-seine fishing and trawler fishing.

## i. Set-Net Fishing

The Food and Agricultural Organization (FAO) defines a 'set net' as 'a single netting wall kept more or less vertical by a floatline and a weighted groundline'.[46] In simpler terms, a set net resembles a badminton net resting on the sea-bottom. The nuisance capacity of set nets is traditionally reduced by the fact that these nets are stationary and limited in size. In addition, fishers used to haul these set nets by hand, which dramatically constrained their size and the depth at which they could be placed. In the early eighteenth century, their size was still relatively small (130 metres in length and 5 metres in height),[47] although it grew to about 1,200 metres in the late nineteenth century.[48] The arrival of the engine in Marseille increased yet again the capacity of set-net fishing. Fishers first invested in small motor boats (with a size of 7.5–10 metres and engine power of 20–70 HP), which they progressively replaced with larger and more powerful boats (with a size of 11.5–12.5 metres and engine power of 50–100 HP) that could carry longer nets further from the coast.[49] Motorboats are now equipped with hydraulic net haulers, which have replaced muscle power when it comes to lifting the nets. In addition, the growth of engine power coincided with the emergence of nylon nets in the 1950s. Before then, fishers had used cotton nets, which they treated regularly in a resin bath in order to avoid putrefaction. One of the key functions of the *Prud'homie* was to organise the treatment of these nets in big cauldrons that it operated for centuries until their dismantling in the early 1960s.[50] Nylon nets represent an attractive alternative to cotton nets, as they are more resistant and do not require regular treatment in a resin bath. The *Prud'homie* tried to curtail the effects of the engine by regulating the size of nets and of the mesh (a large

[46] See Food and Agricultural Organization (United Nations), at www.fao.org/fishery/geartype/219/en (last checked on 10 September 2018).

[47] *Description des Pesches, Loix et Ordonnances des Pescheurs de la Ville de Marseille* (1725), DA 250E2, 171.

[48] See *Annales du Sénat et de la Chambre des députés*, 30 November 1880, 455.

[49] M Bonnet, *La pêche au large aux filets maillants et trémails sur les côtes de Provence*, DA 2331W282.

[50] The *Prud'homie* issued a rule that prohibited fishers from using cauldrons other than its own. See Minutes of the *Prud'homie's* Assembly (20 May 1687), DA 250E4. One of these cauldrons can still be seen in *l'Estaque*. It has been listed as a historical monument by the French Government. See at www.pop.culture.gouv.fr/notice/merimee/IA13000883 (last checked 2 February 2021).

opening in the mesh does not trap smaller fish and is therefore more protective of fish stocks than a smaller mesh size). For instance, the *Prud'homie* tried to limit the size of set nets to 45 pieces (between 3,150 metres and 5,400 metres), but fishers often disregarded the limitation and deployed set nets that were larger than 6,000 metres.[51] All in all, the combination of nylon with engine power led to the growth of set nets by a factor of 60 in three centuries.

## ii. Purse-Seine Fishing

After the demise of the last *madragues* in the early twentieth century, local fishers turned back to the medieval technique of *senches* in order to fish tuna.[52] As explained in chapter 2, *senches* require a high level of coordination among fishers, who are gathered in so-called 'companies'. Each of these companies comprises no fewer than 50 fishers.[53] In the 1950s, four companies of fishers still practised the *senche* in Marseille, but this fishing technique fell into disfavour in the 1960s.[54] The reasons for its demise are unclear. One might surmise, for instance, that the costs of *senches* exceeded their potential returns, as stocks of bluefin tuna declined. Another explanation relates to the emergence of purse-seine boats with powerful engines, allowing fishers to replicate the *senche* technique further away from the coast, with a much tighter crew and fewer boats. An interviewee told me how his father and uncle had imported drawings from San Diego in order to build the first purse-seine boat in Marseille in the mid-1960s. Purse-seine boats (also called 'seiners') operate a 'purse-seine net', which is a large, purse-shaped wall of netting that is used to encircle fish schools (for instance, tuna or sardines). The FAO describes purse seines as 'the most efficient gear for catching large and small pelagic species that is shoaling'.[55] While *senche* requires at least five boats and more than 50 fishers, a single tuna purse-seiner with a crew of 10 to 20 fishers can catch an entire school of tuna, and repeat the same operation several times. These seiners are equipped with engines of 1,600 HP, several hard-hulled motorboats and even helicopters that are used to locate the schools of tuna. Seiners encircle entire schools of tuna with a purse seine carried by a heavy boom and hauled by a 'power block', a mechanised pulley driven by hydraulic pumps connected to the main or auxiliary engine.[56] Figure 4.5 depicts a tuna purse-seiner, with its small motorboats, helicopter and power block above the deck.

---

[51] See, eg, Letter from the Departmental Director for Maritime Affairs to the Regional Director for Maritime Affairs (31 December 1986), DA 2331W282 (mentioning nets of a length up to 6,000 metres). One of my interviewees even reported the use of nets measuring 15,000 metres for tuna fishing.

[52] *Senche* was already practised in the fifteenth century, as explained in ch 2, section III.B.

[53] *Renseignements sur la pratique de la seinche* (ca 1941), NA 19860461/21.

[54] Minutes of the *Prud'homie's* Assembly (15 March 1959), PA.

[55] See Food and Agriculture Organization (United Nations), at www.fao.org/fishery/geartype/249/en (last checked on 10 September 2020).

[56] See Food and Agriculture Organization (United Nations), at www.fao.org/fishery/equipment/powerblock/en (last checked on 10 September 2020).

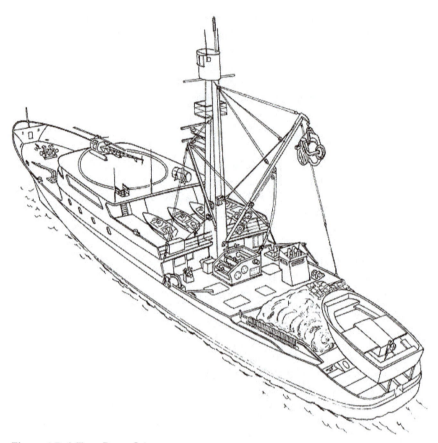

**Figure 4.5**  A Tuna Purse-Seiner
*Source:* Food and Agriculture Organization (United Nations), at www.fao.org/figis/common/format/popUpImage.jsp?xp_imageid=7936 (last checked on 10 September 2020).

Tuna purse-seiners are often held responsible for the decline of bluefin tuna in the western Mediterranean basin. Ellis writes, for instance, that tuna purse-seiners are so 'effective that traditional fishing grounds in the western Mediterranean have been depleted and abandoned in favour of high densities of spawning fish in the eastern part of the sea'.[57] Tuna purse-seiners based in Marseille have played their part in the overexploitation of the tuna stock. Although Marseille remains their home port, tuna purse-seiners sail well beyond the French coast. Interviewees told me how tuna purse-seiners use up their annual quota in a fishing campaign that lasts only a few weeks and brings them to the Balearics and even to the coast of Libya. The tuna are sometimes kept alive and brought

---

[57] R Ellis, *Tuna: Love, Death and Mercury* (New York, NY, Vintage Books, 2009) 63.

to sea farms located in Malta, where they are fattened. They are then exported to Japan and sold in the Toyosu (formerly Tsukiji) market at astronomic prices. The *Prud'homie* is ill at ease regulating an activity that extends well beyond the bounds of its fishery. Everyone considers tuna purse-seiners to be a different breed of fishers than those who operate in Marseille. Because of the high prices of tuna and the international scope of their activities, tuna purse-seiners are frequently considered businessmen rather than fishers. While the *Prud'homie* actively regulated the use of *senches* until the late 1960s, its legitimacy and power seem almost non-existent when it comes to the tuna purse-seiners, whose activities extend well beyond the scope of its jurisdiction (which is loosely defined by territorial waters).

## iii. Trawler Fishing

The previous examples illustrate the ways in which the combustion engine has affected the techniques traditionally used by fishers in Marseille, by encouraging them to use longer nets with increased dragging power and enabling them to reach out to remote fishing grounds. An entirely consistent and even more remarkable evolution concerns the ways in which the engine contributed to the race for power in the operation of dragnets, one of the most popular and controversial fishing techniques in the fishery of Marseille. After the Second World War, one of the most popular forms of dragnet fishing in Marseille, the famous *gangui*, was prohibited due to its destructive impact on the seabed.[58] Simultaneously, the technique of *eyssaugue* was limited to a few 'posts'.[59] The demise of *gangui* and *eyssaugue* for ecological reasons could potentially have led to a renewal of the fishing techniques used in Marseille. However, the fishers unexpectedly turned to even more aggressive techniques involving dragnets, such as trawler fishing, after the prohibition of *gangui* and *eyssaugue*.[60] Some of the boats used for *gangui* were converted into trawler boats after its prohibition in 1949. At that time, these boats had relatively small engines ranging from 20 HP to 38 HP,[61] but their power and size continued to grow in subsequent years. In the 1960s, trawlers measured approximately 15 metres and had an engine power of 150 HP.[62] Twenty years

---

[58] *Arrêté réglementant l'emploi du gangui à poissons dans les eaux de la Prud'homie de Marseille* (1 October 1949), DA 2331W287. The *gangui* quickly reappeared after its prohibition under French law in 1949. For instance, a fisher was accused of fishing with *gangui* during a case brought to the *Prud'homie* in 1961. In the 1980s and 1990s, the use of *gangui* was widespread on the southern coast of France.

[59] Letter from the *Prud'homie* to the Administrator in Chief of Maritime Affairs of Marseille (8 January 1951), MA 100ii264. The last *eyssaugue* fisher of Marseille, Robert Lubrano, practised this technique until the 1990s.

[60] As noted above, some of them quietly returned to their old practices, notwithstanding the fact that they were prohibited.

[61] List of boats used for *gangui* (undated, ca 1949), MA 100ii264.

[62] Letter from a *Prud'homme* to the Administrator of Maritime Affairs of Martigues (23 July 1986), DA 2331W282.

later, they measured approximately 24 metres with an engine power of between 120 HP and 430 HP.[63] In 1981, researchers reported the 'constant rise' in the power of engines and the levelling up of engine power at 430 HP.[64] Currently, the average power of trawlers (of between 16 and 24 metres) operating off the coast of Provence is 437 HP.[65] During an interview, a former *Prud'homme* reported to me the existence of trawlers equipped with engines ranging between 800 HP and 1,500 HP. Thus, the engine power of trawler boats has, on average, increased more than twelvefold over the past 70 years.

Although the *Prud'homie* complained regularly about trawlers, it has done very little to curtail their power. It did try to submit trawlers to its jurisdiction, but this effort failed almost entirely, leading to a case before the Council of State in 1921. In the early 1920s, the Ministry of Marine noted the various issues raised by trawlers equipped with steam engines in the fishery of Marseille, in particular the fact that these steamboats contributed to the 'industrialisation' of the fishery and encouraged fishers to move away from the coast.[66] The Ministry appealed to the Council of State concerning a legal question that had arisen from a dispute between the *Prud'homie* and the owner of two steamboats used as trawlers.[67] The *Prud'homie* requested that this fisher pay the tax that it charged to all of its members, but the fisher refused to pay this tax on the ground that he did not operate his trawlers within the territory over which the *Prud'homie* had jurisdiction.[68] Up until that point, the jurisdiction of the *Prud'homie* had been broadly defined as extending over the 'fishery of Marseille', a territorial delimitation that left ample room for debate. The Council of State settled this matter by ruling that the jurisdiction of the *Prud'homie* was limited to 'territorial waters' (at the time, extending three miles off the coast) and that it lacked jurisdiction over the trawlers that operated beyond the three-mile limit.[69] The concrete result of the Council of State's ruling was that the trawlers did not have to pay the *Prud'homie*'s tax if they operated beyond the three-mile limit. A more important consequence was that the *Prud'homie* could not regulate the activity of these trawlers unless they operated within its territory. This decision marked the starting point of ongoing conflicts between the *Prud'homie* (which tried to regulate trawling) and trawlers

---

[63] Letter from the Director of Maritime Affairs in the Mediterranean to the Minister of Transportation (8 February 1980), DA 2331W286.

[64] Letter from the *Institut Scientifique et Technique des Pêches Maritimes* to the Director General of the Merchant Navy (21 May 1981), DA 2331W286. See also minutes of a meeting held in Sète (29 September 1980), AD 2331W279.

[65] *Etat des lieux et caractéristiques de la pêche maritime professionnelle et des élevages marins en PACA*, (CRPMEM PACA, 2016) 40.

[66] Letter from the Sous-Secrétaire d'Etat au Ministère des Travaux Publics chargé des Ports, de la Marine Marchande et des Pêches to the Vice-Président du Conseil d'Etat (8 April 1921), NA AL/3415.

[67] ibid.

[68] ibid.

[69] Legal Opinion of the Council of State no 178042 (11 May 1921).

(which argued that they did not fall within the territorial jurisdiction of the *Prud'homie*, even though they often trespassed into the *Prud'homie*'s waters[70]).

The introduction of the engine in Marseille increased the productivity of fishers in unprecedented ways. Engines allowed fishers to operate more power-ful boats with much larger nets. This engine-power arms race has had a direct impact on the fish stock, as the ability of trawlers to operate large dragnets (and catch more fish) is directly proportional to the power of their engines. In 1947, the Faculty of Sciences of Marseille assessed their impact by examining the seabed of the Gulf of Lion. After performing 82 dredging operations over a two-and-a-half-year period, the scientists concluded that 'the use of dragnets in the Gulf of Marseille has, since the generalisation of the internal-combustion engine for fish-ing boats, had disastrous consequences for the aquatic fauna of the Gulf'.[71] The scientists emphasised that the 'Posidania meadows' (a spawning ground for fish) had been 'completely devastated' and that the number of fish species and their size (a measure of fishing pressure) had drastically declined.[72] The *Prud'homie* appeared unable to regulate this arms race that culminated with the introduction of the engine. Before exploring the potential reasons for this failure in subsequent chapters, I will first examine two additional examples of technological changes in the fishery of Marseille.

# III.  Dynamite Fishing

This section explores another case study focusing on the use of dynamite in the fishery of Marseille. As with the engine, the persistence of ancient practices facilitated the introduction of dynamite, which has further contributed to the destruction of the marine habitat. Although the *Prud'homie* maintained an offi-cial stance against the use of dynamite, it has also accommodated the practices of many of its members who use it.

## A.  Explosives and Dynamite

Dynamite is one of the most significant inventions of the nineteenth century. In the mid-nineteenth century, scientists already knew the properties of 'high-power' explosives such as gun-cotton and nitro-glycerine, but were unable to control their blasting effect. Nitro-glycerine releases twice as much energy as gunpowder, but its volatility led to many casualties among those who tried to harness its power.

---

[70] In 1983, the *Prud'homie* complained of the 'too frequent incursions' of trawlers within the three-mile zone. See Minutes of a Meeting of the *Prud'homie* (18 March 1983), DA 2331 W275.

[71] *Note sur l'Etat des Fonds Littoraux du Golfe de Marseille* (14 April 1950), DA 2331W287.

[72] ibid.

In the 1860s, Alfred Nobel combined nitro-glycerine with an inert material called kiselguhr and a detonator. This mixture, dubbed 'dynamite', could be used relatively safely. Dynamite famously made its inventor a fortune and was used in a wide array of sectors, including construction, mining, demolition and, of course, the military. It was not long before fishers, too, found a use for Nobel's invention. In fact, the first reported use of dynamite in the fishery of Marseille dates back to 1873, only six years after it was patented in England and Sweden.[73] Dynamite did not appear in a vacuum in Marseille, however, as fishers had already been using other harmful devices with similar, albeit more limited, effects.

## B.  Lethal Weapons in the Fishery of Marseille

For a long time, fishers used poison in order to kill or stun fish on a large scale. Several archival documents report the use of a poisonous plant called *euphorbia* for that purpose. These practices were criticised for the risks they entailed, notably for the end consumers.[74] In order to curtail these risks, the Council of State prohibited the use of poisonous bait in 1725 and 1728.[75] The *Prud'homie* occasionally condemned fishers who poisoned the waters of Marseille,[76] but at other times it condoned or even supported these practices.[77] For instance, in a letter sent to a governmental officer in 1829, the *Prud'homie* defended the use of *titbimale*, a poisonous plant used by fishers that triggers dysentery.[78] In the mid-twentieth century, the fishers discussed the possibility of poisoning the waters in order to curtail the dolphin population.[79] Explosives present the same advantages as poison, but without the health hazard: they kill enormous quantities of fish almost instantly without threatening consumers' health. For this reason, blast fishing became an important practice in Marseille in the late nineteenth and twentieth centuries.[80]

---

[73] Minutes of the Municipal Council of Marseille (7 August 1873), DA 6S10/3.

[74] See, eg, *Description des Pesches, Loix et Ordonnances des Pescheurs de la Ville de Marseille*, AD 250E2, 46.

[75] Decision of the Council of State (25 September 1725), DA 250E5.

[76] Such a case was reported by D Faget, 'Le poison et la poudre. Passé du braconnage halieutique en Méditerranée' in D Faget and M Sternberg (eds), *Pêches méditerranéennes: Origines et mutations Protohistoire–XXIe siècle* (Paris, Karthala, 2015) 169.

[77] *Les pêcheurs de la ville de Marseille et autres pêcheurs de sa banlieue, côtes et villes voisines à M le Maire de la Ville de Marseille*, (11 June 1835), MA 18F6.

[78] Letter from the *Prud'homie* to the Commissaire des Classes (30 August 1829), DA 250E126.

[79] Report of the Association of Fishers of the *Madrague de Montredon* (29 September 1950), MA 100ii264; Memorandum from the Director of Maritime Fisheries to the Deputy Chief of Cabinet of the Minister of the Merchant Navy (14 November 1950), MA 100ii264.

[80] Faget has also insisted on the continuity between poison and dynamite in the south of France. See Faget (n 76) 169.

## C.  Blasting the Fishery: The Use of Dynamite in Marseille

Blast fishing consists of throwing sticks of dynamite into the water and collecting the stunned or dead fish that float to the surface. Another version consists of throwing sticks of dynamite in order to bring the fish (typically pelagic species such as sardines) towards the surface. For more than a century, the fishers of Marseille practised blast fishing on a significant scale. I found numerous reports of dynamite fishing throughout the twentieth century. Already in 1900, the Minister of the Navy reported to the Prime Minister that 'the fishers [of Marseille], attracted by the benefits drawn from such an easy fishing' practise blast fishing.[81] In 1910, blast fishing was accused of bringing 'desertification' to the fishery of Marseille.[82] In 1963, governmental officers reported that several professional fishers used dynamite.[83] My informants confirmed the widespread and persistent use of dynamite by fishers, although they spoke with reluctance and rarely on the record. A fisher told me that his grandfather used dynamite in the mid-twentieth century. A former *Prud'homme* jokingly revealed to me how the indiscriminate use of explosives earned a fisher (and his son) the nickname 'Bam Bam'. Another informant told me that a prominent member of the *Prud'homie* lost an eye while fishing, and how gossips surmised that his accident had been caused by dynamite.

The effects of blast fishing on ecosystems are well known: it indiscriminately kills all species and subjects of various sizes, destroys other marine organisms and devastates the sea-bottom. It is an undeniable cause of overfishing that is used as an easy, but short-sighted, way of increasing productivity in impoverished fishing communities.[84] The fishers of Marseille have always been very well aware of these negative effects. In fact, some of them reacted very strongly against the use of dynamite at various times in the history of the fishery. In 1917, for instance, there was a physical altercation between a group of fishers over the use of dynamite, leaving two of them dead.[85] Because of the negative effects of dynamite on the fishery, one would have expected to see the *Prud'homie* take a strong and active stance against it. At the very least, the *Prud'homie* should have allowed fishers to make very limited and controlled use of dynamite in accordance with its traditional balancing act. However, the response from the *Prud'homie* was much more ambiguous: it did not take any concrete action against blast fishing, while noisily condemning it. In criticising blast fishing, the *Prud'homie* introduced a distinction between two categories of fishers: professional fishers who do not practise blast fishing, and

---

[81] Letter from the Minister of Maritime Affairs to the Prime Minister (19 February 1900), DA 6S10/3.

[82] Minutes of the *Commission départementale des Bouches-du-Rhône* (17 February 1910), DA 6S10/3.

[83] Report of the Maritime Affairs of Marseille (22 February 1963), DA 2331W291.

[84] D Pauly, G Silvestre and IR Smith, 'On development, fisheries and dynamite: a brief review of tropical fisheries management' (1989) 3/3 *Natural Resource Modeling* 307, 323.

[85] See Letter from the Préfet des Bouches-du-Rhône to the Minister of the Interior (24 December 1917), DA 4M2333.

poachers who were actually responsible for the damage caused to the fishery.[86] However, this distinction does not withstand scrutiny and was obviously aimed at condoning the practices of the *Prud'homie*'s constituency. In fact, the *Prud'homie* may have tried to preserve the normative fabric of its community at the expense of reality: it effectively allowed its members to practise blast fishing (a stance that is consistent with the equality norm), while condemning it in the interest of conservation. In practice, blast fishing was not solely engaged in by community outsiders but also involved many professional fishers (including members of the *Prud'homie*). The real response to blast fishing came from other levels of governance. For instance, the state repeatedly tried to control the sale of explosives, patrol the fishery and prohibit the sale of fish caught using dynamite. The *Prud'homie* officially lent its support to the state's efforts, but did not do much in practice.[87] The case of blast fishing is reminiscent of that of engines. The *Prud'homie* seems to have been hard-pressed to fight against a technique that was widely used by its constituents. Rather than engaging in a fight that could be deemed to pose a threat to the fishers' individual right to work, it paid lip service to the preservation of its fishery while doing nothing, or very little, to achieve this goal.

## IV.  Electric Light as Bait

In Marseille, fishers have used light as a way to lure fish for centuries, practising what is known as 'fire fishing' (*pêche au feu*). Although the *Prud'homie* traditionally sought to restrict fire fishing, electricity magnifies its effects in such compelling ways that the *Prud'homie* became increasingly reluctant to restrict the use of this aggressive technique. The arrival of electricity in the fishery of Marseille illustrates yet again the difficulty for the *Prud'homie*, when it came to resisting the shortsighted impulses of fishers faced with an economic bonanza.

## A.  The Tradition of Fire Fishing

Light attracts fish, and fishers have long noticed and taken advantage of this natural attraction. For centuries, fishers set their nets at sunset or sunrise in order to catch sardines as they drifted towards the natural light.[88] Rather than using sunlight, fishers quickly conceived of ways to generate artificial light in order to attract fish. Archival documents from the late fourteenth century refer to fishers

---

[86] See, eg, Letter from the *Prud'homie* to the Préfet des Bouches-du-Rhône (29 August 1917), DA 6S10/3; Minutes of the *Prud'homie*'s Assembly (2 February 1950), PA.

[87] See, eg, Administrative memorandum concerning blast fishing (8 January 1926), DA 6S10/3.

[88] *Description des Pesches, Loix et Ordonnances des Pescheurs de la Ville de Marseille* (1725), DA 250E2, 171–72.

lighting fires onboard their ships in order to lure fish into their nets.[89] Fishers adjusted iron grills at the back of their boats, on which they ignited softwoods at night.[90] The term 'fire fishing' reflects this use of fire as a way to generate light in order to attract fish.

Fire fishing is not only damaging for the fishery, as it attracts a large number of fish, but it is also dangerous for fishers, because fire can attract pirates, who would routinely kidnap fishers for ransom in the late Middle Ages. For instance, the *Prud'homie* prohibited fire fishing in 1458 because it caused 'the capture and loss of fishing boats and their crews'.[91] In 1658, the *Prud'homie* reiterated its prohibition in order to avoid the capture of fishers by 'pirates and privateers'.[92] The focus of the *Prud'homie* on the risks incurred by fishers rather than the potential threats caused to the fish stock might be explained by the fact that the latter threat was, all things considered, relatively benign. However, the emergence of electricity allowed fishers to employ increasingly powerful light-sources, with compounded effects on the fish stock.

## B. The Birth of the 'fée électricité'

The human fascination with the possibilities afforded by the electricity was initially prompted by natural events, such as lightning or electric impulses generated by fish, a species that electricity would ironically contribute to decimating centuries later. Electric catfish (*Malapterurus electricus*) exerted such a fascination on ancient Egyptians that they named their very first pharaoh, Narmer, after this fish.[93] It took several more centuries for humans to learn how to generate light through electricity. Unlike the engine, electricity is not a 'prime mover', as it is generated from another source of energy. Leading scientists such as Benjamin Franklin in the United States, Alessandro Volta in Italy and Michael Faraday in Britain conducted pioneering research to develop electricity as a new source of power. Faraday's research, in particular, led to the mechanical generation of electricity in the nineteenth century. The creation of the filament lamp prompted the emergence of bulb lamps, an economically manageable source of light, in 1879. It took several more decades for electricity to supplant gas as the prime source of lighting in large cities and personal homes. In France, electricity was nicknamed 'fée électricité' or the 'electricity fairy', a term that was meant to capture the miracle of a new technology able to light, heat and propel. As with other technologies,

---

[89] See eg, Deliberation concerning the prohibition of light fishing (17 June 1382), MA BB28.

[90] *Description des Pesches, Loix et Ordonnances des Pescheurs de la Ville de Marseille* (1725), DA 250E2, 48.

[91] ibid 49.

[92] Minutes of the *Prud'homie*'s Assembly (6 August 1658), DA 250E5.

[93] See TAH Wilkinson, 'What a King is This: Narmer and the Concept of the Ruler' (2000) 86 *The Journal of Egyptian Archeology* 23.

it took little time for fishers to devise ways of combining this innovation with existing techniques. In the case of electricity, it soon became obvious that it could advantageously replace fire as a source of light to lure fish. Not only did electricity present none of the risks associated with fire, but it could also generate a virtually unlimited amount of light.

## i. Accommodating Traditional and Modern Techniques: The Emergence of the Lamparo

One historical episode in the fishery of Marseille, which occurred in a context reminiscent of the Catalan migrations in the eighteenth century, illustrates the difficulty that an institution such as the *Prud'homie* has in curtailing the negative social effects of a technology that generates important individual gains. Before and after the Second World War, the fishery of Marseille was once again confronted with an influx of migrants, this time originating from Italy.[94] These Italian migrants typically came from the Lazio region, Naples or Algeria, where their families had settled in the late nineteenth century.[95] Numerous interviewees reported to me how their ancestors left Italy or Algeria for Marseille in the early or mid-twentieth century. They migrated to Marseille (and other places) for a combination of reasons: most of them sought shelter in Marseille when their home country faced a dire economic situation; others left Algeria after its independence in 1962. As with the Catalans, these migrants brought not only their labour force, but also their own fishing techniques. One of these techniques, the so-called '*lamparo*', makes use of light as a way to lure fish. The *lamparo* technique is based on lights that attract pelagic fish (typically sardines or sea breams), which are then encircled within a large net. A fishing treatise from 1909 gives an account of the ways in which fishers of Italian origin practised *lamparo* on the Algerian coast, using iron grills on which they set fire to wood soaked in kerosene.[96] Figure 4.6 represents one of these *lamparos* used in Algeria at the beginning of the twentieth century.

The *lamparo* strongly resembles the fire fishing of the Middle Ages, with the difference that gas and electric lamps progressively replaced fire as a source of light. The *lamparo* made its entry into the fishery of Marseille as a result of two converging social events. As noted above, the first was the arrival of Italian migrants, who brought these techniques with them from the 1930s to the 1960s. A local fisher and former member of the *Prud'homie* told me how his grandfather, an Italian fisher who left Algeria in 1962, evoked surprise and astonishment from the local fishers

---

[94] See F Grisel, 'How Migrations Affect Private Orders: Norms and Practices in the Fishery of Marseille' (2021) 55 *Law & Society Review* 177.

[95] On the migrations of Italian fishers in Algeria, see A Luetz de Lemps, 'Pêcheurs algériens' (1955) 30 *Cahiers d'outre-mer* 161; RH Rainero, 'Les Italiens en Afrique du Nord française' in P Milza (ed), *Les Italiens en France de 1914 à 1940* (Rome, Ecole française de Rome, 1986) 745.

[96] VF Garau, *Traité de pêche maritime pratique illustré et des industries secondaires en Algérie* (Algiers, Imp P Crescenzo, 1909) 37–39.

**Figure 4.6** A *Lamparo* at the Beginning of the 20th Century
*Source: Bibliothèque nationale de France* (BNF Gallica) (VF Garau, *Traité de pêche maritime pratique illustré et des industries secondaires en Algérie* (Algiers, Imp P Crescenzo, 1909) 38).

when he caught two tons of fish using lamps. According to him, some local fishers went on to adopt the *lamparo* with more or less success.

Another reason for the introduction of *lamparo* in Marseille was a state policy encouraging the use of productive techniques in the context of the post-war reconstruction. A high-level official in the French Government, Gilbert Grandval, played an instrumental role in designing this policy in the early 1960s.[97] Grandval relied in his decision-making process on the recommendations of the *Institut scientifique et technique des pêches maritimes* (ISTPM), a research institution specialising in 'oceanographic science'. At a time when France was undergoing rapid economic development and was faced with an influx of populations from its former colonies, Grandval and the ISTPM considered the *lamparo* a suitable method for what they viewed as the 'under-exploited' fishery of Marseille. In an internal note of the French Maritime Directory, a public officer reported that

> when in 1960, Mr Grandval, Secretary General of the Merchant Navy, struck by the discrepancy between poor fishing catches and the figures of the [ISTPM], evidencing high concentrations of blue fish in the Mediterranean, thought about using new methods and recommended the use of lamparo for the fishing of sardines, these newcomers (from southern Italy) did not hesitate and converted themselves to this fishing technique ...[98]

An old fisher who migrated to Marseille from the Italian city of Sperlonga in 1950 explained to me how his family converted their trawler boat to *lamparo* fishing in the early 1960s and imported lamps from Sperlonga for that purpose.

Behind this story lay the unfolding of a regulatory battle between the French state, which supported the introduction of *lamparo*, and the *Prud'homie*, which

[97] On Grandval and his role in post-war politics in France, see ch 5.
[98] Memorandum of the Maritime Affairs concerning Lamparo, DA 2331W291.

**Graph 4.2** The Annual Catch of Sardines in Marseille between 1956 and 1987 (in tons)

took a strong stance against it. I will return to this regulatory battle in chapter 5. What matters here is that the *Prud'homie* lost this battle and that its defeat paved the way for an electric-power arms race among *lamparo* fishers. The administrative state had anticipated this risk by limiting the *lamparos* to the use of four lamps, with 500 watts and 1,000 plugs each, for each boat.[99] However, the *lamparo* fishers soon managed to circumvent this restriction by using several boats instead of one (thus multiplying the number of lamps). In 1963, the journal of the ISTPM reported that the *lamparos* used between 4,000 and 12,000 plugs when fishing (or three times the norm).[100] In the same year, the Director of Maritime Affairs in the Mediterranean reported in a letter to the ISTPM the 'sheer competition' for electric power among fishers.[101] There are also numerous reports that the *lamparo* fishers combined their lamps with dynamite to bring more fish to the surface.

In this context, Gilbert Grandval's belief that *lamparo* could be effective as a fishing technique proved correct. In fact, Marseille quickly became the largest sardine port in France during that time, with a global catch of sardines growing from 200–300 tons per year in the 1950s to 4,000 tons in 1963 and 5,000 tons in 1964.[102] In 1976, the *lamparos* of Marseille still caught about 4,000 tons of

[99] See, eg, Arrêté n° 119 portant règlementation du filet tournant et coulissant dit 'lamparo' et du filet droit dit 'sardinal' dans le quartier de Marseille (25 June 1960), DA 2331W291.

[100] G Kurc, 'La pêche à la lumière en Atlantique' (1963) 113 *Science et Pêche* 1, 5.

[101] Letter from the Director of Maritime Affairs in the Mediterranean to the Chief of Laboratory of the *Institut Scientifique et Technique des Pêches Maritimes* (10 August 1963), DA 2331W291.

[102] C Maurin, 'Situation de la pêche à la sardine dans la région marseillaise' (1965) 143 *Science et Pêche* 1.

sardines.[103] Graph 4.2 shows the enormous increase of the catches of sardines in the early 1960s in Marseille.

However, Grandval probably did not anticipate a fishing arms race to unfold with dire effects on the community of fishers. He also did not anticipate that the *lamparos* would exhaust the resources of sardines on the French Mediterranean coast, considering that the ISTPM had still boasted of rich and unexploited stock in the late 1950s. Grandval's expectations turned out to be plain wrong. Sardines are now too small to be commercialised in Marseille. Fishers typically blame the decreasing quality of plankton (a side-effect of water pollution) and the existence of 'ghost nets' that continue to devastate the fish stock after having been lost in the Mediterranean. However, in the complex exercise of assigning causes to biological effects, one cannot reasonably ignore the responsibility of *lamparo* fishers, who deployed all the technological means at their disposal to capture ever-increasing quantities of sardines. The *Prud'homie* proved unable to restrict these practices, even though it showed genuine concern about this technique at a time when the state repeatedly ignored its warnings and encouraged the fishers of Marseille to practise *lamparo*.

# V. Conclusion

Why was the *Prud'homie* relatively ineffective at regulating the emergence of new technologies in the nineteenth and twentieth centuries, even though it enjoyed enormous powers and credibility among fishers? This chapter suggests that the *Prud'homie* was unable to create and promote an agenda restricting the use of technologies that presented short-term benefits for the community but also threatened the long-term preservation of the fishery. In fact, the *Prud'homie* seemed to favour its members' right to exploit the fishery over its duty to preserve fish stocks. The *Prud'homie* seems to have been overwhelmed by the individual ethos of its members, who paid lip service to the communal norm of preservation while persistently breaching this norm. In the first case, the *Prud'homie* seemed unable and at times even unwilling to restrict the size and use of engines. In the second case, the *Prud'homie*'s official stance against dynamite fishing was undermined by the fact that most of its members used this technique. In the third case, the *Prud'homie* attempted to restrict the use of electrical lamps as a lure for fish, but stumbled in the face of countervailing forces backed by the state, namely, the need to provide jobs and food after the Second World War. In all three cases, the *Prud'homie* seemed unable to design and implement policies that would preserve the long-term interests of its constituents. In addition, each of these three

---

[103] Letter from the Chief of Maritime Affairs of Marseille to the Director of Maritime Affairs for the Mediterranean (11 October 1977), DA 2331W279.

technologies grafted themselves onto older practices, which the *Prud'homie* had previously accepted as a result of political compromises.[104]

The specific nature of the case studies presented in this chapter prevents one from drawing general conclusions. However, one cannot help but notice that, in all these case studies, the *Prud'homie* consistently privileged the norm favouring equality over the norm aimed at preserving the fishing environment. The nature of the former norm could explain the *Prud'homie*'s preference and highlight what might be a fundamental feature of private orders. 'Extrastate' spaces such as private orders often rely on an egalitarian model of social organisation.[105] As a consequence, a formal organisation such as the *Prud'homie* stratifies a society that is essentially horizontal. Because this organisation is embedded in strong cultural traditions of egalitarianism, it is particularly sympathetic towards individual practices, which it strives to accommodate even when these practices contradict another fundamental norm of the community. In the case studies explored in this chapter, the fishers' passion for equality condoned practices that undermined their ideal of conservation. In effect, the *Prud'homie* weighed up both norms and favoured the most important one.[106]

The disjunction that arose between new social practices and the conservation norm will be further explored in chapter 6, which weaves together the material gathered in preceding chapters to draw conclusions about the broader issues at the core of this book. But before that, chapter 5 will examine and discard a further argument in the scholarship on private governance, which traces the failure of private orders back to the inevitable figure of the state.

---

[104] This argument is consistent with the view that technological 'shocks' are often premised on prior technical changes. See M Roe Smith and L Marx (eds), *Does Technology Drive History? The Dilemma of Technological Determinism* (Cambridge, MA, The MIT Press, 1994); WE Bijker, TP Hughes and T Pinch (eds), *The Social Construction of Technological Systems: New Directions in the Sociology and History of Technology* (Cambridge, MA, The MIT Press, 2012).

[105] JC Scott, *The Art of Not Being Governed: An Anarchist History of Upland Southeast Asia* (New Haven, CT, Yale University Press, 2009) 18, 274–77. This is often the case even if these polities also promote discriminatory behaviour against community outsiders and do not present the same guarantees as public orders in terms of transparency and accountability. ED Katz, 'Private Order and Public Institutions' (2000) 98 *Michigan Law Review* 2481.

[106] On the weighing of principles, see R Dworkin, *Taking Rights Seriously* (Cambridge, MA, Harvard University Press, 1977) 26–27.

# Postscript: Provençal Poem by Pierre Molinari (1875), *The Massacre of the Sea Perpetrated by the Tradespeople or the Destruction of Fish*

Pierre Molinari was a local poet, songwriter and novelist from southern France. His poem, *The Massacre of the Sea*,[107] captures several of the themes examined in this book. Molinari relays a well-documented complaint in the second half of the nineteenth century concerning the exhaustion of the fish stock in Marseille. He mentions the greed and short-sightedness of the local fishers, their failure to limit the impact of fishing gear, the use of destructive practices (eg, *tartanes* or *ganguis*) and the difficulties caused by the arrival of fishers from Naples.

Interestingly, Molinari does not utter a word about the *Prud'homie*. However, he does mention the lack of governmental oversight over the fishery of Marseille. The next chapters will explore the complex interrelationships that the *Prud'homie* has maintained with the state, and provide an explanation for its failure to prevent the 'massacre of the sea' vividly captured by Molinari.

| | |
|---|---|
| Braves gens de Marseille, écoutez-moi! | Good people of Marseille, hear me! |
| Voici une poésie pleine de vérités. | Here is a poem full of truths |
| Vous devez avoir remarqué que dans nos pays | You must have noticed that in our lands |
| On ne voit plus de poisson comme autrefois. | Not as much fish can be seen as before |
| Jadis nous mangions le poisson à discrétion, | In the past, we could eat as much fish as we wanted, |
| L'ouvrier pouvait s'en payer, il était à donation. | The worker could afford it, it was free. |
| Jadis on voyait encore des merlans pêchés à la palangre, | In the past, one could still see whiting caught with *palangre*, |
| Les soles, les pagels aujourd'hui ont maigri! | Now, the sole and pageot have shrunk! |
| Et les merlans d'alors avaient bien quatre pans! | And the whiting back then measured about four *pans*![108] |
| Il faut nous contenter du poisson de l'Océan, | Now, we have only fish from the Ocean,[109] |
| Qui le plus souvent nous arrive sans tête, | Which often arrive without their heads, |
| Décapité, de peur de nous donner la peste! | Decapitated, out of fear that they will bring us the plague! |

---

[107] P Molinari, *Le massacre de la mer exécuté par les hommes de métier ou la destruction des poissons, Poésie provençale* (Marseille, Petit Marseillais, 1875). The original text was in the old dialect of Provence. The French translation is taken from *Annales du Sénat et de la Chambre des députés* (1880) 456–59.

[108] One *pan* is about 25cm.

[109] Molinari means that the fish supply is secured through imports from the Atlantic Ocean.

| | |
|---|---|
| Autrefois nous avions des capélans, | We once had capelans, |
| Des rougets, des saint pierre, avec des bélégans. | Red mullet, Peter's fish, with the *bélégans*.[110] |
| Les maquereaux, que nous ne mangeons qu'à trois francs le kilo, | The mackerel that we eat today at three francs a kilo, |
| On en donnait deux pour un sou comme des berlingots. | Could be found two for a *sou* like berlingots.[111] |
| Parfois vous rencontriez quelques belles langoustes, | Sometimes, you would come across some nice rock lobsters, |
| Allez-y maintenant, vous en saurez le prix ! | Go look now, and see how much they cost! |
| Il arrivait souvent qu'au dimanche matin | Often on a Sunday morning |
| On partait en famille pour faire un arlequin (pique nique) ; | We would go on a family picnic; |
| Chemin faisant, on descendait sur le quai | On the way, we would stop off at the pier |
| Pour quarante sous, en chargeait-on des poissons ! | For forty *sous*, we could load up on fish! |
| Allez-y aujourd'hui, ce ne sont que bêtes avariées | Go there now and you'll see only rotting specimens |
| Bonnes à mettre au fumier | Ready to be tossed on the dung heap |
| Coûtant très cher et donnant des nausées | That cost a fortune and make you sick |
| Et qu'il faut jeter aux pourceaux ! | And are fit to be thrown to the pigs! |
| L'ouvrier pouvait en manger: pécairé ! | Then the worker could eat fish: poor thing! |
| Qu'il s'étrangle aujourd'hui avec des haricots ! | Now let him choke on beans! |
| Ah ! si l'on ne prenait que les gros en laissant les jeunes | Ah! If only the big ones were taken while leaving the small |
| L'an d'après il y aurait encor des poissons. | There would still be fish left the following year. |
| La cause de tout ce mal vient de vos tartanes, | The root cause of all this evil are your tartanes |
| Qui ravagent les fonds, détruisent les demeures | That wreck the sea bottoms, destroy the homes |
| Des habitants de la mer et mettent leurs retraites | Of the sea's denizens and cause their hideaways |
| Planes comme des boulevards. | To be torn down like boulevards[112] |
| Je ne sais pourquoi ce siècle de lumière, | I don't know why this century of light, |
| Après tant d'inventions, a fait tant d'ignorants. | After so many inventions, has brought such ignorance. |

[110] *Bélégans* seems to be an old word from the *provençal* dialect that I was unable to translate.

[111] A berlingot is a traditional candy from Provence. *Sou* and *franc* are units of currency: there were 20 *sous* in one *franc*. One can deduce from Molinari's poem that the price of fish soared in Marseille in the 1870s.

[112] Molinari refers to the fact that *tartanes* destroyed the algae and Posidania meadows that provide shelter for the fish.

| | |
|---|---|
| Vous ne pensez qu'à vous, non à vos descendants. | You only think of yourselves, not of your descendants. |
| Oui ! vos enfants, un jour enflammés de colère, | Yes! One day your children, boiling with anger, |
| Mourront de faim en maudissant leurs pères | Will starve while cursing their fathers |

| LA RISSOLE | THE RISSOLE[113] |
|---|---|
| Au mois de mars la pêche à la rissole | In March, fishing with *rissole* |
| Aux pauvres soclets coûte la vie. | Costs the lives of poor *soclets*.[114] |
| Les patrons pêcheurs, toujours en éveil, | The fishers, always awake, |
| Arment des bateaux et partent pleins de joie; | Ready their ships and sail off joyfully; |
| Ils savent où le poisson dépose ses œufs, | They know where the fish lay their eggs, |
| Ils entourent la calanque et prennent poissons et œufs. | They surround the *calanque* and take the fish and the eggs.[115] |
| Pas de matelots avec eux! | No deckhands are with them! |
| Tous patrons, plus grande est la part du butin. | All fishers, they each have a greater share of the spoils.[116] |
| Avec un peu de prévoyance, | With a bit of foresight, |
| Vous auriez pensé à ceux qui viendront après vous; | You would have thought of those who will come after, |
| Vous n'auriez point dit: Tout à nous! | You wouldn't have said: it all belongs to us! |
| Que faire, direz-vous, pour détruire le mal? | What can be done, you will ask, to destroy this evil? |
| Ne pêchez jamais qu'à la palangre avec de gros hameçons, | Only use *palangre* with big hooks, |
| Ou bien avec des filets à la maille du quatre | Or nets with mesh size four |
| Ou du huit ou du dix, mais rien de moins! | Or eight or ten, but nothing less! |
| Qu'on m'interroge, je m'expliquerai, | Ask me and I will explain myself, |
| Car je ne parle pas en homme passionné. | For I am not blinded by passions. |
| Qu'on prohibe la pêche comme on a prohibé la chasse; | Let us ban fishing as we banned hunting; |
| Quand le poisson fait ses œufs, laissez-le tranquille! | When the fish lays its eggs, leave it in peace! |
| Et vos enfants, au lieu de vous maudire, | And your children, instead of cursing you, |
| Après votre mort, vous béniront. | Will sing your praises after your death. |
| Vous me la baillez belle, en accusant les dauphins | You're not fooling anyone, by accusing the dolphins |
| De causer tout le mal, de sauter au milieu des filets, | Of causing all this evil, of jumping into the nets, |
| Et de tout briser! | And breaking everything! |

[113] The *rissole* is a net with tight mesh that was used to catch sardines and anchovies.

[114] *Soclets* are small sardines.

[115] The *calanques* are natural reefs along the coast of Marseille. Molinari seems to use the term to refer to the creeks formed by these reefs.

[116] Molinari refers here to the payment system in place on fishing boats. Fishers were entitled to two shares and deckhands to one share (the *Prud'homie* levied a half-share for itself). See ch 5.

| | |
|---|---|
| Plût à Dieu qu'il y en eût au moins un milliard, | By God, if only there were at least a billion |
| Pour détruire vos filets qui ravagent la mer! | To destroy your nets that ravage the sea! |
| Au printemps, quand les gens de Sainte Marguerite | In the spring, when the people from Sainte Marguerite[117] |
| Débarquent à Marseille, les dents vous en tombent. | Disembark in Marseille, you can't believe it. |
| Après eux, plus rien! | After they're gone, nothing is left! |
| Raclez les fonds, vous ne prendrez que des étoiles (de mer). | Scrape the sea bottoms and you will only catch star(fish). |
| Le Gouvernement qui a tant besoin d'argent, | The Government, which needs so much money, |
| Devrait mettre un impôt sur les patrons. | Should impose a tax on the fishers |
| Ce n'est pas sur le poisson que j'aurais mis la taxe, | I would not place a tax on the fish |
| C'est sur les filets aux petites mailles. | But on the small-meshed nets, |
| Alors on verrait le poisson multiplier, | Then the fish would multiply, |
| Les gros seuls seraient pris, les petits resteraient. | Only the big fish would be caught, the small ones would remain. |
| Ah ! si chaque maille payait cent francs, | Ah! If each mesh brought in one hundred francs |
| De leurs filets ils feraient de beaux feux de joie | They would light beautiful bonfires with their nets. |

### LE GANGUI

### THE GANGUI

| | |
|---|---|
| Lorsque vous calez votre gangui pour pêcher des oursins, | When you set your *gangui* to fish sea urchins, |
| Chaque fois que vous le retirez vous faites des milliers de victimes. | Each time you remove your net, you create thousands of victims. |
| Vous abîmez tout, les œufs, les pères et les mères. | You wreck everything: eggs, fathers and mothers. |
| Le Gouvernement finira bien par y prendre garde! | The Government will eventually pay attention to this! |
| Les œufs, à l'éclosion, ne donnent qu'un alevin déjà mort! | The hatching eggs only bring small fry that is already dead |
| Et vous qui vous dites hommes du métier, | And you who say you are specialists, |
| Vous ne cherchez qu'à priver de poisson le peuple. | You seek only to deprive the people of fish. |

---

[117] Molinari might be referring to the Sainte Marguerite island, off the coast of Cannes.

| LE CALEN | THE CALEN |
|---|---|
| (LA PÊCHE DE NUIT) | (NIGHT FISHING) |
| Voici une pêche infernale | There is a diabolical form of fishing |
| Que les malandrins font pendant la nuit. | That brigands practice during the night. |
| Oh ! ces Napolitains ! par une nuit tranquille, | Oh! These Neapolitans! On a quiet night, |
| Ils s'en vont, armés d'un grand instrument | They go, armed with a large tool |
| Appelé le calen, tout le long du port, | Called a *calen*, along the harbour |
| Râcler les fonds, sous les bâtiments à l'ancre. | To rake the bottoms, under the anchored vessels. |
| Là, ils prennent tout, les gros et les petits. | There, they take everything, all fish both big and small. |
| Cette infamie ne se voit qu'à Marseille. | This outrage can only be seen in Marseille. |
| Partout ailleurs, à Brest, à Rochefort, | Everywhere else, in Brest, in Rochefort, |
| La pêche dans le port est interdite. | Fishing in the harbour is forbidden. |
| Au mauvais temps le poisson y cherche un abri. | The fish find shelter there in bad weather. |
| Ils viennent l'y surprendre et l'assassiner. | [The Neapolitans] surprise them there and murder them. |
| Des étrangers seuls se livrent à cette pêche, | Only foreigners fish this way, |
| Pourquoi ne les force-t-on pas à ne pêcher qu'à la ligne | Why don't we force them to fish only by angling? |
| Qu'ils pêchent à la palangre, ces braves gens-là, | Let them fish with *palangre*, these wonderful people, |
| Ou qu'ils partent ! Nous n'en serons pas fâchés. | Or leave! This wouldn't upset us. |
| Aussitôt ils joueraient du couteau. | But they would soon start stabbing away. |

```
        o
><(((( (°> °
```

# PART III

## Collapse

# 5

# Law and (Private) Order

[W]e must establish ... sworn *Prud'hommes*, who are under the obligation to declare everything that comes to their attention; they are true watchdogs who cost nothing.

Napoleon Bonaparte, 1811[1]

## I. Introduction

This chapter examines the argument according to which private orders cannot function effectively without the support of states. Proponents of this argument, which I call the 'state dependence thesis', view governmental support as necessary to sustain the functioning of private orders. Too much state interference, so the theory goes, would affect the autonomy of private orders, while a lack of state support would undermine their functioning.[2] This view is implicit, for instance, in Stringham's analysis of private governance, or in Bernstein's examination of the ways in which the 'legal system' interfered too heavily with the private order of diamond traders in the 1980s.[3] It is even clearer in Ostrom's argument concerning the necessary 'recognition' of private rules by state authorities,[4] and in Sagy's analysis of the 'proactive role' of 'public orders' in the creation and maintenance of private orders.[5] In other words, according to the state-dependence thesis, the regulatory capacities of private orders would be a bell-curved, Gaussian

---

[1] *Notes de Napoléon dictées en conseil du commerce et des manufactures le 25 novembre 1811*, in *Correspondance de Napoléon Ier publiée par ordre de l'Empereur Napoléon III*, vol 23 (Paris, H Plon, 1868) 38: '[I]l faut établir sur ces points des prud'hommes assermentés, obligés de déclarer tout ce qui vient à leur connaissance; ce seraient de véritables surveillants qui ne coûteraient rien.'

[2] This argument does not exhaust the analysis of how private orders interact with state legal systems. Other authors have held the view that private orders emerge in 'dysfunctional' legal systems. See J McMillan and C Woodruff, 'Private Order under Dysfunctional Public Order' (2000) 98 *Michigan Law Review* 2421.

[3] See eg, EP Stringham, *Private Governance: Creating Order in Economic and Social Life* (Oxford, Oxford University Press, 2015) 194: 'Private governance always functions to varying degrees, but it functions much less effectively the more it is hobbled by government.'; L Bernstein, 'Opting out of the Legal System: Extralegal Contractual Relations in the Diamond Industry' (1992) 21 *The Journal of Legal Studies* 115, 156–57: 'The older arbitrators fear that legal interference in the diamond trade will one day destroy the traditional way of doing business.'

[4] E Ostrom, *Governing the Commons: The Evolution of Institutions for Collective Action* (Cambridge, Cambridge University Press, 1990) 101.

[5] T Sagy, 'What's So Private about Private Ordering?' (2011) 45 *Law & Society Review* 923, 945.

function of state support. Private capacities grow with state support, but diminish as governmental oversight becomes too stringent.

At first sight, the history of the *Prud'homie* seems consistent with this analysis. In fact, the *Prud'homie* has actively sought the support of the state through intense lobbying, thus suggesting that it requires this kind of support to function properly. For instance, the *Prud'homie* plied public officials with gifts (usually tuna),[6] organised festivals for them[7] and touted the merits of its regulatory system in written pamphlets.[8] For the last of these activities, the *Prud'homie* enjoined the services of prominent lawyers such as Portalis, a leader of the bar and the main drafter of the French Civil Code.[9] Through these efforts, the *Prud'homie* ensured that state authorities supported its position in regulatory battles and recognised the sphere of authority that it had patiently accreted over the centuries. Each of these objectives – conflict management and regulatory recognition – finds specific illustrations in the historical record.

A first example concerns the dispute that arose between the *Prud'homie* and Dominique de la Crosse, a favourite of the Queen of France, over the installation of new *madragues* in the fishery of Marseille in the 1670s.[10] In order to improve its prospects over and against de La Crosse, the *Prud'homie* sent two envoys to meet with King Louis XIV in Versailles.[11] After securing the king's support and prevailing against de La Crosse, the *Prud'homie* ordered a painting from an upcoming young artist, François Puget,[12] representing the delegates of the *Prud'homie* bowing at the feet of Louis XIV and imploring him for support.[13] The *Prud'homie* spared no expense with the painting: it spent about 350 livres (the price of a fishing boat) for the artwork, its framing and gilding.[14] The fishers hung Puget's painting on a wall of the *Prud'homie*, displaying their gratitude to Louis XIV, but also their ability to attract support from the most powerful man in France. Today, the *Prud'homie*'s walls are still covered with pictures of its members posing with world leaders, such as former President Chirac or, less expectedly, the Prince of Wales. Several informants told me how a former *Prud'homme* liked to cast doubt on his kinship with a

---

[6] See, eg, Minutes of the *Prud'homie*'s Assembly (8 September 1740), DA 250E4.

[7] See, eg, Document detailing a festival for the visit of the King's brother (January 1743), DA 250E39.

[8] See, eg, Memorial of the *Prud'homie* sent to Mr Chardon against the foreigners (1786), DA 250E36.

[9] See Memorial for the *Prud'homie de pêche* of Marseille (1787), DA 250E8, 146.

[10] See ch 3, section II.C.

[11] The delegates of the *Prud'homie* were Louis Lombardon and Jean Bompard. Lombardon was a *Prud'homme* in 1665 and a prominent member of the community. Bompard was the official writer of the *Prud'homie*.

[12] François Puget was the son of Pierre Puget, a celebrated artist of the 17th century sometimes referred to as the 'French Michelangelo'. François Puget gained fame as one of the most prominent painters in Marseille. Some of his paintings are displayed in the Louvre. Unfortunately, the painting that he made for the *Prud'homie* is now missing. See G Reynaud, 'Du portrait de Louis XIV à l'assomption de la Vierge: Deux œuvres perdues de François et Pierre Puget' (1997) 190 *Provence historique* 587.

[13] Contract between the *Prud'homie* and François Puget (26 July 1677), DA 366E211.

[14] The *Prud'homie* spent 240 livres for the painting (ibid), 52 livres for the framing and 60 livres for gilding the frame (Financial receipt (28 March 1678), DA 366E212).

long-time mayor of Marseille who incidentally shared the same family name. The *Prud'homie*'s efforts to stage its proximity with the current political leadership is a sign of its acumen, but also of the need to draw support from state authorities in order to prevail in conflicts arising within and outside of the fishery.

The second example illustrates more specifically the need for the *Prud'homie* to gain recognition of its powers by the state. This example is drawn from the situation that arose after the beginning of the French Revolution in 1789. At that time, the *Prud'homie* was in a dangerous position, because of its constant support for the monarchy over the past centuries. Additionally, the revolutionaries intended to dissolve guilds and trade associations, such as the *Prud'homie*, for philosophical reasons.[15] Not only did the *Prud'homie* survive the French Revolution, but it also remained untouched by the Statute of 14 June 1791 (*Loi Le Chapelier*) that banned all guilds and trade corporations. In order to achieve this staggering result, the fishers of Marseille applied the same lobbying methods that had proved successful in previous centuries. In July and October 1790, the *Prud'homie* sent delegates who submitted a written memorial to the National Assembly in Paris.[16] This memorial emphasised the democratic nature of the *Prud'homie* and its consistency with 'the principles [of the Revolution]'.[17] The *Prud'hommes* portrayed themselves as 'true arbitrators elected by the general trust and the free will [of the fishers]'. This move was particularly savvy, as the revolutionaries intended to place arbitration at the heart of the French judicial system.[18] On 28 October 1790, the *Prud'homie*'s delegates further developed these arguments in a speech before the National Assembly.[19] Their speech was so eloquent and compelling that a prominent revolutionary (Mirabeau) and the President of the National Assembly (Barnave) credited the *Prud'homie* with having built a system of 'popular justice' well ahead of the Revolution.[20] The *Prud'homie* also took concrete measures to show its conversion to the revolutionary cause, for instance by making a gift of 2,000 livres to

[15] This distaste for guilds and vested interests reflects Rousseau's conception of the general will, a key inspiration for the revolutionaries. See J-J Chevallier, *Les grandes oeuvres politiques: De Machiavel à nos jours* (Paris, Armand Colin, 1970) 109–31.

[16] *Mémoires sur la police de la pêche française* (1790), CCI YC/22/09. The first team of delegates was composed of Tournon (a member of the *Prud'homie*), Floux (a former member of the *Prud'homie*) and Ponsard (the archivist of the *Prud'homie*). The second team of delegates was composed of Imbert, Ardéni (both members of the Prud'homie) and Ponsard.

[17] ibid 15.

[18] See F Grisel, 'The Private-Public Divide and its Influence over French Arbitration Law: Tradition and Transition', unpublished (on file with the author). This analogy was again used in a discussion concerning the constitutionality of the *Prud'homie* in 1796. See *Procès-verbal des séances du Conseil des Cinq-Cent* (10 December 1796), AD 250E9.

[19] See D Rauch, *Les prud'homies de pêche en Méditerranée française à l'époque contemporaine* (Nice, Serre Editeur, 2017) 94–99; Y Bosc, 'La prud'homie des patrons-pêcheurs de Marseille pendant la Révolution française', unpublished (on file with the author).

[20] Rauch (n 19) 98–99. The *Prud'homie* even turned its back on the previous administration by publicly stating that 'the administrations of the Ancient Regime have never granted to this profession [of fishers] the protection that it is entitled to expect' (*Encouragement pour le service de la Marine ou Dépend de la Délibération des Patrons-Pêcheurs de Marseille* (3 October 1790), CCI E/159).

the French 'nation', or by undertaking to ensure freely the security of the port of Marseille and to pay fishers to serve in the conscript army.[21]

By skilfully siding with state authorities, the *Prud'homie* survived this tumultuous period in French history. However, it also showed some difficulties in retaining the support of the state starting in the nineteenth century. How could the *Prud'homie* resist several authoritarian regimes and revolutions but experience problems garnering support from a republican regime? One hypothesis that immediately springs to mind is the progressive reinforcement of state powers over the centuries, which then eventually prevailed over the *Prud'homie*. This potential answer is, in fact, extremely popular among students of the *Prud'homie* and the fishers themselves.[22] According to this view, the *Prud'homie* collapsed in recent times due to the state's efforts to absorb the community of fishers into its own regulatory frame. When asked to explain the *Prud'homie*'s collapse, my informants complained that the administration 'controls everything', that it 'kills the fishers' and that it is 'blind and way too controlling'. Another interviewee told me that the administration 'shoots the *Prud'homie* at point-blank range'. This view is entirely consistent with the state-dependence thesis, which links the effectiveness of private orders to the support of state legal systems.[23]

This explanation has some truth in it, but it captures only part of the reality. While acknowledging the fact that the autonomy of private orders depends on their recognition by state authorities, this chapter places the focus upon private orders, rather than states, in order to explain the former's resilience. In line with the findings in chapter 2, this chapter suggests that states can have a deep interest in sustaining the existence of private orders.[24] A more daring version of the same argument is that private orders may have the capacity to capture regulatory processes in order to sustain their own institutional autonomy.[25] This capacity depends, to a large extent, on the ability of these systems to convince state officials that they are good at performing the tasks for which they are formed. The argument presented in this chapter is consistent with that of Pirie that 'autonomy may represent not so much a lack of interaction with external forces as an active

---

[21] ibid.

[22] See, eg, F Féral, 'Un phénomène de décentralisation contestée: Les Prud'homies de Pêcheurs de Méditerranée' (1986) 133/134 *Economie Méridionale* 95; B Pierchon-Bédry, 'Les Prud'hommes pêcheurs en Méditerranée' in J Krynen and JC Gaven (eds), *Les désunions de la magistrature (XIXe–XXe siècles)* (Toulouse, Presses de l'Université de Toulouse 1 Capitole, 2013).

[23] For instance, Stringham blames states for imposing 'rules and regulations' on private orders 'with little regard for whether they actually benefit market participants'. See Stringham (n 3) 204. See also T de Moor, *The Dilemma of the Commoners: Understanding the Use of Common-Pool Resources in Long-Term Perspective* (Cambridge, Cambridge University Press, 2015) 112.

[24] On this question, see A Greif, *Institutions and the Path to the Modern Economy: Lessons from Medieval Trade*, (Cambridge, Cambridge University Press, 2006) ch 4.

[25] I noted a similar regulatory capture by private actors in the case of international arbitration. See F Grisel, 'Treaty-Making between Public Authority and Private Interest: The Genealogy of the Convention on the Recognition and Enforcement of Foreign Arbitral Awards' (2017) 28 *The European Journal of International Law* 73.

engagement with them',[26] and with Falk Moore's notion of a 'semi-autonomous social field', which captures the complex interactions between internal regulatory processes and the external forces that constrain and frame these processes.[27] In other words, the Bell-curved function of the interactions between private regulation and state powers may not fully account for the complex processes through which private orders and state authorities continuously interact, battle for regulatory prominence or collaborate with each other. The point is that one must not take the state-dependence thesis at face value: beyond the apparent domination of the state lies a much more complex reality, in which private orders create relationships of interdependence with the state.

In support of this argument, this chapter retraces the process by means of which the administrative state progressively gained regulatory powers over the fishery of Marseille, while remaining relatively deferential towards the *Prud'homie*. In fact, the *Prud'homie* managed to preserve alliances with the state for a very long time, and its inability to do so with more distant polities, such as the European Union (EU), provides a useful counterpoint for the analysis. In fact, the EU has been much more effective than the French administration at harnessing the *Prud'homie*'s powers, arguably because the *Prud'homie* was unable to interact meaningfully with the EU in ways that could shield it from regulatory oversight. A major aim of this chapter is thus to highlight the ways in which a long-established organisation, such as the *Prud'homie*, managed to secure collaboration outside its ranks, and how its failure to govern at crucial points in its history undermined its capacity to preserve these alliances. The analysis presented in this chapter offers a more refined version of the state-dependence thesis, according to which private orders are not merely acted upon by public regulators, but can also be actors shaping their own institutional destiny.

## II. The Creeping Codification of the *Prud'homie*

The archives of the *Prud'homie* are replete with formal acts of recognition directed towards it by the successive kings of France.[28] For centuries, the *Prud'homie* largely determined the limits of its own powers, and the kings recognised these powers *ex post facto* in a series of patent letters. The progressive emergence of a centralised state equipped with a specialised administration led it to take a more proactive role, with an increasing level of precision, in the codification of the *Prud'homie*'s

---

[26] F Pirie, 'Legal Autonomy as Political Engagement: The Ladakhi Village in the Wider World' (2006) 40 *Law & Society Review* 77.

[27] S Falk Moore, 'Law and Social Change: The Semi-Autonomous Social Field as an Appropriate Subject of Study' (1973) 7 *Law & Society Review* 719.

[28] The kings of France recognised the *Prud'homie* and its powers in a series of letters patent (*lettres patentes*), which can be found in DA 250E1.

powers. The Great Maritime Ordinance of 1681 and an important decision by the
Council of State in 1738 both illustrate this codification process. As the *Prud'homie*
faced the social challenges described in chapters 3 and 4, the Presidential Decrees
of 1852 and 1859 codified its powers in more restrictive terms.

## A.  The Great Maritime Ordinance of 1681

The strengthening of the administrative state under Louis XIV took a variety of
forms. Colbert, a key actor in the early formation of the French administrative
state and Secretary of the Navy under Louis XIV, codified the rules pertaining to
the regulation of fisheries in the late seventeenth century. This codification led to
the Great Maritime Ordinance, which remained a key pillar of French maritime
policy from its adoption in 1681 until its abrogation in 2006.[29] The fifth and final
book of the Great Maritime Ordinance states in its first provision that fishing is
'unregulated' (*libre*) as long as it is practised with the 'nets and engines permitted
under the current Ordinance'.[30] In other words, everything that was not expressly
prohibited under the Great Maritime Ordinance was allowed. And in fact it regulated some of the oldest fishing techniques in Marseille. For instance, it prohibited
the use of *gangui* and *bregin* from March until May.[31] It also conditioned the operation of *madragues* on 'express authorisation' from the king's administration.[32]
Notwithstanding their importance and potential impact, the *Prud'homie*
simply ignored these prohibitions. For instance, Peysonnel's codification of the
*Prud'homie's* 'fishing laws' of 1725 does not reflect any of the prohibitions set
out in the Great Ordinance.[33] I have not found a single reference in the archival
records to an 'express authorisation' sought by the *Prud'homie* for the exploitation
of its *madragues*. The *Prud'homie* may have held that, while prohibiting certain
fishing practices and seeking to regulate others, the Great Ordinance did not
challenge its authority and implicitly allowed it to keep regulating the fishery of
Marseille. In fact, the Great Ordinance does not explicitly regulate or limit the
*Prud'homie's* jurisdiction. Quite to the contrary, it recognises the right of fishers

---

[29] See *Ordonnance n° 2006-460 du 21 avril 2006 relative à la partie législative du code général de la
propriété des personnes publiques*, Art 7, II, 7°.

[30] Great Maritime Ordinance (August 1681), Book 5, Title I, Art I. Because of this principle of
freedom, the sea was deemed to be a *res nullius*, a space over which anyone could assert rights. See
R Grancher, 'Les communs du rivage: L'Etat, les riverains et l'institution juridique des grèves de la mer
(Manche, XVIIIe–XIXe siècle)' in F Locher (ed), *La nature en communs: Ressources, environnement et
communautés (France et Empire français, XVIIe-XXe siècle* (Ceyzérieu, Champ Vallon, 2020).

[31] Great Maritime Ordinance (August 1681), Book 5, Title II, Art XIII.

[32] Great Maritime Ordinance (August 1681), Book 5, Title IV, Art I.

[33] The Great Ordinance of 1681 appears only once in the codification of the *Prud'homie's* rules by
Peyssonnel. The *Prud'homie* did not seem to consider the prohibitions contained in the Great Ordinance as binding. See *Description des Pesches, Loix et Ordonnances des Pescheurs de la Ville de Marseille*
(1725), DA 250E2, 101. On Peyssonnel's codification, see ch 2, section III.C.ii.

to elect the *Prud'homie*.[34] This ambiguity effectively led to a dual jurisdiction over the fishery of Marseille: the jurisdiction of the *Prud'homie*, on the one hand, and the jurisdiction of the French state that could (and arguably should) implement the prohibitions contained in the Great Maritime Ordinance, on the other hand. The leading commentary on the Great Maritime Ordinance (the so-called 'Valin's Commentary'[35]) acknowledges the existence of this dual jurisdiction, stating that the *Prud'homie*'s police powers over the fishery did not prevent the royal administration from exercising its own police powers, that the *Prud'homie*'s jurisdictional powers did not limit the authority of state courts over 'crimes' and 'delicts' committed in the fishery, and that the fishers and the *Prud'homie* ought to comply with the law.[36] As long as the interests of the *Prud'homie* remained aligned with the king's political agenda, however, the *Prud'homie* ignored the rules set out by the royal administration, even after the state had gained regulatory teeth and the power to overstep the authority of the *Prud'homie*.

## B. The Council of State's Decision of 1738

Chapter 3 describes how the *Prud'homie* faced great financial difficulties when setting up the *madragues* in the seventeenth century. In order to overcome these financial difficulties, the *Prud'homie* started levying a special tax, the so-called 'half-share', in 1725. The term 'half-share' reflects the remuneration system in place on fishing boats: fishers divided their gross income by share, with each crew member being entitled to one share and the captain to two shares. The *Prud'homie* decided to levy half a share for its own budget, a not-insignificant amount, considering the fact that each crew member was entitled to one share. As one might expect, some fishing crews refused to pay the 'half-share' to the *Prud'homie*, which turned towards the state for support in levying its tax. In 1727, the royal court of Aix (*Parlement de Provence*) certified the *Prud'homie*'s decision to create the 'half-share' (another sign that the *Prud'homie* did not neglect the symbolic support of the state).[37] In 1728, the Council of State decided to appoint six fishers in charge of recovering the half-share.[38] The support of the state allowed the *Prud'homie* to

---

[34] The fishers' right to elect the *Prud'homie* was submitted to the supervision of admiralty officers before whom the newly elected *Prud'hommes* were to take an oath. See Great Maritime Ordinance (August 1681), Book 5, Title VIII, Art VI.

[35] René-Josué Valin (1695–1765) is one of the great jurists of the 18th century, who gained particular prominence for his work on maritime law.

[36] RJ Valin, *Nouveau Commentaire sur l'Ordonnance de la Marine du Mois d'Août 1681*, vol 2 (La Rochelle, Légier et Mesnier, 1760) 744.

[37] Decision of the Parliament of Provence (27 January 1727), DA 250E75. The decision mentions that the 'various lawsuits which fishers have been forced to sustain before the Council [of the King] at great expense have greatly increased the expenditures of the group'.

[38] Decision of the Council of the State (6 March 1728), DA 250E75. The First President of the Parliament of Provence appointed the six fishers shortly thereafter, see Ordinance of Cardin Lebret, First President of the Parliament of Provence (27 August 1728), CCI E/159.

rely on a system of physical constraint in order to raise the tax, for instance when a recalcitrant fisher was thrown in jail in 1729 because of his reluctance to pay the half-share.[39]

The key issue that led to another restatement of the *Prud'homie*'s powers arose from the *Prud'homie*'s attempt to levy the half-share from the Catalan fishers who had been migrating to Marseille since the early 1720s.[40] As one might imagine, foreign fishers were even less willing to pay the half-share than their French counterparts. A string of litigation ensued concerning the *Prud'homie*'s powers to levy a tax on foreign fishers. In 1735, the Admiralty of Marseille decided that the *Prud'homie* did not have such powers.[41] The *Prud'homie* swiftly challenged the Admiralty's decision before the Council of State.[42] On 16 May 1738, the Council of State overturned the Admiralty's decision, in a judgment that became a long-lasting precedent for the recognition of the *Prud'homie*'s powers.[43]

The decision of 16 May 1738 is particularly long and detailed: it presents the position of the *Prud'homie* and of the Catalan fishers before enumerating the patent letters issued by various kings in previous centuries.[44] It then recognises in broad terms the *Prud'homie*'s

> right to exercise alone, in the waters of Marseille, police powers over the fishery and to adjudicate in a sovereign capacity, without specific procedure and without writings or lawyers and party representatives, the breaches of its regulations by any fishers, French or foreign, in these waters, as well as any disputes that may arise, in the exercise of this trade, among fishers ...[45]

On this basis, the Council of State prohibits admiralty officers, state courts and judges from interfering in any way with the powers of the *Prud'homie*. The decision of the Council of State is remarkable, as one of the first to recognise the specific powers exercised by the *Prud'homie* over the fishery of Marseille.[46] Pursuant to

---

[39] Letter from the Community of Fishers of Marseille (20 March 1729), DA 250E94. A decision of the Council of the King dated 28 December 1729 entitled the fishers in charge of levying the half-share to seize the boats, nets and the fish stock of recalcitrant fishers (cited in decision of the Council of the King (16 May 1738), CCI E/159, 7).

[40] See ch 3, section III.B.

[41] Decision of the Admiralty of Marseille (9 December 1735). This decision is mentioned, for instance, in the Decision of the Council of the State (16 May 1738), CCI E/159.

[42] Decision of the Council of the State (25 February 1736), DA 250E75.

[43] Decision of the Council of the State (16 May 1738), CCI E/159. This decision was cited, for instance, in Legal Opinion of the Council of State (22 April 1913).

[44] Decision of the Council of the State (16 May 1738), CCI E/159.

[45] ibid ('le droit de connaître seuls, dans l'étendue des Mers de Marseille, de la police de la pêche, et de juger souverainement sans forme, ni figure de Procès, et sans Ecritures, ni appeler Avocats ou Procureurs, les contraventions à ladite police, par quelques pêcheurs, soit Français ou Etrangers, fréquentant lesdites Mers qu'elles soient commises et tous les différends qui peuvent naître, à l'occasion de ladite protection, entre lesdits pêcheurs ...').

[46] The Council of the State maintained these powers in subsequent decisions. See, *e.g.*, Decision of the Council of the State (9 November 1776), CCI E/159 (recognising the *Prud'homie*'s right to exercise police and judicial powers over the fishery of Marseille).

this decision, the *Prud'homie* was free to police, legislate and decide disputes arising in the fishery of Marseille without interference from state authorities. This recognition of the *Prud'homie*'s powers by the Council of State is considerably more specific than the provision of the Great Maritime Ordinance recognising the fishers' right to elect their *Prud'homie*. Accordingly, this decision represented an enormous success for the *Prud'homie*, particularly in its efforts to assert its jurisdiction over foreign fishers. Contrary to a widely held view, it is the *Prud'homie*'s own failure to govern in critical periods of its history that provided the state with grounds to encroach upon its institutional territory.

## C. The Presidential Decrees of 1852 and 1859

As seen in section I, the revolutionaries left the broad powers of the *Prud'homie* untouched.[47] In early 1791, the fishers cheerfully applauded when the newly adopted Statute of 12 December 1790 was read to them.[48] They had good reasons to express joy. The *Prud'homie* is in fact one of the few trade corporations (if not the only one) to have survived the French Revolution. Not only did the Statute of 12 December 1790 maintain the *Prud'homie* in its functions, it also encouraged the replication of the structures of the *Prud'homie* along the whole Mediterranean coast. Article 9 of the Statute allowed other ports on the Mediterranean to create their own versions of the *Prud'homie*.[49] Less than two months later, the *Prud'homie* advised fishers in a neighbouring port (Sète) on the creation of their own *Prud'homie*.[50] Within five months, other *Prud'homies* appeared in Toulon, Sète, St Tropez, Canne, Cassis, Agde, Perpignan, Gruissan, Antibe, Bandol and St Nazaire.[51] The *Prud'homie* now counts 32 counterparts on the French Mediterranean coast. The *Prud'homie* also survived the many regime changes that unfolded over the subsequent decades in France (including two empires, three kingdoms and countless republics). Napoleon, who touted the *Prud'hommes* as 'true watchdogs who cost nothing [to the state]',[52] even created a *Prud'homie* in the Kingdom of Holland,[53] and considered extending the institution throughout his whole empire.[54]

However, growing social conflict in the fishery of Marseille placed the regulatory powers of the *Prud'homie* under strain and encouraged the administrative state

---

[47] *Loi Relative aux Pêcheurs des différents Ports du Royaume, et notamment à ceux de la ville de Marseille* (12 December 1790), DA C4029.

[48] Letter from the *Prud'homie* to the Minister of Marine (2 February 1791), NA C4/181.

[49] *Loi Relative aux Pêcheurs des différents Ports du Royaume, et notamment à ceux de la ville de Marseille* (12 December 1790), DA C4029, Art IX.

[50] Letter from the *Prud'homie* to the fishers of Sète (9 February 1791), NA C4/181.

[51] The decrees creating the new *Prud'homies* can be found in AD 250E9.

[52] *Notes de Napoléon* (n 1) 36–39.

[53] *Décret impérial relatif aux pêches de la morue, du hareng et du poisson frais* (25 April 1812), Arts 12–14.

[54] *Notes de Napoléon* (n 1) 36–39.

to intervene in the management of the fishery. These conflicts arose out of the leniency of the *Prud'homie* towards the dragnets – specifically the *gangui* and *pêche au boeuf* (ox-fishing) – that had been repeatedly prohibited by the state.[55] The *Prud'homie* tried to save face in these debates, arguing that it was in fact acting against ox-fishing and blaming others (namely the fishers of the neighbouring city of Martigues) for using this technique.[56] However, as seen in chapter 4, the *Prud'homie*'s official position did not fool anyone, instead causing a public outcry in Marseille. In particular, an attorney named Laget de Podio filed an official complaint to the mayor and the public prosecutor of Marseille in 1835.[57] In his complaint, Laget de Podio pointed out that several *Prud'hommes* were using dragnets and were reluctant to enforce the legal prohibitions against these nets.[58] Public officials took these complaints very seriously and started re-examining the scope of the *Prud'homie*'s powers over the fishery of Marseille. For instance, the Ministry of Marine formed a committee to investigate the regulation of dragnets in Marseille.[59] But the most effective response came from the Supreme Court (*Cour de cassation*), which used a series of cases to challenge the powers of the *Prud'homie*.

## D.  Challenges to the Powers of the *Prud'homie* before the Supreme Court

### i. *The* Canesse *Case*

The first case illustrates some of the salient issues raised by the 'dual jurisdiction' that arose from the Great Maritime Ordinance of 1681. In 1835, the *Prud'homie* fined a fisher named Canesse for using *gangui*, the type of dragnet that had been prohibited

---

[55] On the development of the dragnets, see ch 4. As stated in section II.A of this chapter, the Great Maritime Ordinance prohibited the use of *gangui* and *bregin* during the months of March, April and May. The royal administration prohibited ox-fishing starting in the first half of the 18th century. See, eg, Ordinance of Cardin Lebret (4 August 1725), AM HH369; Decision of the Council of the State (25 September 1725), AD C2774. Ox-fishing and the *gangui* were again prohibited by a statute of 12 March 1803, see JJ Baudrillart, *Traité général des eaux et forêts, chasses et pêches*, vol IX (Paris, Librairie d'Arthus Bertrand, 1827) 600; *Loi qui prohibe la pêche aux boeufs et celle connue sous le nom de pêche au gangui* (12 March 1803), AD 250E9.

[56] Letter from the *Prud'homie* to the Commissaire des Classes (13 June 1865), AD 250E126; Letter from the *Prud'homie* to the *Prud'homie de Martigues* (21 June 1835), AD 250E126.

[57] See *Les pêcheurs de la ville de Marseille et autres pêcheurs de sa banlieue, côtes et villes voisines à M le Maire de la Ville de Marseille* (Marseille, Marius Olive, 1835); *Mémoire de M Laget de Podio, avocat, au nom des pêcheurs de la ville de Marseille adressé au Procureur du Roi auprès du Tribunal civil de Marseille* (11 June 1835), AM 18F6.

[58] See ch 4.

[59] This committee adopted a regulation restricting the *pêche aux boeufs* (under the control of the *Prud'homie*) in 1738. See *Règlement sur la pêche pour le quartier de Marseille* (2 January 1838), PA. Public officials subsequently 'buried' this regulation, as mentioned in a deliberation of the municipal council of Marseille (5 August 1850), MA 1D79.

under state law a few decades earlier.[60] However, the *Prud'homie* imposed a fine that was negligible (4 francs) when compared with the minimum amount allowed pursuant to statutory law (300 francs).[61] Following the *Prud'homie's* decision, the public prosecutor of Marseille seized local courts, which fined Canesse again with the proper amount under the law.[62] The *Prud'homie* subsequently challenged the decision of these courts before the *Cour de cassation* on two grounds: first, it criticised the lower courts for having breached the principle of *res judicata*, by fining Canesse notwithstanding his previous condemnation by the *Prud'homie;*[63] second, it also claimed that the lower courts overstepped their powers under the Decree of 12 December 1790.

The *Cour de cassation* not only confirmed the decision of the lower courts, but also interpreted the *Prud'homie's* powers in a restrictive manner. The *Cour de cassation* first held that the lower courts did not breach the *res judicata* principle because the decision of the *Prud'homie* could not be considered a 'court' decision. In other words, this decision simply denied that the *Prud'homie* had judicial powers over the fishery of Marseille. The *Cour de cassation* also rejected the charge that the lower courts had failed to recognise the powers of the *Prud'homie* under the Decree of 12 December 1790. It construed these powers as being limited to the enforcement of the *Prud'homie's* rules, not state laws.[64] The *Cour de cassation* therefore interpreted the dual jurisdiction in a way that was detrimental to the *Prud'homie's* powers, thus empowering state courts to apply their laws in the fishery of Marseille. Soon after this decision, the public prosecutor of Aix-en-Provence gave instructions to his subordinates to investigate any breach of the legal prohibition against *gangui* and ox-fishing in Marseille.[65]

## ii. *The* Galiffet *Case*

The second case arose out of a decision of the *Prud'homie* of Martigues (a city neighbouring Marseille) to open by force a fishing trap owned by a certain Mr de Galiffet in 1846.[66] De Galiffet sued the *Prud'hommes* before a criminal court for trespassing on his private property and challenged the *Prud'homie's* decision in another lawsuit before the Supreme Court (*Cour de cassation*). These actions against the *Prud'homie* of Martigues led to two important rulings on the part of

---

[60] See *Cour de cassation*, 9 April 1836, (1836) 32 *Journal du Droit Criminel* 273. The relevant prohibition arose out of the Statute of 12 March 1803 (see n 55).

[61] *Cour de cassation* (n 60).

[62] ibid.

[63] *Res judicata* is a legal principle preventing litigants from being tried twice for the same actions.

[64] *Cour de cassation* (n 60).

[65] This instruction is mentioned in Letter from the *Prud'homie* to the *Prud'hommes de Martigues* (17 July 1836), DA 250E126.

[66] See *Cour de cassation*, 19 June 1847, (1847) 2 *Journal du Palais* 176.

the *Cour de cassation*. In the first ruling, the *Cour de cassation* held that the *Prud'hommes* were not entitled to the legal immunity that judges benefit from under French law, while simultaneously deciding that criminal courts did not have jurisdiction to sanction the *Prud'homie* for trespassing.[67] In the second ruling, the *Cour de cassation* held that it was not entitled to review the decision of the *Prud'homie*, not on the basis that the *Prud'homie* had full and final jurisdiction over disputes arising in its fishery, but because its judgments were at the time rendered orally (a bar against the possibility of appealing court decisions under French law).[68] If the *Prud'homie* had rendered its decision in writing, one could *a contrario* surmise that the *Cour de cassation* would have allowed the appeal.[69]

The *Canesse* and *Galiffet* cases illustrate the growing difficulties concerning the scope of the *Prud'homie*'s jurisdiction, which were compounded by the disastrous effects of the use of dragnets on the fishery of Marseille. In the late 1840s, local authorities gathered several commissions in charge of investigating the effects of dragnets and finding ways to implement fishing laws in Marseille.[70] In 1849, the city council of Marseille criticised the complicit attitude of the *Prud'hommes*, pointing out that 'instead of implementing the prohibitions against dragnets, they were the first ones to breach them'.[71] In fact, the *Prud'homie* remained astonishingly silent on those issues and did not even try to regulate the dragnets, thus giving credence to its critics. These difficulties led to a wide legislative effort purporting to limit the *Prud'homie*'s powers, which culminated in the adoption of the Decrees of 1852 and 1859.

## E.  The Decree of 1852

The Decree of 1852 was the first in a series of statutes aimed at regulating French fisheries.[72] This decree was disastrous for the *Prud'homie*: it temporarily reduced the *Prud'homie*'s powers to virtually nil and established a very strict regulatory regime over the fishery of Marseille. The Decree of 1852 allowed the *Prud'homie* to report violations of state law in signed minutes that had to be transmitted to

---

[67] ibid. The decision of the *Cour de cassation* directly contradicted another decision from the *Cour royale de Montpellier* of 17 March 1846, which granted to a *Prud'homme* of Collioure (Mr Hostalrich) the same legal protection as that owed to public judges under French law. See *Cour royale de Montpellier*, 17 March 1846, (1847) 2 *Journal du Palais* 176.

[68] See *Cour de cassation*, 13 July 1847, (1847) 2 *Journal du Palais* 179.

[69] This incidentally illustrates the effectiveness of the *Prud'homie*'s policy of favouring oral interactions. See ch 2, section III.C.ii.

[70] See *Délibération du Conseil Municipal de Marseille nommant une commission spéciale sur la pêche* (10 November 1848), MA 1D78; *Arrêté du Préfet des Bouches-du-Rhône visant à créer une commission spéciale pour étudier 'les abus de la pêche'* (26 February 1849), CCI MR/45221; Minutes of the Municipal Council of Marseille (24 May 1849), AM 1D78; Minutes of the Municipal Council of Marseille (16 May 1850), MA 1D79.

[71] Minutes of the Municipal Council of Marseille (24 May 1849), MA 1D78.

[72] *Décret sur l'exercice de la pêche côtière* (9 January 1852), CCI MR/45221.

criminal courts for final adjudication.[73] In doing so, the Decree of 1852 not only disregarded the *Prud'homie's* legislative and judicial powers, but also relegated it to the role of a police agent and, most importantly, ignored its oral tradition (a key feature of its independence from state courts, as shown by the *Galiffet* case). The Decree of 1852 also provided for heavy fines and jail sentences in the event of violations of fishing regulations[74] and made the operation of the *madragues* subject to a specific authorisation from the administration.[75] Following the adoption of this decree, five *madragues* were discontinued in Marseille.[76] Unsurprisingly, the Decree of 1852 caused a major outcry in the city. Less than a month after its entry into force, a coalition of fishnet merchants, salt traders and ordinary citizens called for the maintenance of the *madragues* in a written petition.[77]

The turmoil spread within the local administration in charge of implementing the Decree of 1852. Admiralty officers in Marseille complained to their superiors in Paris and asked for guidance on how to reconcile the Decree of 1852 with the *de facto* powers exercised by the *Prud'homie* over the fishery of Marseille.[78] Most admiralty officers strongly favoured the maintenance of the *Prud'homie's* powers, because they were aware of the major outcry that the Decree of 1852 had provoked among local populations.[79] Their supervisors in Paris were, however, less favourably inclined toward the *Prud'homie* and requested a survey of the *Prud'homie's* finances and of its demographic composition in Marseille.[80] These surveys established that the *Prud'homie's* finances were in healthy shape and that the half-share was accepted by the fishers.[81] The *Prud'homie's* longstanding efforts

---

[73] ibid Arts 16–18.

[74] ibid Arts 5–11.

[75] The Decree of 1852 prohibited *madragues*, subject to a specific authorisation from the admiralty administration. Unauthorised *madragues* were to be destroyed, and violators could be subject to a hefty fine and a jail sentence. See ibid Arts 3, 5.

[76] See P Gourret, *Les pêcheries et les poissons de la Méditerranée (Provence)* (Paris, Librairie JB Baillière et Fils, 1894) 249. Two additional *madragues* were discontinued in 1855 and 1876, respectively. See J Billioud, 'La pêche au thon et les madragues de Marseille' (1955) 26 *Marseille: Revue municipale* 3, 16.

[77] Minutes of the Municipal Council of Marseille (3 February 1852), MA 1D81. Another petition was drafted in a neighbourhood of Marseille called *l'Estaque*, where one of the *madragues* was traditionally placed. See Minutes of the Municipal Council of Marseille (5 September 1853), MA 1D81. Some of the fishers of Marseille petitioned the *Prud'homie* and the city of Marseille against the maintenance of the *madragues* (because these *madragues* limited their fishing territory). See Letter of Fishers to the *Prud'homie* (October 1853), DA 250E32; Minutes of the Municipal Council of Marseille (5 September 1853), MA 1D83.

[78] Letter from the Commissaire de l'Inscription Maritime to the Chef du Service de la Marine (14 March 1852), NA F/46/608; Lettre from the Préfet Maritime to the Ministre de la Marine (15 March 1852), NA F/46/608; Report from the Commissaire général de la Marine to the Préfet Maritime (30 March 1852), NA F/46/608; Letter from the Préfet Maritime to the Ministre de la Mer (3 April 1852), NA F/46/608.

[79] ibid.

[80] Memorandum from the Commissaire de l'Inscription Maritime à Marseille (13 August 1852), NA F/46/608; Request for information from the Bureau de l'Inscription Maritime to the Commissaire de l'Inscription Maritime (19 April 1853), NA F/46/608.

[81] ibid.

to balance its budget had finally borne fruit, and probably saved it from regulatory extinction in the 1850s.

## F. The Decree of 1859

Ultimately, the state chose to preserve most of the *Prud'homie*'s powers in another decree adopted in 1859. Once again, the *Prud'homie* showed incredible resilience in surviving regulatory changes. Article 17 of the Decree of 1859 provides a broad codification of the *Prud'homie*'s powers, which has remained the reference text on this matter:

> The powers of the *Prud'hommes* are as follows:
>
> 1° They decide alone, exclusively and without appeal, revision or cassation, all disputes between fishers, arising during fishing, operations and acts that are related thereto, within the scope of their jurisdiction. Accordingly, and in order to prevent, as much as possible, the fights, damages or incidents, they are specifically charged, under the authority of the maritime administration:
>
> To regulate the enjoyment of the fishery and of the maritime public domain between fishers;
>
> To decide on the fishing spots … for each type of fishing;
>
> To establish the order in which fishers shall place their nets during the day and during the night;
>
> Finally, to render all measures of order and precaution, which, because of their variety and multiplicity, are not anticipated in the current decree.
>
> 2° They administer the affairs of the community.
>
> 3° They participate, in accordance with Article 16 of the Decree of 9 January 1852, in the search for and finding of violations in the field of coastal fishing.[82]

On its face, Article 17 contains a sweeping recognition of the *Prud'homie*'s powers. Its first two paragraphs expressly recognise the legislative and judicial powers of the *Prud'homie* over the fishery. Articles 24 and 25 of the Decree of 1859 further recognise the *Prud'homie*'s power to resolve disputes between fishers and to seize the boat and nets of a non-abiding party. However, the third paragraph of Article 17 refers to the *Prud'homie*'s power to 'participate' in the policing of the fishery, thus implying that the core police powers lie with the state. Article 20 of the Decree of 1859 further makes clear that the *Prud'homie* 'receives orders' and 'obeys the injunctions' of the maritime administration when exercising police powers over the fishery. In line with the Decree of 1852, Article 24 of the Decree of 1859 also provides that the *Prud'homie*'s judgments should be made in writing, a hard blow against the oral tradition that the *Prud'homie* had cherished for more than

---

[82] *Décret sur la police de la pêche maritime côtière dans le 5ème arrondissement maritime* (19 November 1859), CCI MR/45221, Art 17.

four centuries. Article 188 of the Decree of 1859 also prohibits one of the most damaging fishing techniques based on dragnets, the *pêche au boeuf* ('ox fishing').

The Decree of 1859 seems to have reflected a form of compromise between proponents of the *Prud'homie* and its critics. This compromise was, on the whole, favourable to the *Prud'homie*, but it also contained ambiguities that the administrative state could use to stretch its own powers to the detriment of the *Prud'homie*. As shown below, the state attempted to limit, but did not fully succeed in limiting, the powers of the *Prud'homie*.

## III. The State Strikes Back

This section focuses on a key historical period when, for the first time in hundreds of years, the state tried to challenge the authority of the *Prud'homie*. This effort began with an attempt to curtail the *Prud'homie*'s powers at the turn of the twentieth century. Based on the evidence presented in this section, I try to complement the 'state dependence' thesis, according to which private orders need the support of state entities in order to operate successfully. The example of the *Prud'homie* illustrates a situation in which the state acquired the capacity to curtail the powers of a private order, but only did so when the private order proved unable to perform its governance functions. This section therefore suggests that states can benefit from the maintenance of private orders and make the conscious decision to support them, even when they have formal authority to rein in their powers. This section will review the attempts of the French state to regulate the *Prud'homie* in the nineteenth and twentieth centuries, and describe the relative indifference of the *Prud'homie* in the face of these regulatory efforts.

## A. A Failed Attempt to Curtail the *Prud'homie*'s Powers

Although the Decree of 1859 was in certain respects ambiguous concerning the scope of its authority, the *Prud'homie* continued to exercise its legislative, judicial and police powers over the fishery of Marseille. In particular, the *Prud'homie* ignored the fact that Article 17(3) of the Decree of 1859 restricted its police powers to 'the search for and finding of violations in the field of coastal fishing'. Although it was entitled to step into the realm of the *Prud'homie*, the state, for the most part, continued to show deference towards the legislative and police powers of the *Prud'homie*.[83] However, some government officials had no qualms about

---

[83] See, eg, *Cour de cassation, Guaitella et Farniolle* (13 July 1865), (1866) 4 *Jurisprudence Générale* 342; *Tribunal civil de Marseille, Soum c. Louis Basso et Consorts*, (1885-1886) *Revue internationale du droit maritime* 503; *Cour d'appel d'Aix-en-Provence, Serra c. Prud'hommes Pêcheurs de Marseille* (16 June 1904), (1904-1905) *Revue internationale de droit maritime* 353.

challenging these powers. For instance, in early 1898, the *Prud'homie* fined a fisher named Joseph Breme for having practised *senche* (a form of tuna fishing described in chapter 2) at a prohibited distance (less than 50 metres from the shore).[84] The Minister of Marine maintained that the *Prud'homie* lacked the jurisdiction to fine fishers, that criminal courts had jurisdiction over the policing of the fishery and that, as a consequence, the *Prud'homie*'s decision was null and void.[85] The decision of the Minister to annul the *Prud'homie*'s fine amounted to a denial of the police powers claimed by the *Prud'homie* (other than as 'watchdogs' in charge of merely 'recording' violations).[86] The Minister effectively adopted an expansive interpretation of the regulatory regime put in place through the Decrees of 1852 and 1859, relegating the *Prud'homie* to the role of a police agent.

Not content with annulling the *Prud'homie*'s fines, the Minister of Marine also began annulling its judgments.[87] The context in which the Minister delivered these blows to the *Prud'homie* is important to consider here. In fact, the archival records of the late nineteenth century are replete with declarations, reports, debates and statements concerning the dire effects of dragnets on the sea-bottom, the need to prohibit these dragnets in the fishery and the inability of the *Prud'homie* to regulate them. For instance, the municipal council of Marseille held a public hearing with a special reporter on the use of dragnets in 1870.[88] During this hearing, the reporter argued that the *Prud'homie* was controlled by dragnet fishers and that it had played an instrumental role in the exhaustion of the fish stock in Marseille, due to its failure to regulate dragnets.[89] In 1872, the municipal council mentioned yet again the active role played by the *Prud'homie* supporting the practice of dragnets.[90]

The administrative state profited from these criticisms of the *Prud'homie*. In 1911, a governmental report noted the 'division' within the community of fishers concerning the need to prohibit dragnets, and advised the administration to 'take advantage' of this division.[91] This is exactly what the Minister of Marine did, in cancelling judgments pronounced by the *Prud'homie*. However, the Minister's attempt to harness the *Prud'homie*'s powers met with some legal limitations. In 1913, the Council of State held that the Minister did not have the authority to annul

---

[84] Letter from the Ministre de la Marine to the Préfet maritime de Toulon (10 March 1898), NA F/46/608.

[85] ibid.

[86] ibid.

[87] See Letter from the Ministre de la Marine to the Vice-Président du Conseil d'Etat (13 February 1913), NA AL3076. The possibility of annulling the judgments rendered by the *Prud'homie* was debated within the Ministry. See Letter from the Ministre de la Marine to the Vice-Amiral Commandant en Chef, Préfet maritime à Toulon (21 December 1901), NA 20160293/112.

[88] *Rapport de Jules Guibert au Conseil Municipal de Marseille pour l'interdiction des filets traînants* (22 June 1870), DA 6S10/3.

[89] ibid.

[90] Minutes of the Municipal Council of Marseille (7 August 1872), DA 6S10/3.

[91] *Rapport du Commissaire spécial près la Préfecture sur la question des arts traînants* (7 January 1911), DA 6S10/3.

judgments of the *Prud'homie*.[92] Remarkably, the Council of State held that, even though the state had gained administrative and police powers over the fishery, the *Prud'homie* still kept 'exclusive jurisdiction' to decide the disputes arising between fishers.[93] In other words, the administrative state was entitled to encroach upon the *Prud'homie*'s legislative and police powers, but not upon its judicial powers. In a final attempt to control the *Prud'homie*'s judicial powers, a member of the parliament introduced a bill aimed at creating an appeals process against the judgments of the *Prud'homie*.[94] This bill failed and, resilient as ever, the *Prud'homie* progressively returned to the exercise of the whole range of its regulatory activities.

In fact, an exhaustive review of the cases decided by the *Prud'homie* between 1946 and 1969 shows that the *Prud'homie* continued to perform its duties, irrespective of whether the state was also able to exercise legislative and police powers over the fishery. Out of the 31 cases brought before the *Prud'homie* during this period, five were disciplinary and 26 concerned disputes between fishers. In three of these 26 cases, the *Prud'homie* also fined fishers for disciplinary reasons. In two of these cases, the *Prud'homie* issued new regulations in order to modify rules that seemed outdated. One can observe that the three functions of the *Prud'homie* – legislative, judicial and disciplinary – remained intertwined and that the *Prud'homie* cared little about the fine lines drawn by the administrative state. A legalistic mind might wonder why the administrative state allowed the *Prud'homie* to exercise the whole range of its powers, even though the state was in a position to limit its administrative and police powers. The archival evidence suggests that the administrative state continued to defer to the *Prud'homie* and rarely encroached upon its powers (except on the rare occasions outlined above). Some Ministers of the Merchant Navy did not hide their inclination for the *Prud'homie*. Two of them even had direct ties with the *Prud'homie*: Henri Tasso (Minister from 1936 until 1938 and Mayor of Marseille from 1935 until 1939) acted many times as the point man of the *Prud'homie* in Paris,[95] and Gaston Defferre (Minister from 1950 until 1951 and Mayor of Marseille from 1953 until 1986) played a similar role by distributing subsidies to the *Prud'homie* and various awards to its members.[96]

---

[92] Legal Opinion of the Council of State no 164420 (22 April 1913).

[93] ibid.

[94] *Proposition de loi ayant pour objet d'instituer un recours contre les décisions des prud'hommes pêcheurs* (26 February 1915), NA 20160293/112.

[95] See, eg, Letter from the Minister of the Merchant Navy to Henri Tasso (23 April 1930), PA; Letter from the Minister of Merchant Navy to Henri Tasso (23 April 1931), PA; Letter from the Minister of the Merchant Navy to Henri Tasso (13 July 1934), PA; Letter from the Minister of the Merchant Navy to Henri Tasso (11 August 1934), PA.

[96] See, eg, Letter from Gaston Defferre to the Under-Secretary of State for the Merchant Navy (5 January 1950), MA 100ii468; Letter from the Minister of Public Works to Gaston Defferre (20 March 1950), MA 100ii468; Letter from Gaston Defferre to the Minister of Public Works (30 June 1950), MA 100ii468; Letter from *Syndicats de pêcheurs professionnels* to Gaston Defferre (5 August 1950), MA 100ii468; Letter from the Minister of the Merchant Navy to the Minister of Budget (8 November 1950), MA 100ii264.

This honeymoon with the administrative state lasted until the late 1950s, when a decisive and purposeful politician, Gilbert Grandval, was appointed Secretary-General of the Merchant Navy, a quasi-ministry whose portfolio included the management of fisheries.

## B.   Grandval and the Decision of the Council of State (1962)

Gilbert Grandval was no fishing specialist. He was a typical civil servant of the early Fifth Republic, who did not go by his real name but, like many former resistance fighters, chose to adopt his wartime nickname after the Second World War. In 1945, Grandval became the military governor and ambassador of the Saarland, a key position in occupied Germany, until 1955. He then became the last representative (Resident-General) of the French Government in Morocco in 1955, a crucial episode in the history of both countries that Grandval described in his memoirs.[97] Grandval was a strong supporter of Charles de Gaulle, and his loyalty was rewarded by the Secretariat-General of the Merchant Navy in the first government of de Gaulle's presidency (from September 1958 until April 1962).

Grandval is often held to be the gravedigger of the *Prud'homie*.[98] My account of Grandval's action is somewhat more nuanced, claiming that Grandval tried, but did not manage, to rein in the powers of the *Prud'homie*. In 1962, Grandval consulted the Council of State to clarify the scope of the powers exercised by the *Prud'homie*. This appeal to the Council of State was not merely a matter of clarification. In fact, Grandval and the *Prud'homie* had reached a stalemate concerning the possibility of allowing the *lamparo* in the fishery of Marseille. As explained in chapter 4, the *lamparo* is a fishing technique based on lights that attract pelagic fish (typically sardines or sea bream), which are then encircled within a large net. The *lamparo* is considerably more efficient – by an order of five to eight times[99] – than the old technique of *sardinal* or *sardinau*.[100] A *lamparo*, when it is properly used, can capture a whole shoal of sardines. The fishers of Marseille had experimented with the *lamparo* in order to improve the food supply during the Second World War, but the *Prud'homie* insisted on – and temporarily succeeded in – prohibiting this aggressive form of fishing after 1945, due to its enormous impact on fish stocks. For instance, in 1948, the *Prud'homie* opposed the reintroduction of *lamparo* in Marseille because of 'the impossibility of controlling it' and the 'unfortunate abuses' resulting from it.[101] The *Prud'homie*'s worries seem

---

[97] G Grandval, *Ma mission au Maroc* (Paris, Plon, 1956).
[98] See, eg, Féral (n 22).
[99] Letter from the Directeur de l'Office Scientifique et Technique des Pêches Maritimes to the Minister of the Navy (11 April 1949), PA.
[100] For a description of the *sardinal* technique, see ch 2.
[101] Minutes of the *Comité local des pêches* (20 June 1948), PA.

to have been well founded: an informant told me how his crew once captured 30 tons of sardines in one go with the *lamparo*. At the same time, Grandval viewed the *lamparo* as a way to modernise fishing and increase productivity levels that were relatively low on the Mediterranean coast. Shortly after his appointment, Grandval came to Marseille to meet with representatives of the fishers, including the first *Prud'homme* (Marius Barbagelata), and to discuss the possibility of introducing *lamparo*.[102] The *Prud'homie* immediately expressed its opposition. In November 1959, Grandval paid another visit to the fishers of Marseille, with the same outcome: the *Prud'homie* once again opposed the introduction of *lamparo*.[103] In a typically top-down manner, Grandval then ignored local critics and issued two decrees allowing *lamparo* in extra-territorial waters (2 December 1959), as well as in the territorial waters of Marseille (14 March 1960). The *Prud'homie* immediately reacted by mobilising the opponents of the *lamparo* in April 1960.[104] In June 1960, another decree permitted and regulated the use of *lamparo* in the fishery of Marseille.[105] Grandval brushed aside the *Prud'homie*'s objections, stating that the *lamparo* did not present 'any risk for the exhaustion of pelagic resources'.[106] Because of the strong opposition mounted by the *Prud'homie*, Grandval saw it as an obstacle to his policy and tried to circumvent its powers. He instructed his administration to investigate the scope of the *Prud'homie*'s powers, as well as its finances, which led to the conclusion that the *Prud'homie* had a 'limited role, rather modest, but nonetheless useful'.[107] This rather positive assessment probably did not please Grandval, who considered that the *Prud'homies* were 'interpreting too broadly their powers arising from Article 17 of the Decree of 17 November 1859'.[108] In July 1961, Grandval requested the local administration to review and annul all the regulations issued by the *Prud'homie* that went beyond the powers set out under the Decree of 1859.[109] But this was still not sufficient for Grandval, who was looking for ways to harness the *Prud'homie*'s powers in the long term. One possible approach was to redefine these powers by modifying the Decree of 1859. This route was risky, since the legislative process would no doubt provide a forum for the *Prud'homie* to defend its age-old role. Another approach would be to seek an interpretation from the Council of State concerning the powers of the *Prud'homie* under the Decrees of 1852 and 1859. The Council of State is not

---

[102] Minutes of the *Comité local des pêches* (15 December 1948), PA.

[103] Minutes of the *Comité régional des pêches* (3 November 1959), PA.

[104] Minutes of the *Fédération des Marins-Pêcheurs de la Méditerranée* (8 April 1960), NA 20160293/112.

[105] *Arrêté n° 119 portant règlementation du filet tournant et coulissant dit 'lamparo' et du filet droit dit 'sardinal' dans le quartier de Marseille* (25 June 1960), DA 2331W291.

[106] Minutes of the *Comité régional des pêches* (11 July 1960), NA 20160293/112.

[107] Letter from Chef du Quartier de Marseille to Directeur de l'Inscription Maritime en Méditerranée (15 February 1960), NA 20160293/112.

[108] Letter from the Secrétaire Général de la Marine Marchande to the Directeur de l'Inscription Maritime à Marseille (11 July 1961), NA 20160293/112.

[109] ibid.

only the highest court in the field of administrative law in France; it also acts as a legal adviser to the French Government. The legal opinions of the Council of State are non-binding but highly authoritative. After liaising with the Council of State and making sure that it was favourably predisposed towards his request,[110] Grandval chose the second route.[111] On 3 November 1961, the Government requested the Council of State to interpret the powers of the *Prud'homie*, with passing reference to the 'infringements [by the *Prud'homie*] leading to the maintenance of conservative and Malthusian practices that are absolutely contrary to the general interest'.[112] It was the first time in more than 500 years of history that the *Prud'homie* faced outright hostility from the administrative state. The Council of State took its duty seriously. It sent a senior member, Louis Pichat, to investigate the *Prud'homie* in Marseille over the course of three months. Grandval personally made sure that the Council of State's envoy had access to documents, archives and contacts at the *Prud'homie*.[113] On 6 February 1962, the Council of State rendered its much-anticipated decision.[114]

Grandval seemed very pleased with the decision of the Council of State. He rapidly drafted a decree incorporating the content of the decision (an unusual procedure that was certainly aimed at giving it a binding character).[115] He even asked the Secretary-General of the Government (the highest administrative officer of the Government) to publish this decree in the official bulletin of the French Government (*Journal officiel*), presenting the decision of the Council of State as 'tightening control' over the *Prud'homie*.[116] However, a closer look at the decision of the Council of State shows that Grandval might have been overly optimistic. In fact, the interpretation of the *Prud'homie*'s powers by the Council of State was very much in line with legislative texts and prior administrative practice. The Council of State first recognised the broad judicial powers of the *Prud'homie* and the impossibility of appealing its decisions. It then considered that the *Prud'homie* must exercise its regulatory powers within the bounds of the law, and that administrative authorities must 'refuse approval' of the *Prud'homie*'s regulations when these regulations contradict the law. Finally, and most importantly, the Council of

---

[110] Memorandum from the Président de la Section des Travaux Publics du Conseil d'Etat (5 October 1961), NA 20160293/112.

[111] Memorandum to the Minister of Public Works and Transportation (9 October 1961), NA 20160293/112.

[112] Letter of the Ministre des Travaux Publics et des Transports to the Vice-Président du Conseil d'Etat (3 November 1961), NA 20160293/112.

[113] Letter from Gilbert Grandval to Louis Pichat (24 November 1961), NA 20160291/112; Letter from Gilbert Grandval to Directeur de l'Inscription Maritime à Marseille (24 November 1961), NA 20160291/112; Letter from Direction des Pêches Maritimes to Louis Pichat (21 December 1961), NA 20160291/112.

[114] Legal Opinion of the Council of State (6 February 1962).

[115] *Arrêté sur la nature et l'étendue des pouvoirs conférés aux prud'hommes pêcheurs de la Méditerranée* (21 February 1962), NA 20160293/112.

[116] Letter from the Secrétaire Général de la Marine Marchande to the Secrétaire Général du Gouvernement (9 March 1962), NA 20160293/112.

State recognised the disciplinary powers of the *Prud'homie*, but held that administrative authorities could annul the *Prud'homie*'s fines when they were pronounced
pursuant to illegal regulations. The Council of State did clarify the powers of the
*Prud'homie* (although it is doubtful that the fishers found the abstruse distinc-
tions made by the Council of State a 'clarification'). The decision of 1962 did not,
however, break new ground as it merely reflected a common interpretation of
the *Prud'homie*'s powers, as reflected, for instance, in Valin's Commentary on the
Great Maritime Ordinance of 1681.[117] For any student of administrative law, it
would have been self-evident that the *Prud'homie* could not adopt illegal rules and
levy fines based on those rules. In fact, while Grandval was rejoicing at 'tightening control' over the *Prud'homie*, the *Prud'homie* showed little sign of caring: on
19 April 1962, the agenda of the *Prud'homie* focused on the risk of pollution from
a nearby factory; on 9 October 1962, it dealt with the violations of its rules by
*lamparo* fishers.[118] Not a single word was uttered against or even about the Council
of State's decision. To all appearances, the *Prud'homie* did not view the decision of
the Council of State as a major threat to its activities.

This decision nonetheless marked the beginning of a period of mutual distrust
between the state and the *Prud'homie*. Various governmental actors whom I inter-
viewed disparaged the *Prud'homie* for being 'incompetent' and 'opaque'. Others
mocked the *Prud'homie* for being part of the 'local folklore'. One of these officers
told me that the administration does not hesitate to impose its regulatory decisions
on the *Prud'homie* in cases of emergency. On the fishers' side, the distrust towards
state authorities is even more obvious. Fishers typically contrast the 'blind' laws of
the state to the 'flexible' regulations of the *Prud'homie*. They complain that state
regulators are 'killing' their fishery. The fishers voice endless complaints against
the administration and mock the absurdity of state regulations. For instance, fishers have recently been enraged by the obligation to state the Latin name of the fish
that they sell in the port of Marseille (to the extent that President Macron himself
declared that they did not have to comply with this obligation).[119] Other fishers
denounce the prohibition against taking onboard anyone who is not an official
crew member, an obligation they resent as an infringement of their basic freedom
and property rights. Despite these bumpy relations, I heard numerous rumours
of collaborative efforts that persist between the *Prud'homie* and state authorities.
Governmental officers occasionally defer to the *Prud'homie*'s regulatory authority
when they need the support of fishers, while the *Prud'homie* discreetly reports
violations of fishing regulations to these officers. When doing so, it typically with-
holds the names of the breachers, but gives sufficient contextual evidence to enable

---

[117] Valin (n 36) 744.

[118] Minutes of the *Prud'homie*'s Assembly (19 April 1962), PA; Minutes of the *Prud'homie*'s Assembly
(9 October 1962), PA.

[119] 'Les poissoniers du Vieux-Port verbalisés pour ne pas avoir apposé le nom latin sur leurs étals'
*Le Monde* (23 June 2018).

the governmental officers to identify them. In addition, the *Prud'homie* usually asks state officers to keep their interventions unofficial and to conceal them from the fishers, a sign of the distrust that has grown between the fishers and the state. The relationship between the *Prud'homie* and the French state therefore seems to be one of interdependence: they do not care much for each other, but their mutual support is still necessary in order to operate effectively.

The relationship of interdependence between the French state and the *Prud'homie* can be contrasted with the *Prud'homie*'s position vis-à-vis the EU. In fact, the *Prud'homie* has not managed to maintain reciprocal ties with the EU, which has in return been much more successful than the French state at imposing its regulations on the *Prud'homie*.

## IV. Fill or Kill: The EU's Regulatory Agenda

'European Union' is a dirty term in the fishery of Marseille. It is no exaggeration to say that most fishers loathe the EU and fear the powers exercised by its officials. Their hostility towards the EU is not surprising: EU regulations have curtailed the activities of fishers in ways that the French state never managed, or even dared to try, to do. In fact, over the course of little more than a decade (1994–2006), the EU forbade fishing techniques that had been in use for centuries in the fishery of Marseille. In addition, the European Court of Justice (ECJ) ostensibly ignores the *Prud'homie* and considers it as being neither a 'court' nor a 'tribunal' for the purposes of EU law. This has made the EU an ideal scapegoat for the fishers of Marseille, who never miss an opportunity to criticise the extent of its powers.

### A. The EU Enters the Game: Regulating the Fishery from Above

The Treaty Establishing the European Economic Community of 1957 (better known as the 'Rome Treaty') is the founding act of the EU. The Rome Treaty listed the creation of a 'common market' for 'fishery products' among the goals of the European Economic Community.[120] However, it was not until 1994 that the fishers of Marseille realised the impact that the European project could have on the management of their fishery. On 27 June 1994, the European Council issued Regulation No 1626/94 'laying down certain technical measures for the conservation of fishery resources in the Mediterranean'.[121] Among these

---

[120] *Traité instituant la Communauté économique européenne* (25 March 1957), Art 38(1).
[121] Council Regulation (EC) No 1626/94 laying down certain technical measures for the conservation of fishery resources in the Mediterranean (27 June 1994).

seemingly innocuous 'technical measures', Article 3(1) of Regulation No 1626/94 prohibits 'the use of trawls, seines or similar nets ... within three nautical miles of the coast or within the 50 m isobath where that depth is reached at a shorter distance'. Ancestral fishing techniques such as *gangui* or *eyssaugue* fell within the broad scope of this provision.[122] The number of boats practising *gangui* dropped sharply as a result of the prohibition,[123] and the fishers consequently tried to lobby the EU to overturn the ban.[124] Despite these efforts, the European Council issued a new regulation in 2006 that put an immediate end to the *eyssaugues* and *ganguis* that were left in Marseille.[125] In sum, the EU managed in a single decade to bring centuries of fishing practices to an end.

A similar process began in 1998, this time for the floating nets that had been used since the fifteenth century to capture tuna (originally known as '*tonnaire de corre*' and more recently as '*courantille volante*' or '*thonaille*').[126] In 2005, 17 boats used this type of net in Marseille.[127] Because they are drifting with the currents, these nets capture more tuna than the traditional set nets.[128] Having restricted the size of these nets to a maximum of 2.5 kilometres, the European Council decided in 1998 to prohibit the use of drift-nets for tuna fishing as of 1 January 2002.[129] In all fairness, the European Council had good reasons to prohibit these nets, which commonly exceeded the maximum size of 2.5 kilometres and threatened the rapidly shrinking stock of blue tuna in the Mediterranean. A fisher who practised the *thonaille* in the late 1990s told me that some other fishers did not hesitate to use up to 15 kilometres of drift-nets. Another one referred to the drift-nets as a form of 'slaughter' and 'bloodshed'.

Tuna fishers seem to have been more effective than the *gangui* and *eyssaugue* fishers in promoting their interests.[130] As a result of their pressure and in the

---

[122] Nineteen boats practised *gangui* in Marseille in 1994 (see Letter from Directeur Interrégional des Affaires Maritimes en Méditerranée to the Ministry of Agriculture (20 May 1994), DA 2331W276). The last *eyssaugue* fisher, Mr Roberto Lubrano di Sbaraglione, unsuccessfully tried to circumvent the EU's prohibition by claiming that *eyssaugue* belonged to the cultural heritage of Provence. See Letter from Directeur Régional des Affaires Culturelles to Directeur Interrégional des Affaires Maritimes (28 February 1994), DA 2331W281.

[123] Report of the *Comité de liaison méditerranéen* (9 June 2000), AN 20160293/180.

[124] The *Comité régional des pêches maritimes* commissioned a scientific report in order to establish the harmlessness of *gangui* and *eyssaugue*. See *Procès-verbal de la table ronde sur la réalisation d'une étude scientifique sur les arts traînants (ganguis, sennes de plage) sous l'égide du CRPMEM-PACA* (26 November 1998), NA 20160293/180.

[125] Council Regulation (EC) No 1967/2006 concerning management measures for the sustainable exploitation of fishery resources in the Mediterranean Sea (21 December 2006), Art 13(1) and (3).

[126] See ch 2, section IV.A.

[127] G Imbert, L Laubier, A Malan, JC Gaertner and I Dekeyser, *La Thonaille ou Courantille Volante*, Final Report to the *Conseil Régional PACA* (30 September 2017) (hereinafter 'Final Report') 155.

[128] See ch 2, section IV.A.

[129] Council Regulation (EC) No 1239/98 amending Regulation (EC) No 894/97 laying down certain technical measures for the conservation of fishery resources (8 June 1998), Art 1.

[130] Several of my interviewees emphasised the great financial resources and lobbying capacity of the tuna fishers.

face of basic common sense, the Regional Council (a local governmental body) commissioned a group of scientific experts tasked with establishing that *thonailles* do not qualify as drift-nets and therefore do not fall under the prohibition set out by the European Council.[131] This report suggests that drift-nets move due to the Coriolis effect generated by the Earth's rotation, and not due to the current.[132] Drawing on the argument that *thonailles* do not qualify as drift-nets, despite a ruling to the contrary by its own Council of State,[133] the French Government dragged its feet in applying the EU ban on drift-nets, resulting in France being condemned by the ECJ.[134] What really matters for our purposes is that the EU banned emblematic techniques in the fishery of Marseille (the *eyssaugue*, the *gangui* and the *thonaille de corre*) in a space of less than 10 years. There is little doubt that these bans were necessary or at least beneficial from the perspective of environmental preservation. From the internal perspective of the community of fishers, however, these bans threw out centuries-old techniques that were a signifi-cant source of income for local fishers, while also disregarding the fine regulatory mechanisms that the *Prud'homie* had been employing for centuries. How did the *Prud'homie* react in the face of these regulatory threats looming over its fishery? The *Prud'homie* of Marseille remained mostly silent, but a textbook case of fishing dispute arose in the neighbouring city of Martigues.

## B. The *Prud'homie*: 'Not a Court or Tribunal'?

On 6 December 2006, a fisher named Jonathan Pilato brought a complaint against fellow fisher Jean-Claude Bourgault before the *Prud'homie* of Martigues. Pilato requested compensation for the loss that he had allegedly suffered as a result of Bourgault's capture of 15 tuna with a *thonaille*.[135] As explained previously, the European Regulation of 1998 prohibited the use of drift-nets for tuna fishing, but local fishers (and the French Government) argued that this prohibition did not apply to the *thonaille*. Bourgault used this argument in his defence before the *Prud'homie*, which referred the question of whether the *thonaille* qualifies as a drift-net under EU law to the ECJ.[136] This move was a bold one, both substantively and procedurally. In terms of substance, it was unlikely that the ECJ would adopt

---

[131] See Final Report (n 127). The fact that tuna fishers influenced the process is suggested by the Council of State. See Decision of the Council of State no 265034 (10 August 2005) (the decision mentions the 'scientific studies that have been called for by the [tuna fishers]').

[132] Final Report (n 127) xxv.

[133] Decision of the Council of State no 265034 (10 August 2005).

[134] Judgment of the Court of Justice of the European Communities (Third Chamber), *Commission des Communautés européennes v République française* (5 March 2009).

[135] Order of the Court of Justice of the European Communities (First Chamber), *Jonathan Pilato v Jean-Claude Bourgault* (14 May 2008), para 16.

[136] The decision of the *Prud'homie*, dated 17 December 2006, is available in NA 20160293/112.

a position favouring the maintenance of the *thonaille*. Procedurally, the eligibility of an entity to refer a question to the ECJ is conditioned upon its qualification as a 'court or tribunal'. The ECJ has developed case law to determine the conditions under which a referring entity can qualify as a 'court or tribunal' under EU law.[137] Among these conditions, it is necessary that the requesting entity be 'independent', that is 'protected against external intervention or pressure liable to jeopardise the independent judgment of its members as regards proceedings before them'.[138] By referring a legal question to the ECJ, the *Prud'homie* of Martigues entitled the ECJ to determine as a jurisdictional threshold whether it was sufficiently independent to qualify as a 'court or tribunal'. This procedural move was risky considering the intricacies of a medieval French institution such as the *Prud'homie*. It was also a cause of embarrassment for the French Government, who felt compelled to support the *Prud'homie*'s preliminary enquiry to the ECJ (if only to defend France's official position concerning drift-nets) while holding no sympathy for the *Prud'homie*'s position behind closed doors. In the words of a high-level official of the Ministry of Agriculture, 'it will be very embarrassing for us to expose the *prud'homies* as fake tribunals, which is more or less what they are'.[139] On 14 May 2008, the ECJ held that the *Prud'homie* of Martigues did not qualify as an independent 'court', notably because its members can be dismissed by the administrative state after a simple preliminary investigation.[140] Although the judgment was specific to the *Prud'homie* of Martigues, there is no doubt that the same reasoning applies to the mother of all *Prud'homies*, that of Marseille.

The *Prud'homie*'s failure to resist EU regulation can be contrasted with its relative success in maintaining its regulatory prerogatives in the French context. These contrasting outcomes suggest the importance of the 'active engagement' mentioned by Pirie in the maintenance of regulatory autonomy.[141] While the *Prud'homie* continues to interact with French authorities – albeit to a lesser degree than in the past – it has very limited contact, if any, with European institutions. During an interview, a high-level official of the European Commission bluntly admitted to having no contact at all with the numerous *Prud'homies* along the French Mediterranean coast, and had no apparent knowledge of the concrete impact of

---

[137] See, eg, Judgment of the Court of Justice of the European Communities, *Nordsee Deutsche Hochseefischerei GmbH v Reederei Mond Hochseefischerei Nordstern AG & Co KG and Reederei Friedrich Busse Hochseefischerei Nordstern AG & Co KG* (23 March 1982).

[138] Order of the Court of Justice of the European Communities (First Chamber), *Jonathan Pilato v Jean-Claude Bourgault* (14 May 2008), para 23.

[139] Email exchange between the Ministry of Foreign Affairs and the Ministry of Agriculture (20–21 April 2007), NA 201602/112: 'Si c'est une position qui sera rendue publique, ça nous gênera fortement, du seul point de vue de la direction des pêches, d'exposer que les prud'homies sont des juridictions en caoutchouc. Ce qui est tout de même un peu le cas, mais nous sommes dans un univers proprement pagnolesque.'

[140] Order of the Court of Justice of the European Communities (First Chamber), *Jonathan Pilato v Jean-Claude Bourgault* (14 May 2008), para 29.

[141] Pirie (n 26).

EU regulations on the ancestral practices of local fishers. The *Prud'homie* did not manage to create ties of interdependence with the EU, and the latter was successful in regulating its fishery.

# V. Conclusion

The starting point of this chapter was provided by an influential narrative in socio-legal scholarship, which I call the 'state-dependence' thesis. According to this thesis, private orders need the support of states in order to operate successfully. The flip side of this argument is that private orders can collapse when states overstep their powers. This chapter has explored how the *Prud'homie* has maintained its regulatory powers for centuries, how the French state has deferred to these powers for a very long time and how the EU has been much more hostile towards the *Prud'homie*. On the basis of this historical material, this chapter has examined a popular argument in the literature – one that is entirely consistent with the state-dependence thesis – according to which the *Prud'homie* has collapsed because of regulatory trespassing by the state. In opposition to this argument, this chapter offers a more nuanced account of the relationships between (state) legal systems and private orders. This line of analysis places the focus on the private order rather than the state in the analysis of governance functions. Instead of viewing the state as an organically developing polity that 'tolerates' and 'supports' the existence of private orders (as per the 'state-dependence' thesis), this chapter suggests that private orders can be extremely resilient and that states defer to their authority (at least until private orders prove ineffective as governance entities). The analysis set out in this chapter also casts light on the complex interactions that exist between the law and private orders, as well as the ties of interdependence that are crucial to consider when analysing these interactions.

A subsidiary question, which has been left relatively unexplored in the literature, concerns the deference displayed by states vis-à-vis private orders.[142] Why do states maintain private polities such as the *Prud'homie*, once compared to a 'small state within the state'?[143] The empirical evidence I gathered suggests that state entities can trade immediate financial benefits (such as donations for the construction of the St Jean Tower (chapter 2)) and long-term political gains (such as the support of an influential group of citizens (this chapter) against the preservation of private orders. From the perspective of the state, the potential benefits of a system of private governance such as the *Prud'homie* can outweigh

---

[142] A noteworthy exception is the scholarship of Avner Greif on merchant guilds. Greif suggests that merchant guilds traded the protection of their property rights against the preservation of future streams of tax income. See Greif (n 24) ch 4. See also, Sagy (n 5) 951 (arguing that states often have a 'vested interest' in the preservation of private orders).

[143] F Escard, *Corporation et Prud'homie des Pêcheurs de Martigues* (Evreux, Herissey, 1896) 21.

its costs, which are relatively negligible as long as the private order performs its duties effectively. Napoleon astutely summed up this calculation in describing the *Prud'homies* as 'true watchdogs that cost nothing [to the state]'.[144] The case of the EU further confirms that the resilience of private orders depends at least in part on their ability to build collaborative platforms with public authorities.

This analysis is of course premised on the ability of private actors to convince state officials of their capacity to regulate. While some scholars argue that governance systems cannot be considered true private orders, so long as they seek and obtain benefits from public entities,[145] the counter-narrative presented in this chapter suggests that the complex interrelationships with these entities might be consubstantial to the life of private orders. In this counter-narrative, the function between state support and the regulatory capacity of private orders is reversed: state support becomes a function of the capacity of private orders to govern (and not the other way around). Unlike the bell-curved Gaussian function mentioned in section I, this new function is linear and ascending: state support grows alongside the governance capacities of the private order. A final question to explore concerns how it is that a private order like the *Prud'homie* has managed to survive at all, having lost much of its legitimacy as a governance entity. Chapter 6 will further investigate the paradox of a private order surviving, despite its failure to discharge the rule-making functions for which it was formed six centuries ago.

><((((°>

[144] ibid.
[145] ibid.

# 6

## Between Facts and Beliefs

## I. Introduction

The *Prud'homie* will soon celebrate its 600th birthday. The remarkable resilience of this institution could lead us to the conclusion that, despite certain shortcomings, its governance mechanisms are fundamentally viable.[1] However, the evidence presented in this book points towards more nuanced findings. While fishers still evoke the *Prud'homie* with a great sense of pride, they no longer resort to any of its governance functions. In other words, the *Prud'homie* has managed to maintain powers that fishers no longer use. This chapter explores the paradox of an organisation that has survived, both symbolically and institutionally, despite having lost much of its practical significance. A classic explanation for this kind of paradox has been referred to as 'institutional path dependence', which refers to the gravitational forces that keep an institution – even an inefficient one – alive indefinitely.[2]

The present chapter seeks to complement this explanation by examining the role played by social norms in the operation of path dependence. It argues that the *Prud'homie* has managed to survive not simply as an effect of institutional gravitation, but more specifically because it is embedded in strong social norms. In fact, fishers still refer today to the same social norms that played a pervasive role over the past centuries. This chapter traces the current situation of the *Prud'homie* back to the constitutive features of social norms, namely their rigidity and their open-endedness.[3] Norms have an incredible propensity to survive due to their rigidity, while enabling a broad range of practices due to their open-endedness. Fishers frequently refer to norms that they constantly breach due to the gap that emerges between evolving practices and persisting beliefs, resulting in what I call 'institutional schizophrenia'. Ultimately, the empirical material presented in this book allows us to reconsider the role of social norms in systems of private

---

[1] The link between institutional resilience and viability is often suggested in the literature. See, eg, TT de Moor, *The Dilemma of the Commoners: Understanding the Use of Common-Pool Resources in Long-Term Perspectives* (Cambridge, Cambridge University Press, 2015) chs 3 and 4.

[2] DC North, *Institutions, Institutional Change and Economic Performance* (Cambridge, Cambridge University Press, 1990) 92–104. Aviram extends the analysis of path dependence to private orders. See A Aviram, 'Path Dependence in the Development of Private Ordering' (2014) 1 *Michigan State Law Review* 29.

[3] See ch 1.

governance and to trace certain potential defects of these systems back to the constitutive features of norms. It will also lead to a finer understanding of the distinction between norms, practices and beliefs.

## II. The Precarious Survival of the *Prud'homie*

This section provides an overview of the *Prud'homie* and of its community over the past few decades. It highlights the latest changes that have occurred, but also the important continuities that have persisted in this community. This section presents material that will be used in section III to trace the weaknesses of systems of private governance back to the features of social norms.

## A. The Community of Fishers in the Past Decades

In this subsection, I examine the changes with which the fishers of Marseille have been confronted since the Second World War. The contemporary history of the community of fishers begins with the bombing of the 'old quarters' of Marseille in 1943, a traumatic event that has left deep marks in the memories of fishers. The story continues with a series of demographic changes arising from significant migrations of foreign fishers and a generational shift with which the community of fishers has been confronted in the past few decades. This empirical evidence shows that, despite important shifts, fishers have remained strongly attached to their social norms.

### i. A Social Trauma: The Bombing of St Jean (1943)

As explained in previous chapters, the community of fishers traditionally lived in 'St Jean' (*le quartier Saint Jean*), a small neighbourhood located in the northern part of the port of Marseille. The fishers of Marseille still mention the old St Jean with great nostalgia more than 70 years after its destruction. Before the Second World War, the streets of St Jean were small and narrow, cultivating a strong sense of belonging among its inhabitants. The ships' boys circulated from house to house every evening in order to announce who would have priority over the various 'posts' in the fishery.[4] However, St Jean fell into decrepitude in the early twentieth century, and progressively became a shelter for petty criminals and prostitutes. The novelist Claude McKay gives a vivid account of this urban decay in the 1920s:

> There was a barbarous international romance in the ways of Marseilles that was vividly significant of the great modern movement of life. Small, with a population apparently too great for it, Europe's best back door, discharging and receiving its traffic to the

---

[4] See ch 2, section III.C.i.

Orient and Africa, favorite port of seamen on French leave, infested with the ratty beings of the Mediterranean countries, overrun with guides, cocottes, procurers, repelling and attracting in its white-fanged vileness under its picturesqueness, the town seemed to proclaim to the world that the grandest thing about modern life was that it was bawdy.[5]

In the 1930s, French authorities started considering the possibility of refurbishing and sanitising the neighbourhood. Their plan came to fruition after the authoritarian regime of 'Vichy' came to power during the Second World War. St Jean was home to a vibrant, cosmopolitan community, and thus a natural target for Vichy propaganda. To make matters worse for the Vichy regime, a major Jewish community lived in Marseille.[6] St Jean met its tragic fate after the Resistance launched a series of attacks in response to the German invasion of Marseille in November 1942. The reaction from the Nazi regime was swift: in early 1943, Himmler ordered the SS to 'purify' the old port of Marseille, and French police took responsibility for doing the dirty work.[7] On 24 January 1943, the police requested the inhabitants of St Jean – about 20,000 people – to leave their homes. In February 1943, the *Prud'homie*'s building and the surrounding neighbourhood were destroyed with dynamite. Only a few buildings were spared, such as the city hall of Marseille and the church of St Laurent, a jewel of Romanesque architecture and the fishers' parish church. In a dramatic event that contributed to the myth of St Jean, the 80-year-old priest of St Laurent rang the bells of the fishers' church during the destruction of the quarter.[8]

Almost 80 years later, the fishers of Marseille still describe the destruction of their 'old quarter' as a social trauma. They evoke this destruction as 'the end of the world'. One of them told me that the 'community exploded' after February 1943. The inhabitants of St Jean, including fishers, were forced out of the neighbourhood in which they had grown up, lived and worked for decades. Some of them even stopped fishing, as they could no longer find accommodation close to the port.[9] Most fishers lost their homes and, to make matters worse, the German army requisitioned some of their boats.[10] The descendant of a family of fishers told me how his grandfather moved from St Jean to a tiny shed in which he lived with seven family members after 1943. Adding institutional confusion to this chaos,

---

[5] C McKay, *Banjo* (New York, NY, and London, Harper & Brothers Publishers, 1929) 69.

[6] In a disgraceful op-ed published in 1941, a Vichy sympathiser chastised 'Marseille the Jew'. See L Rebatet, 'Marseille la juive', *Je Suis Partout* (30 August 1941).

[7] See M Ficetola, *Il était une fois … Saint-Jean: La 'Petite Naples' Marseillaise, avant son Dynamitage en 1943* (Marseille, Massaliotte Culture, 2018) 67–71.

[8] A Sportiello, *Les pêcheurs du Vieux-Port: Fêtes et Traditions* (Marseille, Jeanne Laffitte, 1981) 87.

[9] See the portrait of Pietro, in *Le Temps des Italiens*, available at www.pedagogie.ac-aix-marseille.fr/upload/docs/application/pdf/2013-01/tpsdesitaliensdpgq.pdf (last checked 9 July 2019).

[10] See, eg, Letter from *Directeur de la Caisse Régionale du Crédit Maritime Mutuel* to the *Secrétaire Général de l'Union des Pêcheurs Méditerranéens* (9 May 1944) PA; *Note sur le nombre des bateaux de pêche de la Prud'homie de Marseille* (undated), PA.

the Vichy regime started implementing a policy aimed at replacing 'trade unions' with so-called 'labour communities'. As a result of this policy, the *Prud'homie* was temporarily replaced by a 'community of fishers' in 1942.[11]

The fishers lost their homes, their boats and their age-old institution. They also lost the urban space that had played a key role in the transmission of information within their community.[12] One could hypothesise that the bombing of St Jean undermined the close-knit community of fishers in such a way that it led to the demise of their private order. What is striking, however, is how faithful the fishers remained to their norms in the midst of these dramatic events, and how quickly they returned to their ancestral system of governance after the end of the Second World War. One example is telling in this regard. The dire circumstances of the war affected the food supply to the extent that the fishers raised the possibility of increasing their productivity by using *lamparo*, the aggressive fishing technique described in chapter 4. Only four months after the destruction of St Jean, the fishers discussed the possibility of allowing *lamparo* in Marseille. The minutes of their meeting show how reluctant they were to allow a practice that presumably violated their norm of conservation owing to its grave impact on fish stocks:

> The Community of Fishers remains opposed as a matter of principle to the use of lamparo. It continues to believe that the spatial setting of the coasts of Marseille does not lend itself to a technique that is designed for the fishing of migrating species but captures groundfish, thus causing great damage to the fishers who use fine nets. However, given the exceptionally critical circumstances – fuel in insufficient quantity, fishing restrictions, difficult supplies – the Community allows the communal use of lamparo during the hostilities.[13]

During what was the worst period in their history, the fishers of Marseille nonetheless kept referring to their social norms and allowed the *lamparo* only because of 'exceptionally critical circumstances'. The fact that they had lost their *Prud'homie*, some of their boats and even their houses did not seem to have shaken their inner beliefs. As a matter of fact, the *Prud'homie* reappeared and quickly moved to prohibit the use of *lamparo* in 1945. The resilience of the community's norms also appears when considering the demographic changes that occurred in the post-war period.

---

[11] See, eg, Letter to the *Prud'homie*, dated 16 July 1942, NA 19860461/21. See also D Rauch, 'Les prud'homies de pêche sous l'Etat français: une spécificité méditerranéenne' (2013) 254 *Provence historique* 493.

[12] It should be noted that the St Jean quarter was rebuilt a few years after the end of the Second World War according to plans by the architect Fernand Pouillon. The architectural design by Pouillon is symmetrically opposed to the urban layout of the old St Jean. The neighbourhood is now characterised by large apartment buildings and broad streets, and the *Prud'homie* occupies a building situated on the docks of the port of Marseille. However, the spatial design of St Jean has changed in a way that certainly does not contribute to maintaining the close-knit community of fishers, as the 'old quarters' did.

[13] Minutes of the *Conseil de la Communauté des Pêcheurs de Marseille* (15 June 1943) PA.

## ii. Demographic Changes

The community of fishers has been confronted with two major demographic changes in the past decades. The first was the migration of Italian fishers that unfolded from the late nineteenth century until the mid-1960s. The second has been the decrease in the number of fishers and the changing preferences of the younger generation. This section describes these demographic changes and shows how, in line with what has already been observed, the *Prud'homie*'s social norms persisted during this time period.

From the late nineteenth century until the mid-1960s, Marseille was confronted with significant flows of Italian migrants. These migratory flows were so important that, on the eve of the First World War, around 100,000 inhabitants of Marseille (or a quarter of its population) were Italian.[14] Many of these migrants clustered together in the northern part of the port, specifically in St Jean,[15] which quickly gained the nickname of 'Little Naples'.[16] Many of these Italian migrants were fishers, a trade they continued to practise in Marseille. Their assimilation into the fishers' community went relatively smoothly (at least when compared with the arrival of the Catalan fishers in the eighteenth century).[17] A note drafted by Maritime Affairs in the early 1960s provides further details on the arrival of Italian fishers in Marseille.[18] This note analyses how these fishers brought their own techniques and practices (namely the *lamparo*) in contravention of the *Prud'homie*'s rules.[19] Most of these foreign fishers came from Sperlonga (a small coastal city in Lazio) and constituted a tight-knit group described as the 'Sperlonga clan'.[20] The first migrations from Sperlonga occurred in 1922 and grew over the course of subsequent decades through word of mouth. For instance, one of my interviewees joined his uncles, who had left Sperlonga before the Second World War. It is not entirely clear how many fishers came from Sperlonga. My interviewees described the 'Sperlonga clan' as comprising a 'very high number of fishers' and 'approximately 50 boats'. In order to better assess the size of this population, I reviewed all of the French naturalisation decrees issued between 1925 and 1948. These decrees provide a good proxy for assessing the size of the clan, because French law required fishing crews to include a minimum number of French nationals (and foreign fishers therefore had an incentive to acquire French citizenship as soon as possible after their arrival). The results of my survey are staggering. I counted no fewer than 52 fishers from Sperlonga who settled in Marseille and acquired French citizenship during this period. Together with their families, this population

---

[14] E Temime, 'Les Italiens dans la Région Marseillaise pendant l'Entre-Deux-Guerres' in P Milza (ed), *Les Italiens en France de 1914 à 1940* (Rome, Ecole Français de Rome, 1986) 547–75.

[15] ibid 557.

[16] Sportiello (n 8) 77–81. This nickname is slightly misleading as many of these migrants came from other Italian regions, such as Liguria or Lazio.

[17] See ch 3, section III.

[18] 'La pêche au lamparo au Quartier de Marseille' (1963), DA 2331W291.

[19] ibid.

[20] ibid.

included 182 individuals, all of whom came from Sperlonga. These migrant fishers usually followed a family member who had previously migrated to Marseille. For instance, the Di Lelio family counted no fewer than six fishers who successively arrived from Sperlonga in the 1920s and 1930s. In any case, the 'Sperlonga clan' was sufficiently entrenched to be able to replicate the religious celebration of their hometown in Marseille. The St Leon, named after Sperlonga's patron saint, was so well attended that it soon surpassed the St Pierre, the traditional celebration of the local fishers. It appears that Italian fishers came in clusters that might have attained the critical mass necessary to overturn community norms, thus providing evidence for the argument that a critical mass of newcomers can modify existing social norms.[21] A more fine-grained analysis of the Italian migrations in Marseille suggests, however, that the Italian fishers managed to penetrate the community of local fishers not because of their sheer number, but because of the collaborative relations that they managed to build with the local community.[22] My empirical analysis also suggests that if Italian fishers were able to modify the fishing practices in Marseille, their presence did not affect the longstanding norms of the *Prud'homie*. In fact, fishers from Sperlonga initially worked with trawlers before converting *en masse* to *lamparo* fishing when this technique was allowed in the early 1960s.[23] This is no coincidence: recent migrants were less likely to observe the traditions of the *Prud'homie* and more likely to favour short-term gains over the preservation of the fishery. In fact, these fishers largely ignored the *Prud'homie*'s rules against *lamparo*, for instance by using dynamite on a massive scale. Because trawlers (and arguably *lamparos*) did not have to pay the *Prud'homie*'s tax (they usually fished beyond the three-mile limit that marked the boundaries of the *Prud'homie*'s jurisdiction),[24] these fishers had no qualms about rising up against the *Prud'homie* in defence of their own interests. The arrival of fishers from North Africa after 1962 did not affect their practices. In fact, a former *lamparo* fisher told me how these newcomers, who were often of Italian origin, showed their counterparts how to use dynamite in order to maximise their catch (a prohibited practice).[25] The new migrants from North Africa were no more concerned about the long-term preservation of the fishery than the Sperlonga fishers: a fisher explained to me how his family crossed the Mediterranean sea from Algeria on a fishing boat in 1962, and how they had to 'make up for their losses' once in Marseille.

Thus, the Italian fishers were able to modify social practices by spreading the use of the *lamparo* in Marseille.[26] From the early 1960s until the 1990s, the *lamparo* became a fully-fledged practice in the fishery. Although most of its users were of

[21] See F Grisel, 'How Migrations Affect Private Orders? Norms and Practices in the Fishery of Marseille' (2021) 55 *Law & Society Review* 177.

[22] ibid.

[23] See ch 5, section III.B.

[24] Legal Opinion of the Council of State no 178042 (11 May 1921).

[25] See ch 4, section III.

[26] On the support granted by the French authorities to the *lamparo*, see ch 5.

Italian descent, some local fishers started operating the *lamparo*. It does not appear from the record, however, that the *lamparo* technique affected the social norms of the community of fishers. In fact, the *Prud'homie* continued to defend these social norms by complaining about the dire effects of the *lamparo* at least until the late 1970s.[27] One possible reason why the arrival of Italian fishers did not durably affect the social norms of the *Prud'homie* might be due to their temporal preferences. Unlike other fishers, Italian fishers usually did not encourage their children to pursue their fishing activities (and their children often turned to other professions). The descendant of Sperlonga fishers told me how his father and grandfather discouraged him from becoming a fisher, and how they themselves left the trade as soon as possible to work as a tailor and as a factory worker respectively. Italian fishers saw fishing as a way of making a living, not as an ancestral lifestyle. In fact, the *lamparo* boats progressively disappeared from the fishery of Marseille in the 1990s as the last Italian fishers retired.[28] The same observation applies, albeit to a lesser extent, to local fishers. As was explained in chapter 1, the fishers of Marseille traditionally encourage their sons to become fishers and their daughters to marry other fishers. This social pressure can be quite strong. For instance, an informant told me the story of a community outsider who married the daughter of a fisher and was forced by his father-in-law to become a fisher (which he ended up doing). However, most fishers in Marseille are unanimous in their view that their profession is less popular than it ever has been, and the younger generations are more reluctant to join the ranks of their ancestors. A fisher once confided to me that his neighbour was jealous of him because the neighbour's son was unwilling to carry on the family tradition. The reasons for this disinclination are easy to understand. Fishers make a relatively good living but at a huge personal cost. They work much harder than most people, with hours that often extend into the night and the early morning. In addition, the fishers often blame the regulatory obligations that constrain their work and make it, according to them, less lucrative. Graph 6.1 shows the steep decline in the number of fishers throughout the twentieth century.[29]

This decline has had consequences on the social dynamics of the community. A career as a fisher is less attractive than it used to be, and the sons of fishers are less intent on carrying on the family tradition than in the past. A recent survey indicates that only 32.6 per cent of the fishers on the French Mediterranean coast chose their profession due to 'family transmission'.[30] Some of my interviewees told me that their sons left the trade in order to become a 'policeman' or even a 'judge'. Fishers often consider this departure with a sense of resignation and sadness.

[27] Letter from the *Prud'homie* to the Directeur Général des Affaires Maritimes de Marseille (ca 1977), DA 2331W279.

[28] There were only two *lamparo* boats left in Marseille by 1999. See *Répartition de la flotte de pêche dans la région PACA* (November 1999), NA 20160293/180.

[29] Graph 6.1 only considers the *patrons-pêcheurs* (ie the fishers who own a boat and are allowed to vote for the *Prud'homie*), not their employees.

[30] CRPMEM PACA, *Etat des lieux et caractérisation de la pêche maritime et des élevages marins en PACA*, 2016, 33.

**Graph 6.1** The Community of Fishers in Marseille (1896–2020)

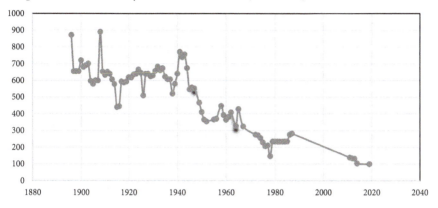

While they understand and often support their children's decisions, the fishers also deplore the end of longstanding traditions. What is even more remarkable is that despite these numerous social shocks – a war, migratory flows and the contraction of their community – the fishers of Marseille have remained strongly attached to their ancestral norms and still consider the *Prud'homie* as the guardian of these norms.

## B.  Whither the *Prud'homie*?

Over the past few decades, the *Prud'homie* seems to have lost most of its regulatory edge. Community members often refer to the uselessness of the *Prud'homie* and to its 'emptiness'. This subsection provides an overview of the *Prud'homie* and of its activities over the past few decades. It describes the near-total abandonment of the *Prud'homie*'s rule-making functions and its subsistence as an important cultural symbol of the fishery. The material presented in this section introduces the argument that the *Prud'homie* has managed to survive because it is embedded in longstanding social norms.

### i.  *The* Prud'homie: *An Empty Regulatory Shell?*

In recent years, the reluctance of the *Prud'homie* to communicate with outsiders has reached new heights, making it more challenging to study. In particular, a halo of mystery and endless rumours swirl around one of its strong men, whom I will call 'John Smith' for reasons of confidentiality. Various sources liken John Smith to 'Attila who leaves nothing behind him', 'a politician who wields the carrot and the stick' and 'a mafia boss' whose arrival has been compared to 'Hiroshima'.[31]

---

[31] My multiple attempts to interview John Smith were unsuccessful.

What is intriguing is that Smith does not reflect the traits of the individuals who traditionally led the *Prud'homie*. Some say that he is not a 'real fisher', and many imply that he has not been properly acculturated to the norms of the *Prud'homie*. How could a newcomer such as John Smith gain power within the *Prud'homie*? A connoisseur of the fishery explained to me that Smith managed to gain leadership at the *Prud'homie* 'because he was not part' of the community and because there was 'no one else' to pick. In fact, Smith is not the first newcomer to have managed this feat. Another outsider, Daniel Dulas, was elected to the *Prud'homie* in the 1990s. Dulas, a jovial man now in his 60s, explained to me how he left the fire department of Marseille to become a fisher in the early 1980s. To make matters worse, he did not originally come from Marseille but from the south-west coast of France. When asked how he achieved becoming a member of the *Prud'homie*, Dulas openly recognised that 'anyone could have been elected' because the position was 'devoid of any substance'.

There are several potential explanations for the diminishing attractiveness of the *Prud'homie*. One obvious answer is that the *Prud'homie* no longer exercises its regulatory functions over the fishery of Marseille. This regulatory impairment affects all the functions traditionally exercised by the *Prud'homie*, namely its judicial, legislative and police functions. For instance, the last judgment of the *Prud'homie* that I have been able to identify through my research dates back to 1969. In this case, a fisher (Louis Vanni) sued another fisher (Marcel Paregno) for having replaced Vanni's net at a fishing post. Vanni further argued that Paregno's brother assaulted him when Vanni complained about Paregno's behaviour. In its decision, the *Prud'homie* restated the rule prohibiting the permanent occupation of a fishing post. This reminder was probably addressed to Vanni, thereby suggesting that he was blocking the fishing post over which Paregno cast his net.[32] The *Prud'homie* then sentenced Paregno to pay compensation to Vanni and reaffirmed that outsiders such as Paregno's brother should not intervene in disputes arising between fishers. I have not seen or heard any trace of a judgment rendered by the *Prud'homie* since 1969. When asked how fishers resolved their disputes nowadays, a community member responded that they no longer turn towards the *Prud'homie* and that they 'figure it out' by themselves. Additionally, the *Prud'homie* seems to have stopped issuing regulations and codifying its rules. The last reference to a codification of the *Prud'homie*'s rules (*règlement prud'homal*) dates back to the late 1980s, when members of the *Prud'homie* discussed a rule limiting the size of nets and mentioned its lack of effectiveness.[33] The *Prud'homie* has also stopped exercising its police powers. Until the late 1990s, the *Prud'homie* still summoned fishers who committed violations and reminded them of the applicable rules, although it refrained from fining them.[34]

---

[32] This decision is entirely consistent with the equality norm that guarantees the right for any fisher to have access to the fishery.

[33] Minutes of the *Prud'homie*'s Assembly (31 March 1987) PA. On this rule, see ch 4, section II.C.

[34] It should be noted, however, that the *Prud'homie* had already stopped fining recalcitrant fishers.

Nowadays, the *Prud'homie* prefers to alert state authorities rather than to discipline fishers itself. Ultimately, the *Prud'homie* no longer exercises any of its powers: it does not legislate, judge or police its members.

Rational-choice analysts would probably claim that the *Prud'homie* has ceased using its powers because it no longer *needs* to do so. In other words, according to this argument, the regulatory challenges that justified the maintenance of the *Prud'homie*'s powers have simply disappeared, and along with them the *Prud'homie*'s exercise of these powers.[35] Such an analysis is consistent with the argument that systems of private governance have great plasticity, and that they evolve and align themselves with the interests of their members.[36] However, this explanation does not account for the fact that the *Prud'homie* has survived despite having lost its practical value. It would have seemed logical from a rational-choice perspective for fishers to dismantle an organisation that is no longer needed. If this line of analysis were true, in other words, there would be no valid explanation for the survival of an organisation such as the *Prud'homie*. In fact, rational actors ought to have consciously stopped paying the transaction costs – fees and time – that are associated with the maintenance of an organisation that has become redundant or useless. There is some apparent truth to this explanation, as indicated by the testimony of a fisher who told me that he stopped paying his dues and left the *Prud'homie* because he saw no use for it. Other fishers also repeatedly confirmed that they saw no use for the *Prud'homie*. However, such an explanation does not account for the formal maintenance of the *Prud'homie* and its persistence as a strong cultural symbol.

## ii. *The* Prud'homie *as a Cultural Symbol*

The variable that seems to be missing from the rational-choice equation is that of belief. The fishers have, in fact, remained strongly attached to the *Prud'homie* as a cultural symbol of their community.[37] While complaining about the 'emptiness' of the *Prud'homie* and the deviance of some of its leaders, the fishers also proudly proclaim their attachment to this organisation as part of their cultural heritage. For instance, some fishers introduce themselves as being from the '*Prud'homie* of Marseille' rather than 'Marseille'. In the debates concerning the regulation of tuna fishing, some fishers suggested that tuna should be branded with the name of the

[35] Some might argue that fishers no longer need the *Prud'homie* because their community has become easier to govern due to its smaller size. On this argument, see, eg, NK Komesar, *Imperfect Alternatives: Choosing Institutions in Law, Economics and Public Policy* (Chicago, IL, The University of Chicago Press, 1994) 69.

[36] ST Qiao, *Small Chinese Property: The Co-Evolution of Law and Social Norms* (Cambridge, Cambridge University Press, 2018) 186–88.

[37] Rational-choice theorists would probably counter that the symbolic role played by the *Prud'homie* still fulfils some underlying social role. However, the functionalist background that sustains most of rational-choice theory shows some limitations here, as fishers do not seem to draw concrete benefits out of the *Prud'homie*'s existence.

*Prud'homie*. Social activists and fishers have even tried to obtain the registration of the *Prud'homies* as part of French cultural heritage and to have them included on UNESCO's list of intangible cultural heritage. The fishers are extremely proud of their organisation and are almost unanimous in praising the traditional regulatory system of the *Prud'homie*. While the fishers have left the *Prud'homie* to the control of community outsiders and no longer participate in its activities, they still value it as a symbol of a glorified past and as the repository, more imaginary than real, of their social norms.

## iii. *The Persistence of Social Norms*

If the analysis of rational-choice theorists held true, the fishers should also have ceased to care about social norms that are no longer needed for governance purposes. Alternatively, these social norms should have evolved in order to reflect the new status quo. Insofar as the community no longer requires a system of private governance, on this account, this normative system should simply disappear or evolve. Such an analysis has potential merits, since it could explain why the fishers no longer use the *Prud'homie*. However, it does not explain why the same norms have persisted in Marseille in the past few decades.

To start with the norm of equality, the fishers still believe that anyone has an equal right to exploit the fishery. By 'anyone', they truly mean any full-fledged fisher (excluding poachers, amateur fishers and so on). While the norm of equality has survived among the fishers, their interpretation of this norm seems to have evolved. Many of my interviewees told me that fishers are fiercely 'jealous' and 'individualistic'. This strong individualism has two sides. First, fishers actively compete with one another in their search for fish. As an old fisher once told me, 'someone who is not jealous is not a fisher'. The flip side of this individualistic behaviour is that fishers seem careful not to encroach upon each other's fishing territory and to maintain distance between them. Fishers are individualistic and jealous, but they respect each other's boundaries. They do not necessarily trust each other, but they seem acutely aware of the common normative background that they share. As mentioned above, the norm of equality that I observed in the archival record is consistent with this individualistic behaviour, although in different ways. In the past, fishers held that they were entitled to a fair share of the fishery and, as a consequence, they tried to share the best fishing posts. The social dynamics have changed insofar as fishers are less likely to compete over the same posts, but their individualistic beliefs remain fundamentally the same: they continue to believe in their equal right to exploit the fishery.

The same can be said of the norm of conservation. The fishers frequently refer to the need to preserve the fishery in the long term. As with the equality norm, however, their interpretation of the conservation norm has evolved over time. In fact, the fishers no longer interpret the conservation norm as implying a duty for them to curtail their own activities. They rarely blame themselves for the decline of the fish stock but often designate water pollution as the culprit. In other words, the conservation norm is no longer framed vis-à-vis the fishers them-selves but is directed towards outside polluters. This shift in the interpretation of the conservation norm has an impact on fishing practices: in the words of my interviewees, the fishers of Marseille 'take whatever they can, as quickly as possi-ble' and no longer make efforts to curtail their fishing practices. This shift does not mean, however, that fishers no longer believe in this norm, simply that their target in the defence of the norm has changed. As noted, the fishers frequently attribute the disappearance of fish to water pollution, arguing, for instance, that the shrink-ing size of sardines is caused by a lower concentration of plankton that is itself due to poor water quality. They are vocal in pointing out the nearby presence of the Rhône estuary on the west side of the fishery and its role in carrying pollutants from chemical plants. They have also complained for decades about the ejection into the sea of so-called 'red mud' produced by a nearby mine located to the east of Marseille.[38] This chemical residue is a by-product of the refinement of bauxite into alumina and poses a known environmental hazard. State officials frequently point out the apparent contradiction between the blame placed by fishers on the polluters and the denial of their own responsibility in the reduction of fish stocks. Some officials even attribute the ecological stance adopted by fishers to a 'fashion', of which they make use in order to shirk their own responsibilities. This contra-diction became apparent, for instance, when fishers protested against the creation of three non-fishing areas along the coast of Marseille, namely the 'Blue Coast Marine Park' (*Parc Marin de la Côte Bleue*), the 'National Park of the *Calanques*' (*Parc National des Calanques*) and the 'artificial reefs' (*récifs artificiels*). These arti-ficial reefs are huge blocks of concrete and metal that have been immersed in the sea in order to foster the development of marine fauna and prevent trawling.[39] I have spoken with public officials in charge of these conservation areas, and they all gave a similar account of the position of fishers towards these areas. In all three cases, the fishers of Marseille opposed the creation of these areas and resented the fact that they could no longer exploit traditional fishing posts.[40] This stance is somewhat paradoxical, as the state created these non-fishing areas in order to repopulate the sea, a goal that is entirely consistent with the *Prud'homie*'s norm of conservation. However, when asked about these non-fishing areas, the fishers seem inclined to recognise the positive effects of these areas on the fish stock.

---

[38] See, eg, Minutes of the *Prud'homie*'s Assembly (19 April 1962), Private Archives. During this meeting, the *Prud'homie* vigorously criticised the mine's decision to dispose of its red-mud residues in the sea.

[39] It is interesting to note that the *Prud'homie* discussed a similar project to immerse shipwrecks in order to repopulate the sea in the 1930s. See, eg, Letter from the *Prud'homie* to the Administrateur en Chef du Quartier Maritime de Marseille (30 November 1935), DA 6S10/3.

[40] The situation was more complex in the case of the creation of the Blue Coast Marine Park, to which the *Prud'homie* seems to have lent its support. See Letter from the *Prud'homie* to the Adminis-trateur en Chef des Affaires Maritimes du Quartier de Marseille (20 March 1984), PA (mentioning the *Prud'homie*'s support for the Park).

One fisher mentioned the opposition of the 'old fishers' to the creation of the Blue Coast Marine Park in 1983 and said, as if to himself, 'what would have happened to us without the park?' (thus suggesting that the park has contributed to the preservation of the fishery). Another fisher expressed his approval of the artificial reefs and confided to me that he himself had sunk a boat wreck in order to foster the growth of young fish. A coast guard in charge of patrolling the artificial reefs told me that fishers were highly critical of one of their colleagues who frequently trespassed into the non-fishing zone. It therefore seems that although their interpretation of the norms of equality and conservation have evolved, the fishers of Marseille still maintain a strong faith in these norms.

The description above allows us to sketch an answer to the question raised in the introduction to this chapter. The *Prud'homie* seems to have survived because it is deeply embedded in the social norms of its community. The behaviour of the fishers has changed: their *Prud'homie* is utterly useless, but they stubbornly repeat their attachment to norms that the *Prud'homie* still symbolises. In fact, individual attempts to abolish the *Prud'homies* have consistently failed. A governmental officer told me how he tried to close down the *Prud'homie* of Cassis (a neighbouring city to the east of Marseille), because fishers no longer ran in its elections. He soon had to backtrack after fishers mobilised their political contacts against the closure of the *Prud'homie*. The fishers rarely take part in the *Prud'homie*'s affairs, but they noisily protest when anyone dares threaten its existence. This finding will serve as a basis for identifying further developments concerning the features of private governance and its limits.

# III.  The Limits of Private Governance

This section identifies the main findings that have been gleaned throughout the preceding chapters. The *Prud'homie* provides an example of an extremely resilient private order that has managed to survive the turmoil of history while losing its concrete efficacy. Based on empirical data, this case study illustrates certain limits that might be generalised to other systems of private governance. My propositions are threefold: first, social norms are a factor of enduring stability, but also of uncertainty, requiring the creation of rules in situations of social conflict; second, the tension between the rigid denomination of norms and their flexible interpretation generates a gap between social norms and practices, which can alter the effectiveness of private governance; third, social norms are not merely a matter of behavioural regularity, but also – and more fundamentally – a reflection of inner beliefs. These propositions capture the basic idea that social norms are factors generating flexibility, but also social inertia. While their meaning often evolves, their rigid denomination constrains beliefs and imaginative forces in ways that affect their capacity to evolve.

## A. Open Norms, Closed Rules

The starting point for my inquiry was the question of why individuals subject themselves to all the difficulties and transaction costs associated with the emergence of formal organisations in circumstances where they could simply rely on social norms. The example of the *Prud'homie* provides the empirical backdrop against which one can identify some of the reasons for which a close-knit community of fishers chose to build a formal organisation in the early fifteenth century. In this case, the social norms of the community seemed too open-ended to provide concrete answers to and to resolve conflicts arising from complex collective-action problems. When confronted with these problems, fishers routinely offered diverging interpretations of their norms at the expense of certainty and peace within the community. Formal organisations such as the *Prud'homie* generate rules that specify the underlying social norms and render them operational. A review of the cases submitted to the *Prud'homie* between 1946 and 1969 suggests continuity in its functions. In the majority of these cases, the plaintiffs complained that the nets cast by the defendants damaged their own nets. The *Prud'homie* then determined who had priority to fish at a given location, and calculated the damages that were owed by the breaching party. Why did fishers claim damages via the *Prud'homie* instead of forgiving one another on the assumption that their loss would cancel itself out, sooner or later (as in Ellickson's 'order without law')?[41] The answer is simple: the normative background shared by the fishers did not provide ready-made answers to complex problems. Without the rule-making activities of the *Prud'homie*, the fishers were left to discuss their respective compliance with social norms *ad infinitum*. For instance, a fisher could endlessly argue that he was 'the one' who was complying with the norm of equality when casting his nets at a location occupied by another fisher, while the latter fisher could reply that he was equally entitled to fish at this location pursuant to the same norm. Elster similarly notes how employees and employers take opposite stances in wage disputes based on the same 'norm of fair wages'.[42] The *Prud'homie* actively generated rules in order to provide concrete answers in these debates. Accordingly, my first proposition is the following: social norms are a factor of enduring stability, but also of uncertainty, requiring the creation of rules when disputes arise.

---

[41] RC Ellickson, *Order without Law: How Neighbors Settle Disputes* (Cambridge, MA, Harvard University Press, 1991) 55–56.

[42] J Elster, *The Cement of Society: A Study of Social Order* (Cambridge, Cambridge University Press, 1989) 126.

## B.  Normative Resilience, Institutional Schizophrenia and Paranomie

On the basis of the longitudinal study of the *Prud'homie*, my research has high-lighted the temporal persistence of the social norms of fishers. Throughout its existence over the past centuries, the *Prud'homie* has almost never failed to proclaim its attachment, at least nominally, to the social norms of its community. This attachment does not mean, however, that fishers or even the *Prud'homie* comply with these norms. Throughout my empirical research, I have noted a form of 'institutional schizophrenia' between the fishers' social norms and their prac-tices. A recurring example is the ways in which fishers have progressively used techniques that threaten the preservation goals that they otherwise proclaim. Two concrete examples illustrate this difficulty. After the fall of the Vichy regime and the departure of German troops at the end of the Second World War, a commit-tee was created in order to reflect on the future of the *Prud'homie*.[43] During a meeting of this committee, the highest-ranking member of the *Prud'homie* (also called the first *Prud'homme*) noisily resigned from his post in order to protest against the policies of the French state.[44] The first *Prud'homme* specifically complained that the state was not supporting the *Prud'homie* in its attempt to prohibit the *lamparo* (thereby signalling the *Prud'homie*'s longstanding attach-ment to the norm of conservation).[45] In a spectacular backlash, other members of the committee called the first *Prud'homme*'s bluff, pointing out that he was equip-ping his own boat for *lamparo* fishing. Before storming out of the meeting, the first *Prud'homme* candidly recognised that he 'was still an opponent of *lamparo* but subsequent to the exhaustion of fish due to the use of this technique, material circumstances had forced him to practice this type of fishing'.[46] Another example delves deeper into the history of the *Prud'homie*. In the late nineteenth century, the first *Prud'homme* wrote a letter to a special commission of the French Senate that was investigating the exhaustion of the fish stock on the Mediterranean coast and its causes. The first *Prud'homme* proudly proclaimed that 'most fishers, in all our deliberations, have always been against dragnets [the main target of public outcry]'.[47] What the first *Prud'homme* failed to specify is that while adopting an official stance against dragnets, the *Prud'homie*'s members were actively engaged in this practice. For instance, a keen observer of the fishery of Marseille wrote that the *Prud'homie* was complicit in dragnet fishing and that it 'turned a blind eye to the violations' committed by fishers.[48]

---

[43] *Procès-verbal d'une réunion d'information portant sur la dissolution des organismes corporatifs* (30 January 1945) PA.

[44] *Procès-verbal de la Commission consultative du quartier de Marseille* (28 Septembre 1945) PA.

[45] ibid.

[46] ibid.

[47] *Annales du Sénat et de la Chambre des députés*, 30 November 1880, 454.

[48] P Gourret, *Les pêcheries et les poissons de la Méditerranée (Provence)* (Paris, Librairie J-B Baillère et Fils, 1894) 322.

These examples illustrate an attitude that I have observed multiple times in archival records and interviews: fishers, and the *Prud'homie* above all, appeal to norms that they themselves continuously breach.[49] In addition, the open-ended character of norms allows them to claim normative compliance when effectively breaching these norms. Examples of this disjunction between social norms and practices abound in the literature.[50] In a landmark book, Diego Gambetta identifies the ways in which prominent members of the Sicilian mafia breach norms while proclaiming their faithfulness to the same norms.[51] In a book on prison gangs, David Skarbeck notes the 'apparent hypocrisy' arising from the proclamation of a norm of fraternity by gang members and their actual disregard for the same norm.[52] Slade similarly observes how the *vory-v-zakone*, an elite and close-knit group within the Russian mafia, 'maintain a type of double-think, paying lip service to the original code while breaking it with abandon'.[53] He cites the case of a *vory* who, very much like the *Prud'homme* in the above example, criticised another group member for engaging in the same kind of 'un-thievish' lifestyle that he himself maintained.[54] Cass Sunstein also gives the imaginary example of John Jones, a convinced environmentalist based in California who fails to recycle his waste.[55] Why are individuals breaching the social norms in which they apparently believe? The answer to this question lies in the nature of social norms. The institutional schizophrenia that can be observed in systems of private governance results from essential features of social norms, namely their open-endedness and their rigidity. Individuals continue to refer to the same norms while construing these norms in ways that accommodate their practices. It is easy for individuals to justify why their practices do not breach the norms in which they otherwise believe.

The current situation in the community of fishers is therefore characterised by a complete lack of regulation coupled with strong, albeit declining, social norms. This situation recalls the one described by Durkheim in a famous chapter

---

[49] Ch 4 also explains how the *Prud'homie* went out of its way to justify the use of destructive techniques such as the *gangui*, while continuously claiming its attachment to the conservation norm.

[50] Bicchieri, Muldoon and Suntuoso note the example cited by Turnbull, whereby the Ik people went out of their way to avoid hunting together in order to avoid complying with a norm of cooperation that would have led them to share the spoils. See C Bicchieri, R Muldoon and A Sontuoso, 'Social Norms' in EN Zalta (ed), *The Stanford Encyclopedia of Philosophy* (2018), available at https://plato.stanford.edu/entries/social-norms/, last checked 27 November 2020. However, it seems like the stronger norm among the Ik people was one of individualism, not of reciprocity, and the behaviour of hunters was in fact consistent with this norm. See TM Turnbull, *The Mountain People* (New York, Simon & Schuster, 1972) 238–39.

[51] D Gambetta, *The Sicilian Mafia: The Business of Private Protection* (Cambridge, MA, Harvard University Press, 1993) 118–26.

[52] D Skarbeck, *The Social Order of the Underworld: How Prison Gangs Govern the American Penal System* (Oxford, Oxford University Press, 2014) 128.

[53] G Slade, 'No Country for Made Men: The Decline of the Mafia in Post-Soviet Georgia' (2012) 46 *Law & Society Review* 623, 643–44.

[54] ibid 643.

[55] CR Sunstein, 'Social Norms and Social Roles' (1996) 96 *Columbia Law Review* 903, 907.

of *The Division of Labor in Society*.[56] Durkheim describes in this chapter the 'pathological' state of societies that are characterised by a demise of 'organic solidarity'.[57] He calls this situation 'anomie', which he describes as a 'debasement of human nature'.[58] Durkheim defines anomie as a situation where the 'relationships between the organs [of the social body] are not regulated'.[59] In an anomic society, according to the Durkheim, the social actor is

> no longer the living cell of a living organism, moved continually by contact with neighboring cells, which acts upon them and responds in turn to their action, extends itself, contracts, yields and is transformed according to the needs and circumstances.[60]

The community of fishers in Marseille presents similarities with Durkheim's anomic society. The fishers are increasingly individualistic and do not seem to follow any rules. When asked how disputes are resolved in the community, a fisher told me that they 'argue and fight'. There is, however, a fundamental difference between Durkheim's description of an anomic society and the current situation in the fishing community of Marseille. Although the fishers do not seem to follow any rules in their mutual interactions, they still refer to the same ancestral norms that are attested in the historical records. In other words, the fishers live in an unregulated bubble, while proclaiming their attachment to longstanding social norms. The analogy with the situation described by Durkheim therefore has its limits. Rather than living in an 'anomic' society, it seems as if the fishers of Marseille are in a situation of 'paranomie', where persisting social norms are belied by the facts on the ground. Paranomic societies are schizophrenic to the extent that they rest on a solid normative foundation that is constantly being contradicted by social practices. These societies are left unregulated, but their members continue to refer to the same social norms.

The case study of the *Prud'homie* suggests that the imaginative force and capacity for change of private orders might be impeded by their own social norms. The argument that private governance based on social norms is responsive to social changes therefore seems incomplete.[61] Social norms do evolve, but they evolve more slowly and less intensively than social practices. The gap between the speed and intensity of changes in social practices, on the one hand, and the speed and intensity of changes in social norms, on the other, is key to

---

[56] E Durkheim, *The Division of Labor in Society* (Glencoe, IL, The Free Press of Glencoe, 1960) 291–308.

[57] ibid 291.

[58] ibid 307.

[59] ibid 304.

[60] ibid 306.

[61] This argument is implicit, for instance, in Ellickson's theory of the 'content of norms' (which is truly a theory of the 'formation of norms'). Ellickson contends that social norms are not an 'exogenous given' but appear in societies fulfilling certain conditions (typically what he defines as close-knit communities). The fact that social norms persist even after the decline in the conditions identified by Ellickson suggests that norms might be stickier and harder to trace back to independent variables than is assumed in his study. See Ellickson (n 41) ch 10.

analysing the evolution of private orders. When this gap is too broad, social norms become a mantra to which social actors pay lip service, while failing to comply with them. The greater the gap between social norms and practices, the less effective a system of private governance will be. This gap does not always persist, and social practices often swing back to what they were, even after undergoing dramatic changes. A famous example is given by Tocqueville in *The Ancien Régime and the Revolution*, which describes the resurgence of a centralised state and a powerful administration after the French Revolution.[62] Another example is the persistence of segregation in the American South after the Supreme Court's decision in *Brown v Board of Education of Topeka* (1954) due to 'social and cultural constraints' that still persist today.[63] These observations lead to my second proposition: the tension between the rigid denomination of norms and their flexible meaning can generate a gap between social norms and practices that undermines the effectiveness of private governance.

## C. The Nature of Social Norms

My first two propositions allow us to reconsider an important debate concerning the nature of social norms. Are norms a product of social practices, or are they a reflection of individual beliefs? Some recent scholarship on private governance tends to equates social norms with dominant social practices. In this view, norms arise from social practices that they merely reflect. As pointed out in the introduction to this book, this view appears from several studies of social life.[64] It is evident, for instance, in Posner's book on social norms,[65] where he argues that norms are 'mere behavioral regularities' that are 'constantly changing'.[66] Posner instantiates the link between social norms and practices through the mechanism of 'signalling'.[67] On his account, social norms become prevalent when they are largely followed by individuals, resulting in the ostracisation of those who 'signal' their lack of compliance with the norms.[68] Posner gives the following example of a social norm generated through 'signalling':

> I once suggested in an essay that the side of the head on which one parts one's hair is arbitrary, and the editor of the volume told me that when he was a child in England,

---

[62] A de Tocqueville, *The Ancien Régime and the Revolution* (Cambridge, Cambridge University Press, 2011).

[63] GN Rosenberg, *The Hollow Hope: Can Courts Bring About Social Change?*, 2nd edn (Chicago, IL, The University of Chicago Press, 1991) 82–85.

[64] See, eg, Shitong Qiao, *Chinese Small Property: The Co-Evolution of Law and Social Norms* (Cambridge, Cambridge University Press, 2018) 186 (arguing that Chinese property norms are more responsive to social change than the law).

[65] EA Posner, *Law and Social Norms* (Cambridge, MA, Harvard University Press, 2000).

[66] ibid 7–8.

[67] ibid 34.

[68] ibid 26.

boys parted their hair on one side, girls on the other side, and any boy who deviated from this norm would be instantaneously ostracized as a 'sissy'.[69]

This example illustrates the potential confusion that arises between social norms and practices. The practice of parting hair on one side is not per se a social norm. The true engine of the 'signalling' described by Posner is not the 'behavioral regularity' of hair-grooming practices but the more deeply ingrained belief in heterosexuality as a marker of masculinity. This belief is not simply determined by 'behavioral regularity' but is framed by deeper social markers, whether religious, cultural or otherwise. It would have been interesting to determine if, in Posner's example, girls who parted their hair on the 'boys' side' suffered from the same 'signalling effects' as the boys did (my intuition is that they did not).

In other words, the view of social norms as a 'behavioural regularity' disregards the fact that social norms appeal to the inner beliefs of individuals.[70] These inner beliefs often coincide with recurring patterns of social behaviour, but this coincidence is a matter of correlation rather than of causation. The theory of private governance and its foundations in rational choice have little to say about beliefs and certainly do not manage to explain their persistence.[71] In fact, the example of the *Prud'homie* suggests that social practices can evolve while norms remain relatively stable. The institutional schizophrenia that I observed in this case study suggests that practices and beliefs are not as strongly connected as is sometimes assumed. To extend the analysis to the example given by Posner, one could hypothesise that a majority of young men continue to nurture homophobic beliefs, while parting their hair on either side. Social practices have evolved, but their underlying norm (ie the ingrained beliefs concerning heterosexuality) has remained the same. In other words, social practices do not always reflect social beliefs. Feeding into this debate, Sunstein notes what he calls the 'disjunction between public acts (including speech) and private thought'.[72] Sunstein specifically argues that individuals may support a social norm not because they believe in this norm, but because they are scared of sanctions if they fail to comply with it. This type of disjunction typically emerges in times of normative settlement. In fact, the analysis presented in this book does not entirely deny the capacity of social norms to evolve, for instance when 'norm entrepreneurs' manage to cause the evolution of beliefs.[73] However, my analysis emphasises the rigidity of social norms and the fact that they are more likely to evolve in their *meaning* than in their professed

---

[69] ibid 24–25.

[70] This view is made explicit by Posner. See ibid 25.

[71] See R Boudon, 'The "Cognitivist Model": A Generalized "Rational-Choice Model"' (1996) 8 *Rationality and Society* 123, 124.

[72] Sunstein (n 55) 929–30.

[73] ibid 929. See also N Fligstein and D McAdam, *A Theory of Fields* (Oxford, Oxford University Press, 2012) 28.

terms. For instance, individuals proclaim their attachment to equality, whether under the guise of promoting the 'separate but equal' doctrine or when fighting discrimination. In other words, the open-ended character of social norms allows for broad flexibility in the interpretation of their meaning, but their rigidity leaves a deep imprint on their formulation. A related question is that of the plasticity of these norms. Do they align themselves with the evolving interests of individuals, or do they maintain their fundamental features throughout time? The answer suggested by my empirical material is once again more nuanced than what one finds in scholarly debates. The social norms of fishers have exhibited important continuities over time, but fishers have twisted their meaning to better fit their individual interests. These norms constrain the activities of individuals as a reflection of their inner beliefs, but they are only one driver of social action – one that might, or might not, prevail over others. These considerations lead to my third proposition: social norms are not merely a matter of behavioural regularity but also and more fundamentally a reflection of inner beliefs.

# IV. Conclusion

The scholarship on private governance credits social norms with many virtues. According to this scholarship, norms are flexible, spontaneous, easy to enforce and inexpensive. They promote economic efficiency by keeping governance lean and responsive to social needs. The law pales when compared with norms: it is blind to social realities, subservient to the rigidities of the legal system and incredibly costly.

The case study examined in this book confirms some of these findings. The system of private governance set up by the fishers of Marseille has been incredibly resilient for several centuries. It has survived many regime changes, the centralisation of state powers in a unified legal system and powerful social forces that have impacted the activities of fishers. This organisation has supplied governance functions normally associated with formal legal systems. However, this case study also highlights the limitations of the social norms on which systems of private governance are based. Social norms are rigid in their denomination and open-ended in their meaning, which drastically limits the capacity of private orders to evolve. Norms are too rigid to sustain imaginative forces and too broad to resolve discrete regulatory issues. Because these social norms can accommodate diverging practices due to their open-endedness (while consistently framing social debates within the community of fishers), the *Prud'homie* progressively found itself unable to regulate practices that obviously breached its social norms. Norms rarely evolve in their formulation, even though their meaning can be interpreted in widely diverging ways.

By offering a glimpse into the life of the *Prud'homie*, this book hopes to cast new light on the virtues of private governance. In doing so, it offers an illustration of how the distinction between law and norms, which sustains much of the litera-ture on private governance, might not be as relevant as is usually assumed.[74] In fact, this distinction creates an artificial wall between law, on the one hand, and society, on the other hand. Removing this wall means considering the law for what it is, namely an integral part of society.[75] In addition, the separation between norms and law neglects to consider some important overlaps between both categories. One can, for instance, observe the enduring influence of socio-legal norms on constitu-tional law debates. In fact, constitutional principles share many features with social norms: they are cast in stone (at least in liberal democracies), but they also lend themselves to creative, potentially diverging interpretations. Constitutional norms constantly require the creation of rules that are narrower than norms, and much easier to alter. Another relevant example is that of the standards such as 'good faith', 'best efforts' or 'the sanctity of contracts' that permeate the field of private law. These principles share the fundamental features of social norms: they are subject to multiple interpretations, but their existence is solidly grounded in the legal system. It seems rather unlikely, for instance, that French contract law does away with the notion of good faith, even though the content of this notion might evolve (and has in fact evolved) over time. Another venue for future research concerns the weight that norms have in the structure and maintenance of these legal systems. It is to be hoped that this task will be taken up by other scholars.

In a nutshell, the *Prud'homie* was born to give concrete meaning to social norms by accreting rule-making functions. The decline of these functions has not affected the resilience of the norms in which the *Prud'homie* is still embedded. A norm is a wondrous thing that irrigates, structures and even governs entire communities. It is also a factor of rigidity that constrains the evolution of these communities.

><((((°>   ><((((°>   ><((((°>

---

[74] This distinction is apparent, for instance, in the debates concerning the impact of law on social norms (see Sunstein (n 55) 967; DM Kahan, 'Gentle Nudges vs Hard Shoves: Solving the Sticky Norms Problem' (2000) 67 *The University of Chicago Law Review* 607) or the impact of social norms on law (see Qiao (n 64) 182). It is also apparent in Lessig's famous analysis of cyberspace governance. See L Lessig, *Code version 2.0* (New York, NY, Basic Books, 2006) 123.

[75] B Latour, *The Making of Law: An Ethnography of the Conseil d'Etat* (Cambridge, Polity Press, 2010) 262. Some might even say, following Durkheim, that legal analysis should be a task for social scientists. See M Fournier, *Emile Durkheim: A Biography* (Cambridge, Polity Press, 2013) 522.

# BIBLIOGRAPHY

Abulafia, O, *The Great Sea: A Human History of the Mediterranean* (London, Penguin Books, 2014).

Acheson, JM, The Lobster Gangs of Maine (Lebanon, University Press of New England, 1988).

——, Capturing the Commons (Lebanon, University Press of New England, 2003).

Aelian, *On the Characteristics of Animals*, vol 3 (Cambridge, MA, Harvard University Press, 1959).

Agrawal, A, 'Sustainable Governance of Common Resources: Context, Method, and Politics' (2003) 32 *Annual Review of Anthropology* 253.

Arnold, ZCM, 'Against the Tide: Connecticut Oystering, Hybrid Property, and the Survival of the Commons' (2015) 124 *The Yale Law Journal* 1206.

Aviram, A, 'A Paradox of Spontaneous Formation: The Evolution of Private Legal Systems' (2004) 22 *Yale Law & Policy Review* 1.

——, 'Forces Shaping the Evolution of Private Legal Systems' in Zumbansen, P and Calliess, GP (eds), *Law, Economics and Evolutionary Theory* (Cheltenham, Edward Elgar Publishing, 2011).

——, 'Path Dependence in the Development of Private Ordering' (2014) 1 *Michigan State Law Review* 29.

Axelrod, R, 'An Evolutionary Approach to Norms' (1986) 80 *The American Political Science Review* 1095.

——, 'The Evolution of Co-operation' (New York, Penguin Books, 1990).

Baudrillart, JJ, *Traité général des eaux et forêts, chasses et pêches*, vol IX (Paris, Librairie d'Arthus Bertrand, 1827).

Berge, E and van Laervohen, F, 'Governing the Commons for two decades: a complex story' (2011) 5 *International Journal of the Commons* 160.

Berkes, F, 'Local-level management and the Commons Problem' (1986) 10 *Marine Policy* 215.

Bermann, PS, 'The New Legal Pluralism' (2009) 5 *Annual Review of Law and Social Science* 225.

Bernstein, L, 'Opting out of the Legal System: Extralegal Contractual Relations in the Diamond Industry' (1992) 21 *The Journal of Legal Studies* 115.

——, 'Merchant Law in a Merchant Court: Rethinking the Code's Search for Immanent Business Norms' (1996) 144 *University of Pennsylvania Law Review* 1765.

——, 'Private Commercial Law in the Cotton Industry: Creating Cooperation through Rules, Norms, and Institutions' (2001) 99 *Michigan Law Review* 1724.

——, 'Beyond Relational Contracts: Social Capital and Network Governance in Procurement Contracts' (2015) 7 *Journal of Legal Analysis* 561.

——, 'Contract Governance in Small-World Networks: The Case of the Maghribi Traders' (2019) 113 *Northwestern University Law Review* 1009.

Bernstein, L, Morrisson, A and Ramseyer, JM, 'Private Orderings' (2015) 7 *Journal of Legal Analysis* 247.

Bicchieri, C, *Norms in the Wild: How to Diagnose, Measure, and Change Social Norms* (Oxford, Oxford University Press, 2017).

Bicchieri, C, Muldoon, R and Sontuoso, A, 'Social Norms' in Zalta, EN (ed), *The Stanford Encyclopedia of Philosophy* (2018).

Bijker, WE, Hughes, TP and Pinch, T (eds), *The Social Construction of Technological Systems: New Directions in the Sociology and History of Technology* (Cambridge, MA, The MIT Press, 2012).

Billioud, J, 'La pêche au thon et les madragues de Marseille' (1955) 26 *Marseille: Revue municipale* 3.

Bosc, Y, 'La prud'homie des patrons-pêcheurs de Marseille pendant la Révolution française', unpublished.

Boudon, R, 'The "Cognitivist Model": A Generalized "Rational-Choice Model"' (1996) 8 *Rationality and Society* 123.

Bouyala d'Arnaud, A, *Evocations du Vieux Marseille* (Paris, Les Editions de Minuit, 1959).

Braudel, F, *The Mediterranean and the Mediterranean World in the Age of Philip II*, vol 1 (Berkeley, CA, University of California Press, 1972).

——, *The Mediterranean and the Mediterranean World in the Age of Philip II*, vol 2 (Berkeley, CA, University of California Press, 1973).

Brin, E, *Le Corps et communauté des patrons pêcheurs de Marseille des origines à la Révolution* (Nogent-le-Rotrou, Daupeley Gouverneur, 1942).

Buti, G, 'Résonances urbaines de conflits de pêche en Provence' (2000) 202 *Provence historique* 439.

Calafat, G, *Une Mer Jalousée: Contribution à l'histoire de la souveraineté (Méditerranée, XVIIe siècle)* (Paris, Seuil, 2019).

Cam, P, *Les Prud'hommes: Juges ou Arbitres? Les fonctions sociales de la justice du travail* (Paris, Presses de la Fondation Nationale des Sciences Politiques, 1981).

Canova-Green, MC, 'L'entrée de Louis XIII dans Marseille le 7 novembre 1622' (2001) 212 *Dix-septième Siècle* 521.

Charbonnel, E, Harmelin, JG, Carnus, F, Le Direac'h, L, Ruitton, S, Lenfant, P and Beurois, J, 'Artificial Reefs in Marseille (France, Mediterranean Sea): From Complex Natural Habitats to Concept of Efficient Artificial Reef Design' (2011) 59 *Brazilian Journal of Oceanography* 177.

Charny, D, 'Illusions of a Spontaneous Order: "Norms" in Contractual Relationships' (1996) 144 *University of Pennsylvania Law Review* 1841.

Cheyette, FL, 'Suum cuique tribuere' (1970) 6 *French Historical Studies* 287.

Clair, S (ed), *Marseille: Archives Remarquables* (Marseille, Nouvelles Éditions Loubatières, 2016).

Clay, K, 'Trade Without Law: Private-Order Institutions in Mexican California' (1997) 13 *Journal of Law, Economics, and Organization* 202.

Coleman, JS, 'Social Capital in the Creation of Human Capital' (1988) *American Journal of Sociology* S95.

——, *Foundations of Social Theory* (Cambridge, MA, Harvard University Press, 1990).

Cooter, RD, 'Three Effects of Social Norms on Law: Expression, Deterrence, and Internalization' (2000) 79 *Oregon Law Review* 1.

Crémieux, AD, *Le VIᵐᵉ Livre des Statuts de Marseille* (Aix-en-Provence, F Chauvet, 1917).

——, *Marseille et la Royauté pendant la Minorité de Louis XIV (1643–1660)* (Paris, Librairie Hachette et Cie, 1917).

De Keyzer, M, Common challenges, different fates. The causal factors of failure or success in the commons: The pre-modern Brecklands (England) and the Campine (Southern Low Countries) compared in Haller, T, Breu, T, de Moor, T, Rohr, R and Heinzpeter, Z (eds), The Commons in a Glocal World: Global Connections and Local Responses (Abingdon, Routledge, 2019).

De Moor, T, *The Dilemma of the Commoners: Understanding the Use of Common-Pool Resources in Long-Term Perspectives* (Cambridge, Cambridge University Press, 2015).

Demsetz, H, 'Toward a Theory of Property Rights' (1967) 57 *The American Economic Review* 347.

De Nicolo, ML, 'Recherches sur l'histoire de la pêche en Méditerranée: Tartanes de Provence, tartanes de Vénétie, trabacs, modèles adriatiques pour la pêche à la traîne et le petit cabotage (XVIIe–XVIIIe siècles)' (2012) 84 *Cahiers de la Méditerranée* 309.

De Ruffi, A, *Histoire de la ville de Marseille* (Marseille, Claude Garcin, 1642).

Dixit, AK, *Lawlessness and Economics: Alternative Modes of Governance* (Princeton, NJ, Princeton University Press, 2004).

Doumengue, F, 'L'histoire des pêches thonières' (1998) 50 *Collective Volume of Scientific Papers (ICCAT)* 753.

Drahozal, CR, 'Private Ordering and International Commercial Arbitration' (2008-2009) 113 *Penn State Law Review* 1031.

Duhamel du Monceau, M, *Traité Général des Pêches*, vol 1 (Paris, Saillant & Nyon, 1769).

——, *Traité Général des Pêches*, vol 2 (Paris, Saillant & Nyon, 1772).

Durkheim, E, *The Division of Labor in Society* (Glencoe, IL, The Free Press of Glencoe, 1960).

Dworkin, R, *Taking Rights Seriously* (Cambridge, MA, Harvard University Press, 1977).

Edelman, LB, 'Rivers of Law and Contested Terrain: A Law and Society Approach to Economic Rationality' (2004) 38 *Law & Society Review* 181.

Eisenberg, MA, 'Private Ordering Through Negotiation: Dispute-Settlement and Rulemaking' (1976) 89 *Harvard Law Review* 637.

Ellickson, RC, 'A Hypothesis of Wealth-Maximizing Norms: Evidence from the Whaling Industry' (1989) 5 *The Journal of Law, Economics, and Organization* 83.

——, 'Bringing Culture and Human Frailty to Rational Actors: A Critique of Classical Law and Economics' (1989) 65 *Chicago-Kent Law Review* 23.

——, *Order without Law: How Neighbors Settle Disputes* (Cambridge, MA, Harvard University Press, 1991).

——, 'Property in Land' (1993) 102 *The Yale Law Journal* 1314.

——, 'Law and Economics Discovers Social Norms' (1998) 27 *The Journal of Legal Studies* 537.

——, 'The Market for Social Norms' (2001) 3/1 *American Law and Economics Review* 1.

——, 'The Evolution of Social Norms: A Perspective from the Legal Academy' in Hechter, M and Hopp, KD (eds), *Social Norms* (New York, Russel Sage Foundation, 2001).

——, *The Household: Informal Order Around the Hearth* (Princeton, NJ, Princeton University Press, 2007).

——, 'When Civil Society Uses an Iron Fist: The Roles of Private Associations in Rulemaking and Adjudication' (2016) 18/2 *American Law and Economics Review* 235.

Ellis, R, *Tuna: Love, Death and Mercury* (New York, Vintage Books, 2009).

Elster, J, *The Cement of Society: A Study of Social Order* (Cambridge, Cambridge University Press, 1989).

——, 'Rational Choice History: A Case of Excessive Ambition' (2000) 94 *The American Political Science Review* 685.

Emran, O and Abraïni, JL, *Dans le Jardin des Pêcheurs* (Marseille, Editions Gramond-Ritter, 2007).

Epstein, L and Knight, J, 'Building the Bridge from Both Sides of the River: Law and Society and Rational Choice' (2004) 38 *Law & Society Review* 207.

Escard, F, *Corporation et Prud'homie des Pêcheurs de Martigues* (Evreux, Herissey, 1896).

Fabre, A, *Les Rues de Marseille*, vol 2 (Marseille, E Camoin, 1867).

Fagan, D, *Fishing: How the Sea Fed Civilization* (New Haven, CT, Yale University Press, 2017).

Faget, D, *Marseille et la mer: Hommes et environnement marin (XVIIIe–XXe siècle)* (Rennes, Presses universitaires de Rennes, 2011).

——, 'Maîtres de l'onde, maîtres des marchés et des techniques: les migrants catalans à Marseille au XVIIIe siècle (1720–1793)' (2012) 84 *Cahiers de la Méditerranée* 159.

——, *L'écaille et le banc: Ressources de la mer dans la Méditerranée moderne XVIe–XVIIIe siècle* (Aix-en-Provence, Presses universitaires de Provence, 2017).

Faget, D and Sternberg, M (eds), *Pêches méditerranéennes: Origines et mutations Protohistoire–XXIe siècle* (Paris, Karthala, 2015).

Falk Moore, S, 'Law and Social Change: The Semi-Autonomous Social Field as an Appropriate Subject of Study' (1973) 7 *Law & Society Review* 719.

Fancello, P and Rossi-Idoux, F, *Marseille des Pêcheurs: A la rencontre d'un patrimoine vivant menacé* (Aix-en-Provence, Edisud, 2002).

Farrugio, H, 'Données historiques sur les anciennes madragues françaises de Méditerranée' (2012) 67 *Collective Volume of Scientific Papers (ICCAT)* 112.

Feldman, EA, 'The Tuna Court: Law and Norms in the World's Premier Fish Market' (2006) 94 *California Law Review* 313.

Féral, F, 'Un phénomène de décentralisation contestée: Les Prud'homies de Pêcheurs de Méditerranée' (1986) 133/134 *Economie Méridionale* 95.

——, 'Un hiatus dans l'administration et la politique des pêches maritimes: les prud'homies de pêcheurs en Méditerranée' (1987) 34 *Norois* 355.

Ficetola, M, *Il était une fois … Saint-Jean: La 'Petite Naples' Marseillaise, avant son Dynamitage en 1943* (Marseille, Massaliotte Culture, 2018).

Fishburne Collier, J, *Law and Social Change in Zinacantan* (Stanford, CA, Stanford University Press, 1973).

Fligstein, N and McAdam, D, *A Theory of Fields* (Oxford, Oxford University Press, 2012).

Fromentin, JM, 'Lessons from the past: investigating historical data from bluefin tuna fisheries' (2009) 10 *Fish and Fisheries* 197.

Galanter, M, 'Justice in Many Rooms: Courts, Private Ordering, and Indigenous Law' (1981) 19 *Journal of Legal Pluralism* 1.

Gambetta, D, *The Sicilian Mafia: The Business of Private Protection* (Cambridge, MA, Harvard University Press, 1993).

Garau, VF, *Traité de pêche maritime pratique illustré et des industries secondaires en Algérie* (Algiers, Imp P Crescenzo, 1909).

Geertz, C, 'The Bazaar Economy: Information and Search in Peasant Marketing' (1978) 68 *The American Economic Review* 28.

Gluckman, M, *The Judicial Process among the Barotse of Northern Rhodesia (Zambia)* (Manchester, Manchester University Press, 1955).

Goldberg, JL, *Trade and Institutions in the Medieval Mediterranean: The Geniza Merchants and their Business World* (Cambridge, Cambridge University Press, 2012).

Gourret, P, *Considérations sur la Faune Pélagique du Golfe du Marseille* (Paris, Cayer, 1884).

——, *Les pêcheries et les poissons de la Méditerranée (Provence)* (Paris, Librairie J-B Baillère et Fils, 1894).

——, *Provence des Pêcheurs* (Nice, Serre, 1981).

Grancher, R, 'Les Usages de la Mer: Droit, Travail et Ressources dans le Monde de la Pêche à Dieppe (Années 1720–Années 1820)', unpublished.

——, 'Les communs du rivage: L'Etat, les riverains et l'institution juridique des grèves de la mer (Manche, XVIIIe–XIXe siècle)' in F Locher (ed), *La nature en communs: Ressources, environnement et communautés (France et Empire français, XVIIe–XXe siècle* (Ceyzérieu, Champ Vallon, 2020).

Granovetter, M, 'Economic Action and Social Structure: The Problem of Embeddedness' (1985) 91 *American Journal of Sociology* 481.

——, *Society and Economy: Framework and Principles* (Cambridge, MA, Harvard University Press, 2017).

Greif, A, *Institutions and the Path to the Modern Economy: Lessons from Medieval Trade* (Cambridge, Cambridge University Press, 2006).

——, 'The Maghribi Traders: A Reappraisal?' (2012) 65 *The Economic History Review* 445.

Grisel, F, 'Treaty-Making between Public Authority and Private Interests: The Genealogy of the Convention on the Recognition and Enforcement of Foreign Arbitral Awards' (2017) 28 *European Journal of International Law* 73.

——, 'Managing the fishery commons at Marseille: How a medieval institution failed to accommodate change in an age of globalization' (2019) 20 *Fish and Fisheries* 419.

——, 'How Migrations Affect Private Orders: Norms and Practices in the Fishery of Marseille' (2021) 55 *Law & Society Review* 177'.

——, 'Arbitration as a Dispute Resolution Process: Historical Developments' in Björklund, A, Ferrari, F and Kröll, S (eds), *Cambridge Compendium of International Commercial and Investment Arbitration* (Cambridge, Cambridge University Press, forthcoming).

——, 'The Private-Public Divide and its Influence over French Arbitration Law: Tradition and Transition', unpublished.

Gueroult du Pas, PJ, *Recueil de vues de tous les differens bastimens de la Mer Mediterranée et de l'Ocean avec leurs noms et usages* (Paris, Pierre Giffart, 1710).

Habermas, J, *Between Facts and Norms: Contributions to a Discourse Theory of Law and Democracy* (Cambridge, MA, The MIT Press, 1996).

Hammel, CJ, *Observations sur les Pêches et les Pêcheurs de la Méditerranée* (Marseille, Feissat Aîné et Demonchy, 1831).

Hardin, G, 'The Tragedy of the Commons' (1968) 162 *Science* 1243.

Hayek, FA, *On Law, Legislation and Liberty: Rules and Order*, vol 1 (London, Routledge, 1982).

Hopkins, AG, *Globalisation in World History* (London, Random House, 2002).

Imbert, G, Laubier, L, Malan, A, Gaertner, JC and Dekeyser, I, *La Thonaille ou Courantille Volante, Final Report to the Conseil Régional PACA* (30 September 2017).

Jolls, C, Sunstein, C and Thaler, R, 'A Behavioral Approach to Law and Economics' (1998) 50 *Stanford Law Review* 1471.

Kahan, DM, 'Gentle Nudges vs Hard Shoves: Solving the Sticky Norms Problem' (2000) 67 *The University of Chicago Law Review* 607.

Kaiser, W, *Marseille au Temps des Troubles: Morphologie sociale et luttes de factions (1559–1596)* (Paris, EHESS, 1991).

Katz, ED, 'Private Order and Public Institutions' (2000) 98 *Michigan Law Review* 2481.

Kennelly, SJ and Broadhurst, MK, 'By-catch begone: changes in the philosophy of fishing technology' (2002) 3 *Fish and Fisheries* 340.

Komesar, NK, *Imperfect Alternatives: Choosing Institutions in Law, Economics and Public Policy* (Chicago, IL, The University of Chicago Press, 1994).

Kramer, RM, 'Trust and Distrust in Organizations: Emerging Perspectives, Enduring Questions' (1999) 50 *Annual Review of Psychology* 569.

Kurc, G, 'La pêche à la lumière en Atlantique' (1963) 113 *Science et Pêche* 1.

Landa, JT, 'A Theory of the Ethnically Homogeneous Middleman Group: An Institutional Alternative to Contract Law' (1981) 10 *The Journal of Legal Studies* 349.

Lapierre, M, *Les Prud'hommes Pêcheurs Marseillais* (Aix-en-Provence, F Chauvet, 1938).

Lara, A, 'Rationality and complexity in the work of Elinor Ostrom' (2015) 9/2 *International Journal of the Commons* 573.

Latour, B, *Reassembling the Social: An Introduction to Actor-Network-Theory* (Oxford, Oxford University Press, 2006).

——, *The Making of Law: An Ethnography of the Conseil d'Etat* (Cambridge, Polity Press, 2010).

Lefebvre, JL, 'Prud'hommes et bonnes gens dans les sources flamandes et wallonnes du Moyen Age tardif ou l'éligibilité dans la fonction publique médiévale' (2002) 2 *Le Moyen Age* 253.

Leley, K, Pelletier, D, Charbonnel, E, Letourneur, Y, Alban, F, Bachet, F and Boudouresque, CF, 'Métiers, efforts and catches of a Mediterranean small-scale coastal fishery: The case of the Côte Bleue Marine Park' (2014) 154 *Fisheries Research* 93.

Leonard, R, *Von Neumann, Morgenstern, and the Creation of Game Theory* (Cambridge, Cambridge University Press, 2010).

Lijphart, A, 'Comparative Politics and the Comparative Method' (1971) 65 *The American Political Science Review* 682.

Lord Smail, D, 'The Consumption of Justice: Emotions, Publicity, and Legal Culture in Marseille, 1264–1423' (Ithaca, NY, Cornell University Press, 2003).

Luetz de Lemps, A, 'Pêcheurs algériens' (1955) 30 *Cahiers d'outre-mer* 161.

Mabile, S, 'L'institution prud'homale en Méditerranée: Une analyse juridique', unpublished.

Macaulay, S, 'Non-Contractual Relations in Business: A Preliminary Study' (1963) 28 *American Sociological Review* 55.

Maggio, T, *Mattanza: The Ancient Sicilian Ritual of Bluefin Tuna Fishing* (Harmondsworth, Penguin Books, 2000).

Marion, AF, *Draguages au Large de Marseille* (Paris, G Masson, 1879).

——, *Esquisse d'une topographie zoologique du Golfe de Marseille* (Marseille, Cayer & Cie, 1883).

Marzagalli, S, 'Maritimity: How the Sea Affected Early Modern Life in the Mediterranean World' in Dabag, M, Haller, D, Jaspert, N and Lichtenberger, A (eds), *New Horizons: Mediterranean Research in the 21st Century* (Paderborn, Ferdinand Schöningh, 2016) 309.

Maurin, C, 'Situation de la pêche à la sardine dans la région marseillaise' (1965) 143 *Science et Pêche* 1.

McMillan, J and Woodruff, C, 'Dispute Prevention Without Courts in Vietnam' (1999) 14 *The Journal of Law, Economics, & Organization* 637.

McMillan, J and Woodruff, C, ' Order under Dysfunctional Public Order' (2000) 98 *Michigan Law Review* 2421.

Méry, L and Guindon, F, *Histoire analytique et chronologique des actes et des délibérations du corps et du conseil de la municipalité de Marseille depuis le Xème siècle jusqu'à nos jours*, vol 1 (Marseille, Feissat Aîné et Demonchy, 1841).

Méry, L and Guindon, F, *Histoire analytique et chronologique des actes et des délibérations du corps et du conseil de la municipalité de Marseille depuis le Xème siècle jusqu'à nos jours*, vol 5 (Marseille, Feissat Aîné et Demonchy, 1847).

Merry, SE, 'Legal Pluralism' (1988) 22/5 *Law & Society Review* 869.

Milgrom, PR, North, DC and Weingast, BR, 'The role of institutions in the revival of trade: the law merchant, private judges and the Champagne fairs' (1990) 2 *Economics and Politics* 1.

Milhaupt, CJ and West, MD, 'The Dark Side of Private Ordering: An Institutional and Empirical Analysis of Organized Crime' (2000) 67 *University of Chicago Law Review* 41.

Mille, J, *Les calanques et massifs voisins: Histoire d'une cartographie 1290–XXe siècle* (Turriers, Transfaire, 2015).

Milza (ed), *Les Italiens en France de 1914 à 1940* (Rome, Ecole française de Rome, 1986).

Mnookin, RH, 'Divorce Bargaining: The Limits on Private Ordering' (1984–1985) 18 *Journal of Law Reform* 1015.

Moore, SF, 'Law and Social Change: The Semi-Autonomous Social Field as an Appropriate Subject of Study' (1973) 7 *Law & Society Review* 719.

Moss Kanter, R, *Commitment and Community: Communes and Utopia in Sociological Perspective* (Cambridge, MA, Harvard University Press, 1972).

Mourlane, S and Regnard, C, *Empreintes Italiennes: Marseille et sa région* (Lyon, Lieux Dits, 2013).

Nash, J, 'Non-cooperative games' (1951) 54 *Annal of Mathematics* 286.

North, DC, 'Institutions' (1991) 15 *The Journal of Economic Perspectives* 97.

——, *Institutions, Institutional Change and Economic Performance* (Cambridge, Cambridge University Press, 1990).

Ogilvie, S, *The European Guilds: An Economic Analysis* (Princeton, NJ, Princeton University Press, 2019).

Olson, M, *The Logic of Collective Action: Public Goods and the Theory of Groups* (Cambridge, MA, Harvard University Press, 1965).

Oppian, *Halieutica or Fishing* (Cambridge, MA, Harvard University Press, 1928).

Ostrom, E, *Governing the Commons: The Evolution of Institutions for Collective Action* (Cambridge, Cambridge University Press, 1990).

——, 'A Behavioral Approach to the Rational Choice Theory of Collective Action' (1998) 92 *The American Political Science Review* 1.

——, 'Collective Action and the Evolution of Social Norms' (2000) 14 *The Journal of Economic Perspectives* 137.

——, 'Reformulating the Commons' (2000) 6 *Swiss Political Science Review* 29.

——, *Understanding Institutional Diversity* (Princeton, NJ, Princeton University Press, 2005).

Ostrom, E, Burger, J, Field, CB, Norgaard, RB and Policansky, D, 'Revisiting the Commons: Local Lessons, Global Challenges' (1999) 284 *Science* 278.

Ostrom, E, Gardner, R and Walker, J, *Rules, Games, and Common-Pool Resources* (Ann Arbor, MI, University of Michigan Press, 1994).

Parsons, T, *The Structure of Social Action: A Study in Social Theory with Special Reference to a Group of Recent European Writers* (Glencoe, IL, The Free Press, 1949).

Patania, L, 'Compte-rendu de la campagne expérimentale de pêche au thon au filet tournant au large des côtes de l'est méditerranéen' (1967) 164/165 *Science et Pêche* 17.

——, *Chronique d'un Itinéraire Singulier* (self-published, undated).

Patania, L and Guillaume, J, *Histoire des Prud'homies de Pêche Varoises, de Leurs Origines à nos Jours* (La Valette-du-Var, Hémisud, 2002).

Pauly, D, Silvestre, G and Smith, IR, 'On development, fisheries and dynamite: a brief review of tropical fisheries management' (1989) 3/3 *Natural Resource Modeling* 307.

Payan d'Augery, C, *Les Prud'hommes Pêcheurs de Marseille et leurs Archives* (Aix-en-Provence, Imprimerie de J Nicot, 1873).

Peyton Young, H, 'The Evolution of Social Norms' (2015) 7 *Annual Review of Economics* 359.

Pierchon-Bédry, B, 'Les Prud'hommes pêcheurs en Méditerranée' in Krynen, J and Gaven, JC (eds), *Les désunions de la magistrature (XIXe–XXe siècles)* (Toulouse, Presses de l'Université de Toulouse 1 Capitole, 2013).

Pirie, F, 'Legal Autonomy as Political Engagement: The Ladakhi Village in the Wider World' (2006) 40 *Law & Society Review* 77.

Pitcher, TJ, 'Fisheries managed to rebuild ecosystems? Reconstructing the past to salvage the future' (2001) 11 *Ecological Applications* 601.

Pizzorni-Itié, F, *L'Histoire du fort Saint-Jean* (Marseille, MUCEM, 2014).

Pomey, P, 'Les épaves grecques et romaines de la place Jules-Verne à Marseille' (1995) 2 *Comptes rendus des séances de l'Académie des Inscriptions et Belles-Lettres* 459.

Portal, F, *La République Marseillaise du XIIIe siècle (1200–1263)* (Marseille, Librairie Paul Ruat, 1907).

Posner, RA, 'Law, Economics, and Inefficient Norms' (1996) 144 *University of Pennsylvania Law Review* 1697.

——, 'Social Norms, Social Meaning, and Economic Analysis of Law: A Comment' (1998) 27 *The Journal of Legal Studies* 553.

——, *Law and Social Norms* (Cambridge, MA, Harvard University Press, 2000).

Qiao, S, *Chinese Small Property: The Co-Evolution of Law and Social Norms* (Cambridge, Cambridge University Press, 2018).

Quiberan de Beaujeu, P, *Louée Soit la Provence* (Arles, Actes Sud, 1999).

Rauch, D, 'Les prud'homies de pêche sous l'Etat français: une spécificité méditerranéenne' (2013) 254 *Provence historique* 493.

——, *Les prud'homies de pêche en Méditerranée française à l'époque contemporaine* (Nice, Serre Editeur, 2017).

Reynaud, G, 'Du portrait de Louis XIV à l'assomption de la vierge: Deux œuvres perdues de François et Pierre Puget' (1997) 190 *Provence historique* 587.

Richman, BD, 'Firms, Courts, and Reputation Mechanisms: Towards a Positive Theory of Private Ordering' (2004) 104 *Columbia Law Review* 2328.

——, 'How Community Institutions Create Economic Advantage: Jewish Diamond Merchants in New York' (2006) 31 *Law & Social Inquiry* 383.

——, *Stateless Commerce: The Diamond Network and the Persistence of Relational Exchange* (Cambridge, MA, Harvard University Press, 2017).

Roe Smith, M and Marx, L (eds), *Does Technology Drive History? The Dilemma of Technological Determinism* (Cambridge, MA, The MIT Press, 1994).

Rose, C, 'The impact of Governing the Commons on the American legal academy' (2011) 5 *International Journal of the Commons* 28.

Rosenberg, GN, *The Hollow Hope: Can Courts Bring About Social Change?*, 2nd edn (Chicago, IL, The University of Chicago Press, 2008).

Runciman, WG and Sen, AK, 'Games, Justice and the General Will' (1965) 74 *Mind* 554.

Sagy, T, 'What's So Private about Private Ordering?' (2001) 45 *Law & Society Review* 923.

Sassen, S, *Territory. Authority. Rights: From Medieval to Global Assemblages* (Princeton, NJ, Princeton University Press, 2006).

Schwarcz, SL, 'Private Ordering of Public Markets: The Rating Agency Paradox' (2002) 1 *University of Illinois Law Review* 1.

Scott, JC, *The Art of Not Being Governed: An Anarchist History of Upland Southeast Asia* (New Haven, CT, Yale University Press, 2009).

Singer, C, Holmyard, EJ, Hall, AR and Williams, TI, *A History of Technology*, vol IV (Oxford, Clarendon Press, 1958).

Singer, C, Holmyard, EJ, Hall, AR and Williams, TI, *A History of Technology*, vol V (Oxford, Clarendon Press, 1958).

Singleton, S and Taylor, M, 'Common Property, Collective Action and Community' (1992) 4 *Journal of Theoretical Politics* 309.

Skarbek, D, 'Governance and Prison Gangs' (2011) 105 *American Political Science Review* 702.

——, *The Social Order of the Underworld: How Prison Gangs Govern the American Penal System* (Oxford, Oxford University Press, 2014).

Sportiello, A, *Les pêcheurs du Vieux-Port: Fêtes et Traditions* (Marseille, Jeanne Laffitte, 1981).

Stern, PC, 'Design principles for global commons: natural resources and emerging technologies' (2001) 5/2 *International Journal of the Commons* 213.

Stone Sweet, A, 'Judicialization and the Construction of Governance' (1999) 32 *Comparative Political Studies* 147.

Strahilevitz, LJ, 'Social Norms from Close-Knit Groups to Loose-Knit Groups' (2003) 70 *The University of Chicago Law Review* 359.

Stringham, EP, *Private Governance: Creating Order in Economic and Social Life* (Oxford, Oxford University Press, 2015).

Sunstein, C, 'Social Norms and Social Roles' (1996) 96 *Columbia Law Review* 903.

Tamanaha, BZ, 'Understanding Legal Pluralism: Past to Present, Local to Global' (2007) 29 *Sydney Law Review* 375.

Temime, E (ed), *Histoire des Migrations à Marseille*, vol 1 (Saint-Rémy-de-Provence, Edisud, 1989).

Tempier, E, *Mode de Régulation de l'Effort de Pêche et le Rôle des Prud'homies: Les Cas de Marseille, Martigues et Le Brusc* (IFREMER, 1985).

Trial, G, 'La Mer et la Pêche en mer sur la côte de Camargue' (1935) 16 *Le Chêne* 69.

Ulen, TS, 'Rational Choice and the Economic Analysis of Law' (1994) 19 *Law & Social Inquiry* 487.

Vandersmissen, J, 'Experiments and Evolving Frameworks of Scientific Exploration: Jean-André Peyssonnel's Work on Coral' in Klemun, M and Spring, U (eds), *Expeditions as Experiments* (London, Palgrave Macmillan, 2016) 51.

Valin, RJ, *Nouveau Commentaire sur l'Ordonnance de la Marine du Mois d'Août 1681*, vol 2 (La Rochelle, Légier et Mesnier, 1760).

Varese, F, *The Russian Mafia: Private Protection in a New Market Economy* (Oxford, Oxford University Press, 2001).

Viaud, R, *Le Syndicalisme maritime français: Les organisations, les hommes, les luttes (1890–1950)* (Rennes, Presses Universitaires de Rennes, 2005).

Von Neumann, J and Morgenstern, O, *Theory of Games and Economic Behavior*, 3rd edn (Princeton, NJ, Princeton University Press, 1953).

Weber, M, *Economy and Society: An Outline of Interpretive Sociology* (Berkeley, CA, University of California Press, 1978).

Weyrauch, WO, 'The "Basic Law" or "Constitution" of a Small Group' (1971) 27 *Journal of Social Issues* 49.

Williamson, OE, 'Calculativeness, Trust, and Economic Organizations' (1993) 36 *Journal of Law & Economics* 453.

——, *The Mechanisms of Governance* (Oxford, Oxford University Press, 1996).

# Videos

Ammar, G and Mondoulet, M, *Gérard Carrodano, Sentinelle de la Méditerranée* (self-produced, 2012).

Bazin, L, *Le partage des eaux* (Aris, 1994).

# Archives

*Archives départementales des Bouches-du-Rhône* (Departmental Archives or DA): 4M2333, 7M239, 9B2, 9B4, 18M29, 250E1, 250E2, 250E3, 250E4, 250E5, 250E6, 250E8, 250E9, 250E10, 250E11, 250E14, 250E15, 250E16, 250E17, 250E18, 250E19, 250E20, 250E21, 250E22, 250E23, 250E25, 250E30, 250E31, 250E32, 250E35, 250E36, 250E39, 250E40, 250E41, 250E57, 250E69, 250E75, 250E76, 250E94, 250E126, 250E147, 250E168, 250E169, 250E177, 250E191, 250E195, 250E196, 250E197, 250E203, 250E207, 250E211, 250E213, 250E216, 250E224, 250E226, 250E227, 250E229, 250E235, 250E243, 250E250, 250E255, 250E256, 250E257, 250E258, 250E273, 250E274, 250E276, 363E177, 366E211, 366E212, B5012, 2225W1, 2225W2, 2331W268, 2331W269, 2331W271, 2331W272, 2331W273, 2331W275, 2331W276, 2331W277, 2331W279, 2331W281, 2331W282, 2331W284, 2331W286, 2331W287, 2331W288, 2331W291, 2331W336, 2331W337, C2335, C2774, C4026, C4027, C4028, C4029, PHI529/1.

*Archives de la Chambre de Commerce et d'Industrie de Marseille* (CCI): E/159, L/19/62/192, L/19/62/193, L/19/62/194, MR/4552, MR/45221, YC/22/09.

*Archives municipales de la ville de Marseille* (Municipal Archives or MA): AA1, AA5, AA25/1, AA30, AA44, AA63, AA68, AA69, AA70, BB18, BB19, BB20, BB21, BB22, BB23, BB25, BB26, BB27, BB28, BB32, BB33, EE29/2, EE182, EE183, HH369, HH370, HH371, HH372, 1BB282, 1BB1608, 5ii17, 5ii19, 5ii35, 18F1, 18F3, 18F5, 18F6, 78Fi36, 100ii262, 100ii264, 100ii468.

*Service historique de la défense, Toulon* (Army Archives or AA): 12P/6/39, 13P/10/3, 13/P/10/6, 13P/10/10, 13P/10/15, 13P/10/16, 13P/10/17, 13P/10/18.

*Service historique de la défense, Vincennes* (Army Archives or AA): CC5/374, CC5/599.

*Archives nationales de France* (National Archives or NA): C4/181, MAR/A/4/1, MAR/C4/176, MAR/C4/177, MAR/C4/178, MAR/C4/179, MAR/C5/27, MAR/C5/28, MAR/C5/29, MAR/G/92, 19860461/21, 19860461/24, 20160293/91, 20160293/112, 20160293/113, 20160293/180, 200220138/1, AL/3076, AL/3415, F/46/212, F/46/608.

*Archives privées* (Private Archives or PA).

><((((°>

# INDEX

Lightning Source UK Ltd.
Milton Keynes UK
UKHW021057300622
405173UK00002B/20